School & College
CURRICULUM
DESIGN

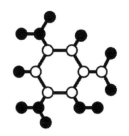

Book One:
INTENT

Matt Bromley

Spark
BOOKS

DEDICATION

I am lucky: my job affords me the opportunity to visit countless schools and colleges in the UK and overseas. Ostensibly, I do so to share my expertise and experience which, let me tell you, gives me a sense of imposter syndrome. I'm particularly surprised when a school or college invites me back because they wish to hear more! But in so doing, I get to talk to and learn from so many wonderful colleagues – teachers, leaders, support staff all – who are dedicated to the education profession and determined to make a difference for the pupils and students in their charge.

It is fair to say my thoughts and ideas are continually reshaped and refined as a consequence of these inspiring interactions. Sometimes, my opinions are solidified because I see and hear hard evidence of their truth. At other times, my opinions are challenged and changed as they meet with the resistance of reality.

I therefore dedicate this book to the thousands of hard-working people who work in education every day and who have helped shape the ideas I share within these pages. They can take the credit; I will accept the blame for any errors or omissions.

CONTENTS

INTRODUCTION

This is the first of three guides to the school and college curriculum design process.

Taken together, this series will navigate you through the process of redesigning your school or college curriculum, in order to ensure it is broad and balanced, ambitious for all, and prepares pupils and students for the next stages of their education, employment and lives.

Our journey begins here in Book One with **curriculum intent** – the *'Why?'* and the *'What?'* of education. Book Two, meanwhile, tackles **curriculum implementation** – the *'How?'* of education. And Book Three concludes with **curriculum impact** – the *'How successfully?'* of education.

In *Part One* of this book on intent, we'll explore what the term 'curriculum' means and argue that a curriculum is a composite of at least four different elements: the national, the basic, the local, and the hidden curriculums. We shall also define the words 'broad' and 'balanced' and explore what a broad and balanced curriculum looks like in practice.

We will examine the primacy of the curriculum over teaching, learning and assessment, and defend curriculum's role as the master, rather than the servant, of education.

We will consider the purpose of education and, by so doing, determine the intended outcomes of an effective curriculum.

We will explore the vital role senior leaders must play in the curriculum design process whilst simultaneously defending the rights of middle leaders and

1

teachers – those with subject specialist knowledge – to create their own disciplinary curriculums with freedom and autonomy.

We will also explore the importance of creating a culture of high aspirations where each pupil is challenged to produce excellence. We will consider the centrality of social justice to effective curriculum design – using the curriculum as a means of closing the gap between disadvantaged pupils and their more advantaged peers.

In *Part Two* of this book, we will examine *why* designing a knowledge-rich curriculum matters because, contrary to popular opinion, pupils can't 'just Google it'. We will then discuss *what* knowledge matters most to our pupils' future successes and how to identify the 'clear end-points' or 'body of knowledge' of our whole-school or college - and indeed subject-specific - curriculums.

We will discuss ways of ensuring our curriculum is ambitious for all, including through a mastery approach whereby we set the same destination for all pupils and students, irrespective of their starting points and backgrounds, rather than reducing the curriculum offer or 'dumbing down' for some. We will talk, too, of modelling the same high expectations of all, albeit accepting that some pupils will need additional and different support to reach that destination.

In *Part Three* of this book, we will discuss how to assess the starting points of our curriculum, both in terms of what has already been *taught* (the previous curriculum) and what has actually been *learnt* (our pupils' starting points – their prior knowledge, and their knowledge gaps and misconceptions).

We will explore the importance of curriculum continuity, too, and consider the features of an effective transition process. And we shall look at ways of instilling a consistent language *of* and *for* learning.

In *Part Four* of this book, once we have identified both our destination and our starting point, we shall plot a course between the two, identifying useful waypoints at which to stop along the way – what we might term 'threshold concepts' – through which pupils must travel because their acquisition of these concepts (be they knowledge or skills) is contingent on them being able to access and succeed at the next stage.

We will explore the importance of having a planned and sequenced curriculum, ensuring we revisit key concepts several times as pupils travel through our education system but, each time, doing so with increasing complexity, like carving a delicate statue from an alabaster block, each application of hammer and chisel revealing finer details and, in the case of curriculum sequencing, more - and more complex - connections to prior learning (or schema) that, in turn, will help pupils to learn more and cheat the limitations of their working memories in order to move from novice and towards expert.

We will explore how these 'waypoints' or threshold concepts may be used as a means of assessment so that curriculum knowledge – rather than something arbitrary such as scaled scores, national curriculum levels, GCSE grades or passes/merits/distinctions – is what we assess, by means of a progression model.

In *Parts Five* and *Six* of this book, we will turn to the subject of differentiation – arguing (as I say above) that all pupils deserve access to the same ambitious curriculum, no matter their starting points and backgrounds, and no matter the opportunities and challenges they face in life.

Of course, as I also say above, some pupils will need more support and will need more time in order to reach the designated end-points of our curriculum, and not all will do so, but we should not 'dumb down' or reduce our curriculum offer for disadvantaged, vulnerable or SEND pupils because by so doing we only perpetuate the achievement gap and double their disadvantage. Rather, we should ensure that every pupil is set on course for the same destination, albeit the means of transport and journey time may differ.

First, in *Part Five*, we will define excellence and explore the importance of 'teaching to the top'. We will look at how to model high expectations of all pupils. And we will look at ways of 'pitching' learning in pupils' 'struggle zones' (delicately positioned between their comfort zones and their panic zones where work is hard but achievable).

Then, in *Part Six*, we will look at ways of diminishing disadvantage - accepting that if we want to offer all pupils the same ambitious curriculum, we must also identify any gaps in their prior knowledge and skills, and support those pupils with learning difficulties or disabilities to access our curriculum and have a fair – if not equal – chance of academic success.

We will look at the role of cultural capital in closing the gap, arguing that vocabulary instruction (particularly of Tier 2 words) is a useful means of helping disadvantaged pupils to access our curriculum, but that this, in and of itself, not enough. Rather, we will assert that cultural capital takes myriad forms and, as such, we should also plan to explicitly teach pupils how to speak, read and write in each subject discipline, and fill gaps in their world knowledge.

We will also look at how to make a success of in-class differentiation and additional interventions and support. And we will look at how to develop pupils' literacy and numeracy skills in order to help disadvantaged learners to access our curriculum. Finally, we will examine ways of developing pupils' metacognition and self-regulation skills to help them to become increasingly independent, resilient learners.

This book, therefore, follows a six-step process of curriculum design as follows:

1. Agree a vision

2. Set the destination

3. Assess the starting points

4. Identify the way-points

5. Define excellence

6. Diminish disadvantage

We will begin our curriculum journey shortly but first a note on the text...

A NOTE ON THE TEXT

This series is entitled 'School and College Curriculum Design' because it is aimed at leaders and teachers in primary, secondary and further education settings.

At times, I will refer to 'pupils and students' in order to make clear that my advice applies equally to young children and to adult learners. I will also make explicit reference to the schools and further education and skills inspection handbooks, articulating the differences in language and focus.

However, for the sake of brevity and clear communication, I will often default to the language of 'pupils' and 'schools'.

I wish to make clear, therefore, that all of the advice contained within this book relates to schools *and* FE colleges, even if the language I sometimes use does not.

Of course, at times I will talk about strategies specific to schools such as the Pupil Premium but the advice – if not the illustrated example – is, I think, relevant to all.

I have worked extensively – as a teacher, leader and advisor – in all three phases – primary, secondary and FE. I have enacted the advice I proffer in this series of books in all three phases and I know it can work. Yes, there are differences, of course; but all three phases have more in common than that which divides them.

THE OFSTED CONTEXT

At the time of writing, the school and college curriculums are hot topics in England thanks in part to Her Majesty's Inspectorate. Ofsted published a new Education Inspection Framework (EIF) which came into effect in September 2019.

Although teachers and education leaders in England cannot ignore Ofsted (to do so would, in my view, be foolish rather than brave), we should never forget that Ofsted are not why we do what we do. As teachers and leaders, we do what we do for our pupils and students and if we do what is right for them, acting with integrity at all times, we should have nothing to fear from Ofsted.

Nor are Ofsted the reason for this book – indeed, the manuscript began life long before Ofsted consulted upon and published its EIF – although, perhaps shamefully, in the final draft of this book I 'borrowed' (at my publisher's request) Ofsted's 3I's of intent, implementation and impact as a means of articulating the curriculum design process.

Having said this, the new inspection framework does, I think, provide a logical way of thinking about curriculum design and its focus on 'the real substance of education' is to be commended.

The purpose of the new framework, Ofsted says, is to discourage schools from narrowing their curriculum offer – perhaps in the form of running a three-year GCSE or closing down certain subjects.

The EIF is also intended to end practices such as teaching to the test – being blinkered by what Amanda Spielman calls the 'stickers and badges' of qualification outcomes at the expense of a more rounded education that better prepares pupils for the next stages of their education, employment and lives.

Finally, the EIF aims to tackle social justice issues, ending educational disadvantage and affording every child, no matter their starting point and background, an equal opportunity to access an ambitious curriculum and to succeed in school and college. This final aim is, in part, achieved by providing disadvantaged children with the knowledge and cultural capital they need to succeed in life.

So, before we embark on our own curriculum journey, let us take a pitstop to consider the Ofsted context…

The new key inspection judgments

There are four key judgment areas in the new EIF:

1.   Quality of education
2.   Behaviour and attitudes
3.   Personal development, and
4.   Leadership and management

In addition, as before, schools will receive an 'overall effectiveness' grade.

The old judgment pertaining to 'outcomes for pupils' has therefore been scrapped, making clear that test and/or exam results are no longer paramount and that schools in difficult circumstances which might not achieve good headline outcomes can nevertheless provide a good quality of education and serve their pupils well.

The 'teaching, learning and assessment' judgment has also gone.   This implies that the focus will be on a whole school's provision – its curriculum – and how that curriculum is delivered and assessed, not so much on an individual teacher's classroom practice.

Both 'outcomes for pupils' and 'teaching, learning and assessment' have been subsumed within a new judgment called 'quality of education' which places the quality of the school curriculum centre-stage.

For the purposes of this series we will focus on the 'quality of education' judgment and its definition of curriculum according to its **intent, implementation** and **impact**…

Intent is "a framework for setting out the aims of a programme of education, including the knowledge and understanding to be gained at each stage".

Implementation is a means of "translating that framework over time into a structure and narrative within an institutional context".

Impact is the means of "evaluating what knowledge and understanding pupils have gained against expectations.

We might therefore conclude that:

- Intent is concerned with *curriculum design* and provision, the emphasis being on providing a broad and balanced curriculum for all pupils;
- Implementation, meanwhile, is about *curriculum delivery*, in other words on teaching, assessment and feedback, crucially that which leads to long-term learning; and
- Impact is about *pupil achievement* as assessed by external test and/or exam results and by using progression and destinations data, recognising that good outcomes are not just measured in qualifications but in how well pupils are developed as citizens.

I could go further and define the 3I's even more simply as:

- Intent = *why and what?*
- Implementation = *how?*
- Impact = *how successfully?*

Each of the 3I's, Ofsted says, will not be graded separately but evidence for each will be aggregated into an overall grade for the 'quality of education'.

It is worth noting that 'quality of education' is considered a leading judgment – in other words, it will form the bulk of inspection activity, provide the majority of the evidence used to grade a school, and as such – put simply - if the quality of education is not judged to be 'good' then every other judgment and indeed 'overall effectiveness' are unlikely to be.

Before we home in on what Ofsted has to say about the curriculum, let's examine some of the mechanics of inspection…

Preparation for inspection

In the draft handbook, Ofsted proposed that, for section 5 (full) inspections, inspectors would arrive on site the day before inspection activity began in order to prepare. But, following feedback from senior leaders, Ofsted have said that, rather than be on site, all preparation will continue to be carried out off site and the notice of inspection will remain at half a day.

However, Ofsted also said that their pilots convinced them that they could enhance the way that inspectors prepared for inspection. Accordingly, under the 2019 EIF inspectors will increase considerably the amount of time they spend speaking to leaders about the education provided by the school during the normal pre-inspection telephone call.

Indeed, this phone call – which will take place in the afternoon before an inspection, after '*the* call' has been made, will now last for approximately 90 minutes.

Inspectors will use this conversation to understand:

- the school or college's context, and the progress the school has made since the previous inspection, including any specific progress made on areas for improvement identified at previous inspections
- the headteacher's or college nominee's assessment of the school's current strengths and weaknesses, particularly in relation to the curriculum, the way teaching supports pupils to learn the curriculum, the standards that pupils achieve, pupils' behaviour and attitudes, and personal development
- the extent to which all pupils have access to the school's full curriculum
- a discussion of specific areas of the school (subjects, year groups, and so on; and in the case of FE colleges, the types of provision on offer) that will be a focus of attention during inspection.

This call will, Ofsted says, give inspectors and headteachers/nominees a shared understanding of the starting point of the inspection. It will also help inspectors to form an initial understanding of leaders' view of the school's progress and to shape the inspection plan.

The method of inspection

In tandem with the final EIF, Ofsted outlined its methodology for inspection. Inspection activity will, it said, take three forms:

1. **Top-level view**: inspectors and leaders will start with a top-level view of the school's curriculum, exploring what is on offer, to whom and when, leaders' understanding of curriculum intent and sequencing, and why these choices were made.

2. **Deep dive**: next, they will be a 'deep dive' which will involve gathering evidence on the curriculum intent, implementation and impact over a sample of subjects, topics or aspects. This, Ofsted says, will be done in collaboration with leaders, teachers and pupils. The intent of the deep dive is to seek to interrogate and establish a coherent evidence base on quality of education.

3. **Bringing it together:** finally, inspectors will bring the evidence together to widen coverage and to test whether any issues identified during the deep dives are systemic. This will usually lead to school leaders bringing forward further evidence and inspectors gathering additional evidence.

Top level view

This will largely take place during the initial 90-minute phone call between the lead inspector and headteacher/nominee and, as I say above, will focus on the school's context, the headteacher's assessment of the school's current strengths and weaknesses, the extent to which all pupils have access to the school's full curriculum, and specific areas of the school (subjects, year groups, aspects of provision, and so on) that will be a focus of attention during inspection.

Deep dive

The deep dive, meanwhile, will take place throughout the inspection visit and will include the following elements:

- an evaluation of senior leaders' intent for the curriculum in any given subject or area, and their understanding of its implementation and impact
- an evaluation of curriculum leaders' long- and medium-term thinking and planning, including the rationale for content choices and curriculum sequencing
- visits to a deliberately and explicitly connected sample of lessons
- the work scrutiny of books or other kinds of work produced by pupils who are part of classes that have also been (or will also be) observed by inspectors

11

- a discussion with teachers to understand how the curriculum informs their choices about content and sequencing to support effective learning
- a discussion with a group of pupils from the lessons observed.

Ofsted says that, during deep dives, context will matter. Carrying out lesson visits or work scrutiny without context will, they accept, limit the validity of their judgements.

It is important that, in order to make lesson visits and scrutiny more accurate, inspectors know the purpose of the lesson (or the task in a workbook), how it fits into a sequence of lessons over time, and what pupils already knew and understood. Conversations with teachers and subject leads will, they say, provide this contextual information.

Ofsted also says that a sequence of lessons, not an individual lesson, will be their unit of assessment – accordingly, inspectors will need to evaluate where a lesson sits in a sequence, and leaders'/teachers' understanding of this.

As has been the case for some years – though perhaps not widely known – inspectors will not grade individual lessons or teachers.

Ofsted says that work scrutiny will form a part of the evidence inspectors will use to judge whether or not the intended curriculum is being enacted. They'll ask: Do the pupils' books support other evidence that what the school set out to teach has, indeed, been covered?

Work scrutinies, Ofsted says, can provide part of the evidence to show whether pupils know more, remember more and can do more, but only as one component of the deep dive which includes lesson visits and conversations with leaders, teachers and pupils.

Coverage is a prerequisite for learning, Ofsted says; but simply having covered a part of the curriculum does not in itself indicate that pupils know or remember more.

Work scrutinies cannot be used to demonstrate that an individual pupil is working 'at the expected standard' or similar, and it is not valid – Ofsted admits – to attempt to judge an individual pupil's individual progress by comparing books from that pupil at two points in time.

Ofsted says that inspectors can make appropriately secure judgments on curriculum, teaching and behaviour across a particular deep dive when four to six lessons are visited, and inspectors have spoken to the curriculum lead and teachers to understand where each lesson sits in the sequence of lessons.

The greater the number of visits, therefore, the more inspectors can see the variation in practice across a deep dive. However, there is a point after which additional visits do little to enhance the validity of evidence. Since an inspection evidence base will include multiple deep dives, the total number of lessons visited over the course of the inspection will substantially exceed four to six.

Ofsted says that inspectors should review a minimum of six workbooks (or pieces of work) per subject per year group and scrutinise work from at least two-year groups in order to ensure that evidence is not excessively dependent on a single cohort. Normally, inspectors will repeat this exercise across each of the deep dives, subjects, key stages or year groups in which they carry out lesson visits.

In a research paper published in June 2019, Ofsted admitted to concerns with regards the reliability and validity of some of its proposed methods of inspection including lesson observations and work scrutiny, particularly in secondary schools and in FE. We can expect, therefore, further revisions or clarifications on their approach once the new framework is being routinely used to inspect providers.

Bringing it together

At the end of day one, the inspection team will meet to begin to bring the evidence together. The purpose of this important meeting is to:

- share the evidence gathered so far to continue to build a picture of the quality of education, identifying which features appear to be systemic and which are isolated to a single aspect
- allow the lead inspector to quality assure the evidence, and especially its 'connectedness'
- establish which inspection activities are most appropriate and valid on day 2 to come to conclusions about which features are systemic
- bring together evidence about personal development, behaviour and attitudes, safeguarding, wider leadership findings, and so on, in order to establish what further inspection activity needs to be done on day 2 to come to the key judgements.

Inspecting the curriculum

According to the inspection handbooks, inspectors will take a range of evidence, including that held in electronic form, into account when making judgments.

This, Ofsted says, will include official national data, discussions with leaders, staff and pupils, questionnaire responses and work in pupils' books and folders.

Gathering evidence

Before we consider what inspectors will want to do and see both before and during an inspection, I think it equally valuable to clarify what inspectors will not do and see because this can bust some unhelpful myths…

What Ofsted does NOT want

Ofsted make clear that inspectors will not grade individual lessons, create unnecessary workload for teachers, routinely check personnel files (although inspectors may look at a small sample), or advocate a particular method of planning, teaching or assessment.

Likewise, Ofsted will not require schools to provide any written record of teachers' verbal feedback to pupils, individual lesson plans, predictions of attainment and progress scores, assessment or self-evaluation (other than that which is already part the school's business processes).

Ofsted will not require performance and pupil-tracking information, monitoring of teaching and learning and its link to teachers' professional development and the teachers' standards (other than that which is already part of the school's normal activity), specific details of the pay grade of individual teachers who are observed during inspection, or processes for the performance management arrangements for school leaders and staff.

What's more, Ofsted does not expect schools to carry out a specified amount of lesson observations, use the Ofsted evaluation schedule to grade teaching or individual lessons, ensure a particular frequency or quantity of work in pupils' books or folders, take any specific steps with regard to site security (in particular, inspectors do not have a view about the need for perimeter fences), or carry out assessments or record pupils' achievements in any subject, including foundation subjects in primary schools, in a specific way, format or time.

Ofsted does not expect secondary schools to be at similar stages of EBacc implementation as any other schools. They do not expect any schools or colleges to provide additional information outside of their normal curriculum planning, or to produce a self-evaluation document or summary in any particular format.

Ofsted does not specify that tutor groups/form time must include literacy, numeracy or other learning sessions, nor does it dictate the frequency, type or volume of marking and feedback, or the content of, or approach to, headteacher/principal and staff performance management.

So far so pragmatic. It is, I think, helpful that Ofsted has set out – and so explicitly – what it does not want or expect to see in order to dispel myths and prevent unhelpful leadership practices from emerging.

What Ofsted does want

As well as any publicly available information about the school, inspectors will look at a summary of any school self-evaluations and the current school improvement plan (including any planning that sets out the longer-term vision for the school, such as the school or the trust's strategy).

They will expect schools to have to hand at the start of an inspection the single central record, a list of staff and whether any relevant staff are absent, whether any teachers cannot be observed for any reason (for example, where they are subject to capability procedures), whether there is anyone working on site who is normally employed elsewhere in the MAT (where relevant), and maps and other practical information.

They'll also want copies of the school's timetable, a current staff list and times for the school day, the Pupil Premium strategy, any information about previously planned interruptions to normal school routines during the period of inspection, records and analysis of exclusions, pupils taken off roll, incidents of poor behaviour and any use of internal isolation, records and analysis of bullying, discriminatory and prejudiced behaviour, either directly or indirectly, including racist, sexist, disability and homophobic/bi-phobic/transphobic bullying, use of derogatory language and racist incidents.

Ofsted also wants a list of referrals made to the designated person for safeguarding in the school and those who were subsequently referred to the local authority, along with brief details of the resolution, a list of all pupils who have open cases with children's services/social care and for whom there is a multi-agency plan, up-to-date attendance analysis for all groups of pupils, documented evidence of the work of those responsible for governance and their priorities, including any written scheme of delegation for an academy in a MAT, and any reports from external evaluation of the school.

What Ofsted will do

During an inspection, inspectors will gather further evidence by observing lessons, scrutinising pupils' work, talking to pupils about their work, gauging both their understanding and their engagement in learning, and obtaining pupils' perceptions of the typical quality of education in a range of subjects.

Discussions with pupils and staff will also be used as evidence (as will – in primary schools – listening to pupils read), and inspectors will look at examples of pupils' work for evidence of progress in knowledge, understanding and skills towards defined endpoints.

The lead inspector will invite the headteacher or nominee, curriculum leaders and other leaders to take part in joint observations of lessons. Inspectors will not take a random sample of lesson observations. Instead, they will connect lesson observation to other evidence. Lesson observation will be used for gathering evidence about 'implementation' and how lessons contribute to the quality of education. And observations will provide direct evidence about how behaviour is managed within individual classrooms.

The lead inspector will also invite curriculum leaders and teachers to take part in joint scrutiny of pupils' work. Inspectors will not evaluate individual workbooks or teachers. Inspectors will connect work scrutiny to lesson observation and, where possible, conversations with pupils and staff. Work scrutiny will be used for gathering evidence about the 'impact' of the quality of education. Inspectors may also use work scrutiny to evaluate pupils' progression through the curriculum.

Those are the mechanics of inspection under the 2019 EIF. Now let's focus on the role that the curriculum will play in future inspections…

What Ofsted say about curriculum design

As I said earlier, Ofsted defines curriculum in terms of its intent, implementation and impact. Let's take a closer look at each of the '3I's' in turn…

1. Intent

When inspecting 'intent' in <u>schools</u>, inspectors will look to see whether or not the curriculum builds towards **clear 'end points'**. In other words, they will want to see clear evidence of what pupils will be expected to know and do by each of these end points, be they the end of a year, key stage or phase.

In FE settings, rather than clear end-points, inspectors will look to see if curriculum managers and teachers have identified the **'body of knowledge'** students will be expected to acquire. Ofsted defines this 'body of knowledge' as the technical, vocational and life skills that a learner needs so that they will thrive in the future and not be left behind. It's worth a college considering how this body of knowledge has been influenced by the provider's local context and by the typical gaps in learners' knowledge and skills. It's also worth considering the extent to which the college takes account of the knowledge, skills and behaviours that learners bring with them.

Inspectors will also want to see evidence that the school's and college's curriculum is **planned and sequenced** so that new knowledge and skills build on what has been taught before, and towards those defined end points.

As well as being clearly sequenced and building towards a clear end-point, Ofsted says that the curriculum should also **reflect the provider's local context** by addressing typical gaps in pupils' and students' knowledge and skills.

The curriculum should remain as broad as possible for as long as possible, too, and, in schools, pupils should be afforded the opportunity to study a strong academic core of subjects, such as those offered by the English Baccalaureate (EBacc). In colleges, we might assume that inspectors will want to see that students are afforded the opportunity to study a well-rounded study programme which includes English and maths, employability and enrichment.

In schools, inspectors will want to see evidence that there are **high ambitions for all pupils**, whether they be academic, vocational or technical in nature. And Ofsted will want to see that the school does not offer disadvantaged pupils or pupils with SEND a reduced curriculum.

In FE settings, meanwhile, inspectors will seek to assure themselves that the provider intends to **include all its learners in its high academic, technical and vocational ambitions**. They will also seek to assure themselves that the provider offers disadvantaged learners or those with SEND, including those who have high needs, a curriculum that remains ambitious and meets their needs.

In FE, it is also expected that the provider's curriculum intent will have regard to the needs of learners, employers, and the local, regional and national economy as necessary

Curriculum narrowing

Talking of a reduced curriculum, inspectors will be particularly alert to signs of narrowing in the key stages 2 and 3 curriculums in primary and secondary schools. In other words, if a school has shortened key stage 3, inspectors will look to see that the school has made provision to ensure that pupils still have the opportunity to study a broad range of subjects in Years 7 to 9.

At the heart of an effective key stage 4 curriculum, Ofsted says, is a strong academic core: the EBacc. On this point, the schools inspection handbook may invite some contention. It restates the government's response to its EBacc consultation, published in July 2017, which was a commitment that a large majority of pupils should be expected to study the EBacc. Indeed, it is therefore the government's ambition that 75% of Year 10 pupils in state-funded mainstream schools should be starting to study EBacc GCSE courses nationally by 2022, rising to 90% by 2025. Including this information in the handbook implies that Ofsted will expect schools to be working towards these goals and will have some explaining to do if they fall short. However, as I said above, Ofsted will not expect all schools to be at similar stages of implementation.

Cultural capital

There are several explicit mentions of 'cultural capital' in the schools inspection handbook. Ofsted says that inspectors will judge the extent to which schools and colleges are equipping pupils with the knowledge and cultural capital they need to succeed in life. Ofsted's definition of this knowledge and cultural capital matches that found in the aims of the national curriculum: namely, that it is "the essential knowledge that pupils need to be educated citizens, introducing them to the best that has been thought and said and helping to engender an appreciation of human creativity and achievement".

In FE settings, Ofsted argues that the curriculum is a powerful means to address social disadvantage, giving learners access to the highest levels of knowledge, skills and experience. As such, the curriculum should be based on a firm agreement about what education and training should provide for each learner.

We will return to cultural capital in more detail in Chapter Twenty-Three.

2. Implementation

Under curriculum implementation, inspectors will seek evidence of how the school curriculum is taught at subject and classroom level. They will want to see how teachers enable pupils to understand key concepts, presenting information clearly and promoting appropriate discussion, how teachers check pupils' understanding effectively, identifying and correcting misunderstandings, and how teachers ensure that **pupils embed key concepts in their long-term memory** and apply them fluently.

Further, they will want to see if the subject curriculum that classes follow is designed and delivered in a way that allows pupils to transfer key knowledge to long-term memory and it is sequenced so that **new knowledge and skills build on what has been taught before** and towards defined end points.

In FE settings, Ofsted argues that teachers need sufficient subject knowledge, pedagogical knowledge and pedagogical content knowledge to be able teach learners effectively. Ofsted recognises that there will be areas in which staff are not yet experts, so inspectors will explore what leaders are doing to support staff to ensure that no learner receives poor teaching.

Effective teaching and training should, Ofsted argues, ensure that learners in FE settings **know more and remember what they have learned** within the context of the approach that teachers have selected to serve the aims of their curriculum. Consequently, learners will be able to apply vocational and technical skills fluently and independently. Effective teachers also check learners' understanding effectively, identifying and correcting misconceptions.

In both schools and FE settings, inspectors will want to see evidence that teachers use assessment to check pupils' understanding, and they will evaluate how assessment is used in the school or college to support the teaching of the curriculum, but – crucially – not in a way that substantially increases teachers' workloads. By including reference to the report of the Teacher Workload Advisory Group, 'Making data work', which recommends that school leaders should not have more than two or three data collection points a year, Ofsted rather implies – I think – that it will expect schools to follow this advice or have a solid rationale for not doing so.

In practice, effective implementation involves high quality teaching that leads to long-term learning. We will explore implementation in Book Two of this series but here is a brief summary…

What is long-term learning?

One of the central tenets of a quality curriculum is the provision of long-term – or deep - learning.

John Sweller's 'Cognitive Load Theory' (2011) posits that, "If nothing has altered in long-term memory nothing has been learned." The educational psychologist Paul Kirschner, meanwhile, defines learning as a change in long-term memory.

For its part, Ofsted argues that:

- Progress means knowing more and remembering more
- Knowledge is generative (or 'sticky'), i.e. the more you know, the easier it is to learn
- Knowledge is connected in webs or schemata
- Knowledge is when humans makes connections between the new and what has already been learned

We might, therefore, meaningfully define long-term learning as the acquisition of new information (knowledge, skills and understanding) and the application of that information at a later time and in a range of contexts.

The theory being this: for pupils to succeed, particularly on linear courses with terminal assessments after a year or two, they must be able to retain information over the long-term. They must also be able to apply what they've learnt in one context to other contexts such as in an exam, in the workplace and in life.

How can we help pupils to achieve long-term learning?

The process of learning is the interaction between the environment (new information coming in from the outside) and the long-term memory (new information being stored away for later use).

The long-term memory is where new information is stowed and from where it can be recalled when needed, hence long-term learning is a change in long-term memory. If something new does not enter the long-term memory, we cannot say it has been learnt. However, for information to enter and be stored in long-term memory, it must first be processed in the short-term (or 'working') memory.

In order to ensure a pupil achieves long-term learning, teachers need to gain the attention of – and help learners to cheat the limited space in – working memory, and improve the strength with which information is stored in, and the ease and efficiency with which it can later be retrieved from, long-term memory.

In order to do this, teachers need to:

1. Create a positive learning environment.
2. Make pupils think hard but efficiently.
3. Plan for deliberate practice.

We will take a look at each of these three steps in detail, and turn the theory into classroom practice, in Book Two.

Now let's turn to the third and final 'I' of the Ofsted framework…

3. Impact

Under impact, inspectors will gather evidence to help them judge whether the most disadvantaged pupils in the school – as well as pupils with SEND – are given the knowledge and cultural capital they need to succeed in life.

Ofsted says that national assessments and examinations are useful indicators of the outcomes pupils in the school achieve, but that they only represent a sample of what pupils have learned. As such, inspectors will balance these with their assessment of the standard of pupils' work from the first-hand evidence they gather on inspection.

Ofsted says that learning in schools must build towards a goal. As such, at each stage of pupils' education, they will want to see evidence that they're being prepared for the next stage of education, training or employment, and will consider whether pupils are ready for the next stage.

In FE settings, inspectors will make clear that there need be no conflict between teaching a broad, rich curriculum and achieving success in examinations and tests. A well-constructed, well-taught curriculum will lead to good results because those results will reflect what learners have learned.

In FE, as in schools, national tests and examinations are therefore a useful indicator of the outcomes learners achieve, and inspectors will balance these with their assessment of the achievement of learners drawn from the first-hand evidence they gather on inspection about non-qualification activity and the progress that learners make from starting points.

As in schools, Ofsted says that learning in further education settings must build towards a goal. At each stage of learners' education, they are being prepared for the next stage of education, training or employment or independence. Inspectors of FE provision will consider whether learners are ready for the next stage by the time they leave the provider or provision that they attend. Inspectors in FE will also consider whether learners are ready for the next stage and are going to appropriate, high-quality destinations.

If, having read the last few paragraphs, you're getting a strange sense of déjà vu, then you should: Ofsted, like me, believe schools and FE have more in common than apart and so apply the same rationale and indeed standards to all phases of education – hence the eerily similar language used in both inspection handbooks.

We will explore assessment in more detail in Book Three of this series.

Measuring outcomes

In terms of the evidence of impact, inspectors say they will use nationally-generated performance information about pupil progress and attainment – that which is available in the IDSR – as well as first-hand evidence of how pupils are doing, drawing together evidence from the interviews, observations, work scrutinies and documentary review described above. They will use nationally-published information about the destinations to which its pupils progress when they leave the school, and – in primary schools – they will listen to a range of pupils read.

Ofsted will not want to see internal assessment data such as that used to track progress in-year. Ofsted says that this is because inspectors do not want to add to school leaders' and teachers' workload by having them produce lots of data for the purposes of inspection. Unsaid but also a probable factor in this decision, is the belief that some schools will present 'massaged' data that isn't accurate or helpful.

In the final version of the EIF and inspection handbooks, Ofsted softened its position with regards a school's and college's internal data. They clarified that they would be interested in hearing the conclusions headteachers/principals and school and college leaders had drawn from their own data but would not want to see the data itself.

As such, it's recommended that senior leaders extrapolate their own data and have clear findings to share.

What has Ofsted previously opined about curriculum?

Before we move away from Ofsted and begin our six-step process of curriculum design, I think it worthwhile mining some recent inspection evidence because this might prove useful when considering what Ofsted regards as strengths and weaknesses of school and college curriculums…

Evaluations of recent inspection reports show that, in the past, Ofsted has regarded the following – which I have taken the liberty of paraphrasing - as strengths:

- Leaders review the curriculum regularly and check the impact on outcomes for all pupils, then remodel it to help all pupils perform well
- Leaders are attuned to research findings, as well as reforms to national curriculum and qualifications, and use this to inform how their local curriculum is developed to improve outcomes and pupils' personal development
- CEIAG is integral to the curriculum and pupils' progression, and the curriculum helps pupils to experience and learn about their options for their future
- There is a recognition that challenge is for all not just the most able pupils.

Conversely, Ofsted has noted the following – which, again, I have paraphrased - as weaknesses:

- Coordination of numeracy and literacy across the curriculum is poor and, as such, pupils struggle to read and access learning
- Support from middle leaders to develop pedagogy is poor – notably in mixed ability classes in Key Stage 3
- Pupils in Key Stage 3 repeat work from primary school which leaves them bored and frustrated by the lack of challenge
- There is a lack of understanding and coherence in assessment, and a lack of oversight
- Expectations of pupils are low
- The timetable is fragmented and poorly planned, leading to a lack of coherence across the curriculum
- Leaders are slow to tackle issues as a result of teacher vacancies and lack innovation to sustain a good curriculum despite teacher shortages.

Beyond Ofsted

Now that we have a good understanding of the Ofsted context, let us focus instead on what is in the best interests of our pupils rather than inspectors.

In order to do this, as I explained in the introduction, we will explore my six-step plan for curriculum design. Here's a quick reminder:

1. Agree the vision
2. Set the destination
3. Assess the starting points
4. Identify the waypoints
5. Define excellence
6. Diminish disadvantage

We will start, sensibly enough, with Step 1, which is to 'agree the vision'...

PART ONE

AGREE THE VISION

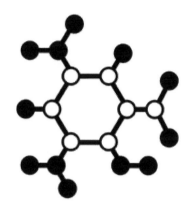

CHAPTER ONE
WHAT IS A CURRICULUM?

What is a curriculum? It's a simple question, isn't it, and, surely, before we can embark upon the complicated process of curriculum design, we must first understand what a curriculum actually is? After all, you wouldn't try to manufacture a widget without first knowing what a widget looks like, what it does, and how it works.

So, yes, it is indeed a simple question. But, unfortunately, the answer is not quite so simple...

For too long in our schools and colleges the curriculum has been synonymous with a timetable (the lessons we teach in structured blocks) and yet surely it is much more than this?

In a blog in October 2017 Ofsted's National Director, Sean Harford, said that "Without [the curriculum], a building full of teachers, leaders and pupils is not a school. If pupils don't get the benefit of a rich and deep curriculum then they will have learnt too little and made little progress."

Harford bemoaned the fact that, in recent years, "there has been a lack of reflection on the design, content and implementation of curriculums" and that, even today, there is "a lack of coherent debate and discussion about the curriculum."

To help reshape the discussion, Ofsted proffered a working definition of 'curriculum'. The curriculum, Ofsted said, is "a framework for setting out the aims of the programme of education, including the knowledge and understanding to be gained at each stage" - what the inspectorate, in the EIF, now calls 'intent'.

The curriculum is also a means of "translating that framework over time into a structure and narrative, within an instructional context" - what Ofsted calls 'implementation'.

And the curriculum is also a means of "evaluating what knowledge and understanding pupils have gained against expectations" - what Ofsted calls 'impact'.

Even with this more detailed definition, many may regard the FE curriculum as synonymous with an awarding body specification and the school curriculum solely through the lens of the *national* curriculum. A curriculum is much more than what is prescribed in an exam specification or in the national curriculum – as we will discover shortly – but first let's define what is meant by the 'national curriculum'…

The national curriculum

We can trace the evolution of the national curriculum in England back to a speech by Sir James Callaghan at Ruskin College, Oxford, in 1976. Certainly, this speech signalled the state's intention to assume a greater role in deciding, not just funding and facilities, but what was taught in its schools.

In his so-called 'Great Debate' speech, Callaghan argued that education should "equip children to the best of their ability for a lively, constructive place in society, and also to fit them to do a job of work. Not one or the other but both."

It took until the Education Reform Act of 1988 for Callaghan's dream to be realised. The 1988 Act led to the publication of a national curriculum which was officially introduced in schools in 1989.

The original national curriculum was a substantial document and contained attainment targets, programmes of study, and assessment arrangements. When it was first published, prime minister Margaret Thatcher famously decried she "never meant it to be this big". As such, each subsequent review of the national curriculum – including in 1995, 2008 and 2013 (with updates in 2014), has seen the documents slimmed down and simplified.

The current version of the national curriculum says that "Every state-funded school must offer a curriculum which is balanced and broadly based and which promotes the spiritual, moral, cultural, mental and physical development of pupils at the school and of society, and prepares pupils at the school for the opportunities, responsibilities and experiences of later life."

Furthermore, the national curriculum provides pupils with "an introduction to the core knowledge that they need to be educated citizens. It introduces pupils to the best that has been thought and said; and helps engender an appreciation of human creativity and achievement."

With this last sentence, the curriculum borrows from Matthew Arnold who said that "a good modern society can only come about when all of its citizens are educated in "the best that has been thought and said in the world".

In conclusion, then, the purpose of the national curriculum is to set out the principles, aims and content of the subjects to be studied by pupils in primary and secondary schools, and to ensure all pupils nationally encounter the same content and material that's considered important.

As such, the national curriculum, though certainly more insightful than a timetable, is still not the entirety of a school's curriculum; it is only those aspects afforded to all pupils nationally.

Dylan Wiliam, in his SSAT pamphlet, 'Principled Curriculum Design' (2013), said that "In recent years in England, discussion of the school curriculum has been all but absent. This neglect has been largely driven by the adoption in 1988 of a national curriculum for schools in England and Wales. Many teachers, leaders and policymakers assumed that because the government had specified what schools were required to teach, then no further discussion of the issue of curriculum was necessary."

Wiliam argued that this belief is mistaken for two reasons:

"The first is that the legal framework of the national curriculum specified only what schools were legally required to teach – any school was entirely free to teach whatever it wished in addition to the prescribed national curriculum.

"The second is that the real curriculum – the lived daily experience of young people in classrooms – requires the creative input of teachers. For example, the national curriculum may require that students learn about negative numbers, but the kinds of analogy that a teacher might use to teach this topic (e.g. heights above and below sea level, temperatures above and below zero, positive and negative bank balances, and so on) must be chosen with an understanding of the students, their experiences, and a range of other contextual factors."

The real curriculum, then, is created by teachers, every day.

In fact, the 'real' curriculum in maintained schools consists of at least three distinct elements of which the national curriculum is but one:

1. *The national curriculum* which, as I explained above, is that prescribed by statute and consists of the core and foundation subjects.

2. *The basic curriculum* which describes the statutory requirements for curricular provision beyond the national curriculum, comprising the requirements in current legislation for the teaching of RE (within the guidelines of the local Standing Advisory Committee for Religious Education), sex education, careers education, and opportunities for work-related learning. These are compulsory requirements, but schools are able to determine for themselves the specific nature of this provision.

3. *The local curriculum* which is one that schools are free to adopt in order to complement the national and basic curriculums with other curricular elements that are determined at school or community level. Often, these will reflect the individual nature of the school and its community, and perhaps its subject specialism(s).

Tim Oates et al (2011) argued that "Education can be seen, at its simplest, as the product of [an] interaction between socially valued knowledge and individual development. It occurs through learner experience of both of these key elements. The school curriculum structures these processes."

The QCA (2000), meanwhile, offered a broader definition which included "everything children do, see, hear or feel in their setting, both planned and unplanned."

The unplanned parts of the curriculum are often referred to as the 'hidden curriculum', a term first used by Jackson (1968). Jackson argued that what is taught in schools is more than just the formal curriculum and that schooling should be understood as a socialisation process whereby pupils receive messages through the experience of being in school, not just from what they're explicitly taught in lessons. The hidden curriculum, therefore, includes learning from other pupils, and learning that arises from an accidental juxtaposition of the school's stated values and its actual practice.

When designing a curriculum, therefore, we need to think carefully about all the ways in which pupils learn, not solely in structured lessons but also in the space between lessons and in the behaviours and values of the adults working in the school. As John Dunford (2012) puts it, "The school curriculum is not only the subjects on the timetable; it is the whole experience of education."

The curriculum, therefore, can be found, not just in a policy statement, and certainly not in the timetable or even in the national curriculum, but in the subjects and qualifications on the timetable, in the pedagogy and behaviours teachers and other adults use, in the space between lessons when pupils interact with each other, in approaches to managing behaviour, uniform, and attendance and punctuality, in assemblies and extra-curricular activities, and in the pastoral care and support offered to pupils… in short, in the holistic experience every child is afforded in school.

As well as the national, basic, local and hidden curriculums, it may be helpful to think in terms of the intended, enacted and real curriculums. The intended curriculum is that which is planned and written down in curriculum statements, schemes of work, lesson plans, resources and so on. The enacted curriculum is that which is actually taught and transmitted to pupils by teachers in lessons. And the real curriculum is that which is received and learnt by pupils, both in and out of lessons. Together, they form a pupil's whole experience of education.

Curriculum vision

Once you have clearly defined what is meant by the term 'curriculum' in your school or college, the next step, I think, is to agree and articulate a clear and shared vision setting out what you think is important and what you regard as the purpose of education.

The vision should, I think, comprise a list of the broad and rich learning experiences each pupil in the school can expect in each subject as well as outside of lessons.

This vision should make reference to the hidden curriculum and be cognisant of the fact that pupils' learning is not confined to the classroom; they learn from each other and from the way in which all the adults in school behave.

The reason I recommend you start the process of curriculum design with a vision is because this vision will provide the benchmark against which all subsequent decisions about curriculum content, structure, sequence, monitoring, evaluation and review can be tested.

As such, I do not advocate the writing of a vision statement which is then locked away in a dusty drawer, but of engaging in a meaningful debate about why your school exists and what it seeks to achieve for its pupils and community, and why these purposes and aims are important.

Finnish education experts attribute much of their success to the driving force and guiding power of their curriculum vision which is: to improve access to previously under-represented groups excluded or restrained by poverty, ethnicity, [and] gender, [and] to provide for broader meta-cognitive and interpersonal skills requiring deeper learning to meet the needs of an emerging knowledge society with more sophisticated labour requirements and built-in instability.

Here are some questions to consider when drafting your vision:

- What are the desired outcomes of our curriculum? Are academic outcomes – including high grades and value added - enough on their own? What of progress from individual starting points? What else do we desire for our pupils?
- What will excellence look like? Will it always look this way? Will it be the same for all pupils?
- What does social, moral, spiritual and cultural development mean for our pupils?
- What does employability mean for our pupils? How can we support its development at all stages of education and beyond school?
- What do we really believe about our pupils, their potential, and their destiny? How does this translate in practice? How can we ensure high expectations – and high challenge – for all pupils not just the higher performing, compliant ones?
- What, ultimately, is the purpose of education at our school? Why?

It is, I think, the last question on the list that will influence your curriculum vision the most and yet it is perhaps the most difficult question of all… so, I would advise you start here and we will return to this vital question in Chapter Four. First, though, let us consider what is meant by the term 'a broad and balanced curriculum'…

CHAPTER TWO
WHAT IS A BROAD AND BALANCED CURRICULUM?

In the previous chapter I explained that we might meaningfully define the 'curriculum' as a pupil's or student's holistic experience of education – the national, basic, local and hidden curriculums; the intended, enacted and real curriculums. But what might make it both broad and balanced?

In June 2017 the Chief Inspector of Schools, Amanda Spielman, gave a speech at the Festival of Education in which she advocated a broad and balanced school curriculum. All too often, she argued, schools lose sight of the real substance of education: "Not the exam grades or the progress scores, important though they are, but instead the real meat of what is taught in our schools and colleges: the curriculum."

She said that, although education had to prepare young people to succeed in life and make their contribution in the labour market, "to reduce [it] down to this kind of functionalist level is rather wretched." Education, she argued, "should be about broadening minds, enriching communities and advancing civilisation," and "ultimately, it [should be] about leaving the world a better place than we found it."

So, a broad and balanced curriculum is, or at least to begin with, about ensuring pupils are prepared for the next stages of their education, employment and lives… that they are developed holistically, and leave school or college skilled and knowledgeable employees and well-rounded, healthy and active citizens of the world.

But what else?

The 2002 Education Act requires schools to provide a 'balanced and broadly-based curriculum' – a phrase echoed in the national curriculum – which: promotes the spiritual, moral, cultural, mental and physical development of pupils at the school and of society, and; prepares pupils at the school for the opportunities, responsibilities and experiences of later life.

Although only maintained schools are required to teach the national curriculum, all schools – including independent schools and academies – must meet the requirements of the Education Act. However, there are no legal requirements for any school about the methods of delivery of the curriculum or the amount of time allocated to each subject.

Colleges are not governed by the national curriculum but by government policies and acts of parliament which dictate, for example, that students who did not achieve a standard pass of grade 4 in GCSE English and/or maths must continue to study the subject(s) until the age of 18. Colleges are also governed by funding arrangements (for example, the coalition government of 2010, and Conservative government of 2015 focused sector funding on apprenticeship provision and a current review of FE is likely to recommend the abolition of several vocational programmes) and, in most cases, through the instrument and articles of government.

So, within these rather vague legal frameworks, how can schools and colleges ensure that their curriculums are broad and balanced and will, therefore, produce well-rounded young people who can succeed in life and work as well as stand up to the increased scrutiny of Ofsted post-2019?

The regulatory standards for independent schools provide a useful way of thinking about breadth. The standards require schools to provide a curriculum that gives pupils experience in the following areas: linguistic, mathematical, scientific, technological, human and social, physical, and aesthetic and creative, so that it promotes spiritual, moral, social and cultural development.

A broad curriculum, therefore, might be regarded as one in which there are enough subjects on a pupil's timetable to cover all these experiences. Narrowing the curriculum for less able pupils or stretching GCSE study into Key Stage 3 clearly runs counter to this definition of breadth. A broad curriculum offers *all* pupils a wide range of subjects for as long as possible.

A balanced curriculum, meanwhile, might be regarded as one in which each subject is not only taught to all pupils but is afforded sufficient space on the timetable to deliver its distinct contribution. The danger here is that some subjects, such as art, music, and languages, are squeezed out of the timetable by English, maths and science. It is not uncommon for English to have five or more lessons on the timetable per week and art just one, or for the arts to operate on a carousel whereby design technology is only taught for one term of the year.

In his Ofsted blog, Sean Harford said that in 10 out of the 23 secondary schools inspectors visited as part of their consultation on the curriculum, school leaders admitted to "reducing key stage 3 to just 2 years". Whilst this might work for subjects where concepts are revisited at deeper levels (such as English and maths), "it doesn't work for all subjects, especially those that pupils drop before GCSE."

Amanda Spielman, in her speech at the Festival of Education, bemoaned this increasing "cannibalisation" of Key Stage 3 into Key Stage 4: "Preparing for GCSEs so early," Spielman said, "gives young people less time to study a range of subjects in depth and more time just practising the tests themselves." We have, she said, "a full and coherent national curriculum and [it is] a huge waste not to use it properly."

All children should study a broad and rich curriculum, she said, and yet "curtailing key stage 3 means prematurely cutting this off for children who may never have an opportunity to study some of these subjects again."

In short, Spielman said that schools had "a tendency to mistake badges and stickers for learning itself... [and put their own interests] ahead of the interests of the children in them."

"We should be ashamed," she said, "that we have let such behaviour persist for so long."

The 2019 Education Inspection Framework, as we have already seen, seeks to put an end to this behaviour and encourage schools – with the carrot and stick of inspection - to develop broader, more balanced curriculums that better prepare pupils for the future.

Though now outdated, the 2014 Common Inspection Framework (CIF) might provide some clues as to how Ofsted defines a broad and balanced curriculum...

In the CIF, inspectors were told to evaluate:

1. The design, implementation and evaluation of the curriculum, ensuring breadth and balance and its impact on pupils' outcomes and their personal development, behaviour and welfare.

2. How well the school supports the formal curriculum with extra-curricular opportunities for pupils to extend their knowledge and understanding, and to improve their skills in a range of artistic, creative and sporting activities.

3. How well the school prepares pupils positively for life in modern Britain and promotes the fundamental British values of democracy, the rule of law, individual liberty and mutual respect for, and tolerance of those with different faiths and beliefs and for those without faith.

When designing and delivering a curriculum, therefore, we might infer from this the following:

- We should consider the curriculum in its widest sense – it takes place in and between lessons, in subjects and in extra-curricular activities, and it develops pupils' skills in a range of areas including in the arts and sport, and – although important – it is not solely concerned with the pursuit of academic outcomes.
- We should ensure our curriculum prepares pupils, not only for the next stage of their education and training, but also for their lives as active citizens and for success in the world of work, developing employability skills and work-ready behaviours, and educating pupils on their career options.
- We should think carefully about how, once we've designed the curriculum, we will implement and evaluate it in order to ensure it delivers its stated aims and continues to be relevant.

In FE settings, I think it useful to consider breadth and balance in the guise of the 16-18 study programme which already requires young learners to study, not just a main qualification, but also English and maths, and to engage in meaningful work experience (including a work placement) and enrichment opportunities.

The development of English and maths skills, and employability and wider (enrichment) skills must be integral to the programme of study each learner pursues and not regarded as 'add-ons' or distractions from the main academic, vocational or technical qualification. If this is to happen, the shape of the study programme must be made clear to learners and teachers and their importance articulated loud and clear and often. What's more, the employability and enrichment opportunities must be relevant and meaningful to the main aim.

Further, what's good for young people is good for all and so a rounded study programme should be afforded to all learners in a college, irrespective of age, level of study, and area of study.

So far, we have defined the word 'curriculum' and described what a broad and balanced curriculum might look like in practice. Now let's consider *why* the curriculum is so important...

CHAPTER THREE
WHY DOES THE CURRICULUM MATTER?

The curriculum, as I have already said, is in the ascendency – in part because of its centrality to the new Ofsted inspection framework. Indeed, one of the best things about the new Ofsted framework is the fact that, after decades in exile, it's helped the curriculum be crowned king once more.

The curriculum - it's intent, implementation and impact - is front and centre in the new 'quality of education' judgment, which is the leading judgment. And the curriculum runs through all other areas of the framework like the letters in a stick of rock, notably in the 'personal development' judgment (whereby the curriculum is the means by which schools prepare pupils for the next stage of their lives) as well as in 'leadership and management'.

This – I think – is a positive step because, for too long, assessment means, methods and outcomes, not the curriculum, have held the sceptre in education.

Outcomes have been paramount – not just to Ofsted inspections but to the way the Department for Education measures educational effectiveness and indeed how they judge individual schools (including in the national league tables) and also to the way in which many schools and colleges are run.

Outcomes data (test and exam results, qualification pass rates and achievements, retention, value added scores and high-grade achievements) have been the primary means by which school and college effectiveness has been judged. Outcomes have often been the focus for senior leaders, too; underpinning teachers' performance management, and driving teaching and interventions.

The *means* of assessment have also trumped the *meaningfulness* of assessment - for example, national curriculum levels became the primary method of describing pupil learning and progress in primary schools and at key stage 3, and yet describing a pupil as a '5a' or '4b' in, say, English, makes little sense because a level cannot possibly do justice to a pupil's grasp of complex curriculum content nor does an arbitrary level provide any useful information for pupils and their parents/carers about what a child can and cannot yet do and what that child does and does not yet know. The levels were never designed to be used in the ways they came to be used.

Assessment has been at the wheel for far too long, drunkenly swaying all over the road. But now, having failed the breathalyser and unable to walk the line, it's handed the keys to the curriculum, our new designated driver.

The real substance of education

HMCI Amanda Spielman has said that, with her new inspection framework, she wants to stop teaching to the test and focus on the real substance of education. Put another way, she wants to shift the emphasis from qualifications outcomes - though still important – onto the curriculum.

In this brave new world, assessment becomes - quite rightly - the servant and not the master of our education system.

I personally hope that, in light of this, schools not only spend time on developing their curriculum provision, re-professionalising teachers and middle leaders as subject specialists crafting ambitious and exciting curricula that reflect the nature of their subject disciplines and their schools and colleges, but that this also allows the curriculum to dictate the means of assessment, not vice versa.

In other words, our methods and means of assessment should be driven by the curriculum and therefore inform us if pupils are making progress through that curriculum, rather than be based on dubious, arbitrary numbers or letters.

When the national curriculum levels were scrapped, schools had the opportunity to design an assessment system that was meaningful and yet many schools replaced levels with levels-in-all-but-name. For example, some schools starting using GCSE grades from Year 7 and yet not only was this demotivating to pupils (because they started on, say, a grade 3), it was - if you really think about it - a nonsense. GCSE grades are designed to assess pupils' achievements at GCSE not in key stage 3. In short, if you use grades 1-9 to assess pupils in Year 7 then you're using a car to cross the Atlantic or an ocean liner to navigate the M25.

If curriculum dictates assessment, however, it will tell you who has and who has not yet mastered certain aspects of that curriculum. For example, who does and does not know certain key concepts - or 'end points' to use the Ofsted parlance.

In fact, once you've identified the 'end points' of your curriculum (which we will do in Part Two of this book) these can be converted into curriculum statements or learning intentions which provide a ready-made means of assessment (as we will see in Part Four).

For example, if one such end-point of the English Language curriculum is that pupils have mastered the concepts of, say, explicit and implicit meanings (which is the first bullet under Assessment Objective 1 for GCSE English Language), then we could devise a set of curriculum statements - or checkpoints - through which they each must travel.

For example, they might first be taught to define the words 'explicit' and 'implicit', then be taught how to identify both explicit and implicit meanings in a non-fiction text. Next, they might be taught to explain why a writer has chosen to imply something rather than state it outright, and perhaps several different ways in which a writer could imply something. Then, they might be taught how to analyse the effects of explicit and implicit meanings on the reader. And so on and so forth.

Each of these 'threshold concepts' can become a simple 'can do' curriculum statement, assessed simply as 'yes' or 'no' - for example, "I can define the words 'explicit' and 'implicit'". This yes/no assessment tells us something meaningful and useful - concrete not abstract. It shows us how well and how quickly a pupil is travelling through our curriculum towards clear end-points. It shows us what pupils do and do not yet know and provides us and indeed them - with tangible information on which we and they can act. It can inform our whole-class teaching, too - telling us what we need to go back and re-teach or re-cap.

As well as providing meaningful, actionable information to and about each pupil, the data can be aggregated to provide useful information about the effectiveness of the curriculum. For example, we can ascertain at any point, what proportion of pupils have acquired the expected standard or reached the stage we had planned for and predicted. If they haven't, we know we need to revisit our curriculum model and the teaching strategies we have employed in order to ensure more pupils make better progress in future.

These end-points and threshold concepts will and should look different in each subject, of course. In Science, they may take the form of key (or 'big') questions; in Geography, they may be features of the natural or human landscape. It is important, therefore, that senior leaders allow their subject specialists the freedom to devise both a curriculum and a means of assessing that curriculum in a way that best suits the nature of the subject. We will explore this further in Chapter Five.

Having said this, senior leaders can ask some common questions of all subject leaders, such as:

- **What do you expect pupils to know?**

- **When do you expect pupils to know this?**

- **Why do you want pupils to know this?**

- **How will you know when pupils know this?**

- **What next?**

But senior leaders need to avoid the temptation to provide standardised pro forma for all their subject specialists to complete. And senior leaders need to accept that all subjects cannot conform to a whole-school curriculum and assessment mould.

We will explore meaningful assessment in Book Three of this series but, whilst we're on the subject, briefly, what else can we do to improve our assessment practices and ensure they are the servants of our curriculum rather than its master...?

Assessing the curriculum: Purpose, process and validity

Any discussion about improving curriculum assessment should, I believe, focus on three things:

1. Purpose

2. Process

3. Validity

Purpose

As a handy rule of thumb, whenever we ask teachers to engage in any form of assessment, we should ask ourselves: Why? What is the point of this assessment? How will this assessment - and the data we collect from it - help pupils to make better progress and improve the quality of education at our school?

If an assessment or data collection exercise is solely for management purposes (to produce a report to governors, say; or to generate pretty graphs to impress colleagues in meetings) rather than to actually help pupils make progress, then it should stop.

Of course, I know that it's not always as simple as this…

A teacher's time is finite and sometimes we also need to stop doing things that are indeed in pupils' best interests rather than for management purposes in order to afford us the time to do other things that are more impactful to pupils, or to cut a teacher's workload and make their jobs more manageable. As Dylan Wiliam sagely says, the essence of effective leadership is stopping teachers doing good things to give them time to do even better things.

Process

As well as considering the *purpose* of assessment, we should think about the *process* by which teachers are expected to assess, input data, and report the outcomes of assessment.

Here, it is useful we ask ourselves whether the process is as efficient as it can be or unnecessarily burdensome.

Consider also: when and how often are teachers expected to assess and input data? Are teachers expected to engineer a test for pupils or can data be gathered in a more holistic, synoptic way? How is the data inputted, directly into software or can teachers supply it in written form for the admin team to input? If it requires the use of technology, do all teachers have easy access to it? What will be the outcome of this data collection exercise? What will be done with the data afterwards and by whom?

As well as considering the time implications of data collection, it is wise to consider the extent to which teachers are trained in using the systems – including what you might consider basic spreadsheets as well as commercial software – and the extent to which they have the requisite skills to assess, record and analyse data, as well as act upon that data. Again, we should think about the opportunity cost, too. How long will it take a teacher to input this data and what else could they be doing with their time that might have a bigger impact on our pupils?

Validity

Finally, we should consider how valid the data they garner from assessments will be. By this, I don't mean how useful the data will be (we covered this under 'purpose', after all) but rather how accurate and useable it will be. In other words, although we may have confidence that the data will be very useful in helping pupils to make better progress (for example, by identifying 'at risk' pupils who require additional interventions, and by 'stretching' the higher-performing pupils to high grade achievement and good value added scores), the actual data we mine might not be as accurate as we hope and so all our subsequent actions may be futile or misguided.

To help answer this question of accuracy, we may wish to consider once again whether or not teachers have the requisite skills to be able to assess and provide data. Have we triangulated previous teacher assessments with actual validated outcomes? Have teacher assessments proven accurate in the past? Were some teachers' predictions way off-mark and, if so, have we identified any training needs? Have teacher assessments helped to predict eventual outcomes and therefore been useful in terms of identifying those pupils who are at risk of underachievement? Did the subsequent interventions prove effective? Sometimes we keep doing what we've always done because that is easy but, sometimes, we keep doing the wrong things. We should not be afraid to be bold and question seemingly unquestionable practices.

We may also wish to consider what is actually being assessed and if indeed that thing is assessable in a meaningful way. What, for example, are we comparing a pupil outcome to? Are those two things indeed comparable? Is the data we draw reliable and defensible? Is it, for example, possible at this stage to assess progress, or might we be measuring a poor proxy for progress? If assessments are used to measure progress over time, such as on a 'flight-path', is progress in this topic and subject actually linear? Should we be able to see nice neat contrails heading for the skies? Or is progress messier than this because pupils need to go backwards before they can go forwards, or because different things are being assessed in different topics at different times? Succeeding in topic one might not, for example, mean that pupils will do even better in topic two because the knowledge and/or skills being taught in each may be different and/or unrelated.

To conclude, the curriculum is king, and this is a good thing because the curriculum needs to take precedence over teaching and assessment. What's more, assessment should not be based on arbitrary measurements divorced from curriculum content but should measure how well and how quickly a pupil travels through our curriculum and how successfully they learn – in other words, the extent to which they know more and can do more than they could previously.

If we are to take full advantage of this golden opportunity in our schools and colleges to design an effective, relevant, exciting and ambitious curriculum, then we should also ensure that we make our methods and means of assessment meaningful and useful.

CHAPTER FOUR
WHAT IS THE PURPOSE OF EDUCATION?

So far in this book we have defined what we mean by the word 'curriculum' and explained what a broad and balanced curriculum looks like. We have explained *why* the curriculum matters so much and how to ensure that our assessment systems measure a pupil's journey through the curriculum in a meaningful and useful way.

Another important aspect of Step 1 in the six-step process of curriculum design I'm sharing in this book – 'agree the vision' – is to articulate the purpose of education in our schools and colleges as well as in each of the subject disciplines we teach within these institutions.

You may find the following questions useful when debating the purpose of education in your school or college:

- Why do we exist as a school or college?
- What makes us different?
- What are the opportunities and challenges our pupils and students face because of their geographical/demographical/socio-economical context?
- How does our school or college reflect the local community and jobs market we serve?
- What is our specialism or focus? Why? Will this change?
- How does our community *inform* what we do and how do we *involve* that community in designing and delivering our curriculum?
- What is it we intend to teach our pupils and students?

- What do we expect them to know and be able to do by the time they leave?
- Why do we teach each of the subject disciplines and vocations we teach?
- Why do we teach this particular qualification at this particular level?
- Why do we teach this particular module or topic?
- Why do we teach this content at this point?
- Why do we teach this before we teach this?

I cannot answer these questions for you, of course, because every school and college are different. I would therefore advise you to hold discussions with all your stakeholders on this subject. To help provoke and inform these discussions, however, I would like to use the remainder of this chapter to explore a bigger question: What is the purpose of education at all?

Why do we educate?

Is the purpose of education to prepare young people for the world of work or is it to instil in them an appreciation of the arts and sciences? Is it to develop character traits – such as resilience and empathy – in order to increase a pupil's employability, or is it to indoctrinate young people into our shared culture and history?

Is education a means to an end, or learning for learning's sake?

Thomas Gradgrind, the headmaster in Charles Dickens' novel Hard Times, famously said: "Teach these boys and girls nothing but Facts. Facts alone are wanted in life. Plant nothing else, and root out everything else. You can only form the minds of reasoning animals upon Facts: nothing else will ever be of any service to them."

Like Gradgrind, I believe that teaching facts is important, but I don't believe we should teach "nothing but facts" because facts learned in isolation are of limited value. Rather, we should teach facts and then teach our pupils how to apply those facts in a range of different contexts and make myriad connections between them. Teaching pupils how to convey their learning from one context to another is the difference between educating someone and simply training them to perform a task repeatedly. It is, if you like, the difference between learning and performance. Actually, I'd go even further in my definition of education...

Whilst I believe that education is about teaching pupils facts and teaching them how to apply those facts in a range of different contexts, as well as making connections between them, I also think that education is about creating new connections. In other words, education is not just about passing on existing knowledge, but it is also about creating new knowledge and forging new understandings. W B Yeats put it best when he said that education was not about the filling of a pail but about the lighting of a fire.

According to Gert Biesta in his book 'The Beautiful Risk of Education' (2015), there are (at least) three domains in which education can function and thus three domains in which educational purposes can be articulated. One is the domain of qualification, which has to do with the acquisition of knowledge, skills, values and dispositions. The second is the domain of socialisation, which has to do with the ways in which, through education, we have become part of existing traditions and ways of doing and being. The third is the domain of subjectification, which has to do with the interest of education in the subjectivity or "subject-ness" of those we educate. It has to do with emancipation and freedom and with the responsibility that comes with freedom.

Education, so argues Biesta, is not just about the reproduction of what we already know or of what already exists, but is genuinely interested in the ways in which new beginnings and new beginners can come into the world not just how we can get the world into our pupils. And this is the crucial point: if we view education - as opposed to training - as a way of creating new knowledge not just of 'passing on' existing knowledge, and as a means of developing people who will in turn create new things, then we must encourage risk-taking and experimentation in lessons. Education cannot conform, it cannot inflexibly follow a prescription if it is to focus on how we help our pupils to engage with, and thus come into, the world.

Aristotle said we should never think of education solely as a process of production...

Aristotle made the distinction between two modes of acting, poiesis and praxis - making action and doing action. Poiesis is about the production or fabrication of things, it is about "how something may come into being which is capable of either being or not being" and about things "whose origin is in the maker and not in the thing made". Poiesis is about the creation of something that did not exist before. Praxis is the domain of the variable - the world of human action and interaction.

While education is clearly located in the domain of the variable, it is concerned with the interaction between human beings not the interaction between human beings and the material world. Education is precisely what production (or poiesis) is not because we teachers cannot claim to 'produce' pupils. We educate them. We help them to change, to become something new and different. What's more, we help them to see and interact with the world in new and different ways.

Sharon Todd - in her book Learning from the Other (2003) - argues that teaching only has meaning if it carries with it a notion of 'transcendence', that is to say, if it is understood as something that comes from the outside and adds to rather than just confirms what is already there - in other words, education must create new knowledge and understandings not simply 'pass on' existing knowledge. Todd quotes Levinas who makes the claim that "teaching is not reducible to maieutics [the Socratic mode of enquiry, but] comes from the exterior and brings me more than I contain".

In other words, in the act of teaching - through education - we achieve far more than simply 'passing it on'; we create new meanings and new understandings. And often this creation is the result of the interaction itself, it is the very process of teaching that leads to new beginnings being forged. In other words, teaching is essential rather than accidental to learning. Indeed, as Kierkegaard (1985) argues, teaching is about more than simply presenting pupils with something they do not yet know, rather it is about presenting pupils with something that "is neither derivable from nor validated by what [they] already know" but truly transcends what they already know.

Todd and Kierkegaard both argue that teaching must have meaning beyond the facilitation of learning. In other words, teaching must have a meaning that comes from the outside and brings something radically new as in Climacus's idea of teaching as "the truth giving" and Levinas's understanding of teaching as a relationship in which I receive from the other "beyond the capacity of the I" - to emancipate pupils. Indeed, the idea that the purpose of education is to emancipate pupils - to free them as individuals - played an important role in the establishment of education as an academic discipline. Allow me to explain...

Emancipation means to "give away ownership" (ex: away; municipium: ownership). Immanuel Kant defined enlightenment as "man's release from his self-incurred tutelage" and argued that the "propensity and vocation to free thinking" was not a contingent, historical possibility but should be seen as something that was an inherent part of human nature; it was man's "ultimate destination" and the "aim of his existence". To block one's progress towards enlightenment was therefore "a crime against human nature" and a human being could only become human through education.

From this, we can trace the idea that education is not about the insertion of the individual into the existing order but is, instead, about developing autonomy and freedom.

Education, I suggested, is not a process of transportation of information from one mind to another - simply dumping knowledge from teacher to pupil - but is a process of meaning and interpretation that involves discussion and debate and the creation of new knowledge and understandings. And it is surely logical to argue that existing knowledge should be discussed and interpreted not simply imparted from one mind to another because, as John Dewey wrote (in his book Experience and Nature, 1929), "consciousness, thinking, subjectivity, meaning, intelligence, language, rationality, logic, inference and truth only come into existence through and as a result of communication". Moreover, "when communication occurs... all natural events are subject to reconsideration and revision; they are re-adapted to meet the requirements of conversation, whether it be public discourse or that preliminary discourse termed thinking."

Dewey seems to agree that education is a social art - more than mere production or reproduction. In Democracy and Education (1916), he said that in education "a being connected with other beings cannot perform his own activities without taking the activities of others into account [because] they are indispensable conditions of the realisation of his tendencies". Communication, he argued, should be understood as "a process of sharing experience until it becomes a common possession". In other words, education is the "participation in a common understanding".

In short, education is about a warm human interaction. It is about a connection between a teacher and a pupil, and between a pupil and her peers. It is indeed about learning the best that has been thought and said - Gradgrind's "nothing but facts" - and then learning how to apply those facts in a range of different contexts and making connections between them. But it is also about the domain of the variable, concerned with the interaction between human beings. It is about helping pupils to change, to become something new and different and to see and interact with the world in new and different ways. It is something that comes from the outside and adds to rather than just confirms what is already there; it comes from the exterior and brings more than it contains.

It is along these lines that Dewey suggested a crucial difference between education and training. Training, he said, is about the situations in which those who learn do not really share in the use to which their actions are put; they are not a partner in a shared activity. Education, on the other hand, is about those situations in which teachers and pupils share or participate in a common activity, in which they have a shared interest in its accomplishment. In those situations, participants' ideas and emotions are changed as a result of their very participation: a pupil "not merely acts in a way agreeing with the action of others, but, in so acting, the same ideas and emotions are aroused in [the pupil] that animate others". It is not therefore transmitted from one person to another. It is because people share in a common activity that their ideas and emotions are transformed as a direct result of the activity itself. In Democracy and Education, Dewey says that to have the same ideas about things that others have is "to attach the same meanings to things" - something that is brought about through communication and conjoint action.

Here's the crux of the argument: Dewey rejects the idea that a pupil can simply discover the meaning of the world through careful observation from the outside - or by being taught "the best which has been thought and said". Instead, Dewey suggests that pupils learn from the practices in which they take part, they learn by participating in a shared experience. In other words, it is only through the act of learning and engaging in classroom activity that they discover the meaning of the world; meaning cannot be derived without this interaction.

Dewey also makes the point that participation has the potential to generate a particular kind of learning - namely, learning that leads to a transformation of ideas, emotions, and understanding of all who take part in an activity in such a way that a common or shared outlook emerges. Dewey is not alone - Ernst Von Glasersfeld, Jean Piaget, and Lev Vygotsky all emphasise the importance of pupil activity and their theories of the constructivist classroom are based on the assumption that pupils must construct their own insights, understandings and knowledge, and that teachers cannot do this for them.

The purpose of education and the curriculum

Let's bring this discussion back to the curriculum…

Biesta (2015) argues that the purpose of education is to "recognise [each pupil's] unique characteristics and potentials, and [to develop] their ability to act autonomously and independently" Education, Biesta argues, is also a means of socialising "pupils into ways of thinking and acting, vis-a-vis educational disciplines [and of teaching] subject-specific bodies of knowledge, skills and values which will qualify students to take on active roles in society".

Macintyre (2002), meanwhile, believes the purpose of education is to create "an educated public" which is "constituted by educated generalists, people who can situate themselves in relation to society and to nature, because they know enough astronomy, enough geology, enough history, enough economics, and enough philosophy and theology to do so."

If the purpose of education is to 'pass on' the "best that has been thought and said" (as is stated in the national curriculum as we discovered in Chapter One), who decides what constitutes the 'best'?

Michael Young (2014) talks of 'powerful knowledge' as a type of knowledge that "allows those with access to it to question it and the authority on which it is based and gain the sense of freedom and excitement that it can offer". Young argues that facts alone do not constitute 'powerful knowledge'. So how do we decide what powerful knowledge is? Young says that "the knowledge on which maths or history as GCSE subjects is based has a form of universality derived from two sources: 1. How mathematics has been developed by specialists in the universities, and 2. How school maths teachers select and sequence mathematics content in ways that their theory and experience tell them is appropriate for the majority of pupils at different ages."

Meanwhile, in his SSAT pamphlet on 'Principled Curriculum' (2013), Dylan Wiliam sets out four purposes of education which you may find useful in terms of articulating the goals of your own curriculum. These four 'purposes' are as follows:

1. **Personal empowerment:** Arguably the most important aim of education is to allow young people to take greater control of their own lives, perhaps best exemplified by the work of Paulo Freire. The idea is that rather than simply enculturating young people into the existing systems, education is the means by which people 'deal critically and creatively with reality and discover how to participate in the transformation of their world' (Shaull, 1970).

2. **Cultural transmission:** Another reason that is often given for educating young people is, in Matthew Arnold's words, to pass on from one generation to the next, 'the best that has been thought and known in the world' (Arnold, 1869). Those who do not know what people are expected to know are regarded as ignorant – not stupid, but simply lacking the knowledge expected of them.

3. **Preparation for citizenship:** Democratic citizenship arguably works only if those who are voting understand the choices they are given, and education

therefore has a vital role to play in preparing citizens so that they can make informed decisions about their participation in democratic society (Council of Europe, 2010).

4. ***Preparation for work:*** As a number of reports from the Organisation for Economic Cooperation and Development have shown, more educated workers are more productive (e.g. Hanushek & Woessman, 2010). Educational achievement is therefore inextricably linked with economic prosperity.

Returning to Michael Young, he says that the purpose of education "is to enable all students to acquire knowledge that takes them beyond their experience. It is knowledge which many will not have access to at home, among their friends, or in the communities in which they live. As such, access to this knowledge is the right of all pupils as future citizens."

Young is therefore arguing that the purpose of education, and therefore the goal of our curriculum, is to achieve social justice and improve social mobility.

We know that the attainment gap widens as children travel through our education system. Indeed, disadvantaged pupils fall two months further behind their peers each academic year and by the end of secondary school the gap is nearly twenty months.

Young argues that all pupils have an entitlement to knowledge that takes them beyond their own experiences. It's important to note that the 'powerful knowledge' that Young argues all pupils should be taught is distinct from the commonsense knowledge they gain through everyday experience. Rather, it is *systematic* in that it is based on concepts that are related to each other in groups we call disciplines rather than rooted in real-life experience, and is *specialised* in the sense it is developed by experts in clearly defined subject groups who work in fields of enquiry with socially and historically fixed boundaries.

We will return to the concept of 'powerful knowledge' and indeed to social justice later. We will also extol the importance of these subject disciplines and argue that the curriculum should be designed by the experts in each specialism. But first let us consider what role senior leaders can play in the curriculum design process…

CHAPTER FIVE
THE ROLE OF SENIOR LEADERS

In truth, the process of curriculum design is largely within the purview of middle leaders and teachers because subject specialists must design a curriculum that befits their discipline.

An English curriculum is distinct from a Maths curriculum, which is distinct from a Science curriculum and so on. The key concepts are different and will likely take different forms; the ways in which experts in each field think differ, too – for example, if you apply a scientific way of thinking to the study of Theology, it will fail, and vice versa.

Language and its meanings also differ in each subject – for example, to 'analyse' something in English is not quite the same as to 'analyse' something in History, Maths or Science.

The shape of the curriculum in each subject discipline is different, too – some are linear, some helical or spiral in nature – and so the time it takes pupils to progress through a curriculum and the path they must take is, by definition, different.

In some subjects, we may see a neat line of progress as pupils incrementally increase their knowledge and skills and build upon their prior learning. In other subjects, pupils will likely go backwards as well as forwards, or will succeed in one topic but then be required to learn a different, unconnected set of skills and knowledge, which means any attempts to extrapolate progress between the two points is meaningless. For example, a pupil may excel in football in term one, but might not be as adept at tennis in term two, and so their progress, if a line is drawn between the two terms, may look negative when in fact we are comparing apples and oranges.

In short, each subject *is* a subject in its own right precisely because of the differences between it and other subjects, and so subject specialists must be allowed to design a curriculum that works in their discipline. As a secondary English specialist, I can design an English curriculum for key stages 3, 4 and 5, but I could not do so for Science or indeed for my own subject at key stages 1 and 2 without first deepening by knowledge of how pupils learn the knowledge and skills required at this level. Only subject specialists are equipped with the depth of knowledge and understanding to make decisions about curriculum design.

Remember what Michael Young said about powerful knowledge in the previous chapter: it is *systematic* in that it is based on concepts that are related to each other in groups we call disciplines rather than rooted in real-life experience; and is *specialised* in the sense it is developed by experts in clearly defined subject groups who work in fields of enquiry with socially and historically fixed boundaries.

It would be easy, therefore, for senior leaders to feel impotent, disenfranchised and divorced from the process.

However, I think senior leaders have five key roles to play:

Firstly, it is the responsibility of senior leaders to **agree the vision** for their whole school or college curriculum. This, as we have already explored, involves defining what is meant by the term 'curriculum' and making decisions about the national, basic, local and hidden curriculums.

Secondly, senior leaders – particularly the curriculum and timetable leads – are key to determining how broad and balanced the whole school or college curriculum will be and why. They must make decisions about **which subject disciplines and vocations matter most** and **which subjects are afforded the most time** on the timetable. For example, senior leaders must be attuned to their community and learner needs and if their school population predominantly has English as an additional language (EAL), they may decide to timetable more English lessons.

Thirdly, senior leaders **articulate the purpose of education** in their school or college – and therefore guide middle leaders in determining the broad 'end-points' (schools) or 'body of knowledge' (FE) to be taught. For example, senior leaders must have an overview of what qualification types and levels are offered in their school or college, and must ensure that their offer meets local needs (including learner needs, employer needs, community needs, etc) and that each entry-point to their curriculum leads to a higher level of study and/or into meaningful employment rather than to a series of dead-ends. Only senior leaders have the necessary oversight of the whole school or college curriculum to be able to make these decisions.

Senior leaders can also help their middle leaders and subject specialists to determine the 'end-points' or 'body of knowledge' they plan to teach within their subjects by asking some broad questions about their curriculums such as those which follow:

Why?

- Why teach this subject? Why does it matter? In what way is it or will it be useful?
- Why teach this qualification? Why this level of study?
- Why (for examined courses) use this awarding body and this specification?
- Why teach this module/topic? Why is this knowledge more important than this?
- How does this subject relate to other subjects? How will you make the links explicit?

What?

- What do you expect pupils/learners to know and be able to do at the end of the topic/scheme/term/year/course/school or college?
- Why is this knowledge important? Who decides and why?
- What knowledge and skills will be most useful to pupils in the future? Says who? Is this likely to change?
- What knowledge gaps (inc. vocabulary) might some pupils need to have filled before they can access the curriculum? How will you identify the gaps and the pupils? How and when will the gaps be filled?

When?

- When do you expect pupils/learners to have acquired this knowledge/skills?
- Why then?
- What must be taught before and after this knowledge/skills? Why?

- How will the learning be sequenced? Is this a logical order?
- How will the curriculum build increasing complexity over time?
- Does each entry-point to the curriculum lead to a higher level of study and/or into meaningful employment? (If you offer a Level 1 course, do you also offer a suitable Level 2 course, and so on?)

How?

- How will this knowledge/skills be taught to ensure long-term learning? Will all teachers teach in this manner? How will you know?
- How will prior knowledge be activated? How will pupils be helped to transfer knowledge/skills from one context to another, and from the classroom to life/work?
- How will retrieval practice be built into the curriculum to ensure prior learning is kept active?
- How will the curriculum be spaced and interleaved to aide long-term retention?

Fourthly, senior leaders **create the culture** in which a curriculum flourishes. This, I think, has three layers:

1. **The staff culture;**

2. **The pupil and student culture; and**

3. **The learning culture.**

Finally, and perhaps most critically of all, senior leaders are the gatekeepers and defenders of staff skills and time. They have a duty to **provide appropriate training** to staff to ensure they are skilled at curriculum thinking, and they have a duty to **provide protected time** for staff to engage in the time-consuming task of designing, delivering and reviewing the curriculum in their subjects.

With a just focus on teacher workload, senior leaders must do all they can to prevent this renewed focus on curriculum design adding to teachers' workloads and must decide what to stop doing in order to carve out the time for teachers to focus their energy on 'the real substance of education'.

Over the course of the next three chapters, we'll now take a closer look at some of these five aspects of senior curriculum leadership: In Chapter Six we will look at creating the culture; in Chapter Seven we will look at teacher professional development; and in Chapter Eight we will look at teacher workload...

CHAPTER SIX
CREATING THE CULTURE FOR CURRICULUM TO THRIVE

One of the key aspects of senior curriculum leadership I outlined in Chapter Five was creating the culture in which a curriculum can flourish. There are – I think – three layers to this culture: the staff culture; the pupil or student culture; and the learning culture. Let's take a look at each in turn…

1. The staff culture

In 'Rule Makers, Rule Breakers', the psychologist Michele Gelfand asks what ultimately drives human behaviour. Do ideals, symbols and beliefs lead people to act as they do? Or are our motivators less ethereal: money, fear, thirst for power, circumstance and opportunity, with culture only an afterthought?

Gelfand comes down firmly on the side on the culturalists: "Culture is a stubborn mystery of our experience and one of the last uncharted frontiers." And the most important ingredients of culture, she argues, are the social norms, the often-informal rules of conduct, the dos and don'ts that emerge whenever people band together.

And it is this notion of 'people banding together' that is so crucial to the sort of staff culture in our schools and colleges that will help our curriculum to flourish because the kind of workplace environment we want to foster is one of collaboration not competition… let me explain why…

In a paper pithily entitled 'Organisational Blueprints for Success in High-

Tech Start-Ups: Lessons from the Stanford Project on Emerging Companies' by James N. Baron and Michael T. Hannan, published in the California Management Review in 2002, the authors proposed five different models of organisational structure: the star model; the engineering model; the commitment model; the bureaucratic model; and the autocratic model.

The only culture that was a consistent winner - lasting the course and sustaining success - was the one built on <u>commitment</u>. In fact, "commitment" organisations outperformed every other type of organisation in almost every meaningful way. Organisations which followed the "commitment" model were focused on creating a culture in which people happily worked for the same company their whole careers.

Leaders in 'commitment' cultures want to create a strong family-like environment. They want employees to be bound to their organisation by a sense of personal belonging and identification; in other words, by a love of their school and what they do.

In commitment cultures, there is a sense of trust among staff and leaders that entices everyone to work harder and stick together through the setbacks that are inevitable. There are also higher levels of teamwork and psychological safety in these cultures.

So, what does 'commitment' look like in practice in schools and colleges?

In the best schools and colleges, the staffroom remains a hub - it is busy with staff sharing and listening; offloading and laughing. Conversely, in the least successful schools, the staffroom is either non-existent or deserted; instead, staff work in departmental silos or, worse, alone in their classrooms.

In the best schools and colleges, I would argue, the canteen and corridors are calm, friendly places - respected and kept clean by everyone. People are polite, greeting you with a smile; and they are purposeful, focused on learning and teaching. In the least successful schools, meanwhile, there's a threatening atmosphere of chaos and confusion. There are no-go areas, behaviour isn't tackled because there is no leadership from the top: rather, behaviour is regarded as a teacher's responsibility and if they can't manage it, they alone are to blame.

In the best schools and colleges, leaders develop a 'no-blame' culture. They believe that, just because someone has made a mistake, this doesn't mean they should suddenly forget the important contribution which the same colleague makes every day. In fact, in such situations, they know that staff need to feel supported and trusted to learn from their mistake and to move on. When things are going well, meanwhile, the best leaders are generous with their praise and recognition.

Let's take a closer look at no-blame cultures…

No-blame cultures have proven vital to the success of organisations. In 'Black Box Thinking' (2015), Matthew Syed says that the most successful organisations in the world - and he uses the example of aviation - show a willingness and tenacity to investigate the lessons that often exist when we fail, but which we rarely exploit. A no-blame culture, Syed argues, is about creating systems and cultures that enable organisations to learn from errors, rather than being threatened by them.

After all, practice - which we teachers tell our pupils is a vital part of the learning process - is all about harnessing the benefits of learning from failure while reducing its cost. As Syed says, "It is better to fail in practice in preparation for the big stage than on the big stage itself." Or, as Eleanor Roosevelt put it, we should "learn from the mistakes of others [because we] can't live long enough to make them all [ourselves]".

Syed says the 'paradox of success' is that is it build upon failure. Everything we know in, say, aviation, every rule in the rule book, every procedure we have, we know because someone somewhere died. As Syed phrases it: "We have purchased at great cost, lessons literally bought with blood that we have to preserve as institutional knowledge and pass on to succeeding generations. We cannot have the moral failure of forgetting these lessons and have to relearn them."

And yet we can only learn from failure if there is an openness to admit to mistakes. If staff feel threatened of owning up to errors, they are less likely to do so and so that rich seam of intelligence will be lost to us, we'll keep on making the same mistakes over and again. Only if we operate a no-blame culture will colleagues willingly admit when they get it wrong and then we can work together to get it right next time.

This is why the best teams seemingly make the most mistakes. They don't; they just admit and record them more willingly and more often. Closeted teams who fear failure and blame, don't record their mistakes and so appear, to the outside, to be more successful. This is why the world of medicine appears more infallible than the world of aviation: doctors, particularly in the US where there is a litigious culture, rarely admit to making surgical mistakes. Rather, whenever things go wrong in the operating theatre, it's about inherent risk and factors outside their control. Pilots, meanwhile, alive through testimony and dead through black boxes, openly articulate what they did wrong so that the profession can learn from it and make flying safer and safer.

Senior leaders in the best schools and colleges, then, build trust and openness, and thus develop autonomy, mastery and purpose. They build for the future; they develop sustainable models by investing in their people and reducing attrition.

In terms of curriculum design, senior leaders need to create a culture in which middle leaders and teachers are encouraged to honestly self-reflect and admit to mistakes. They need to review the effectiveness of their curriculum and make changes to it without fear. A curriculum must be a living, breathing thing – constantly under review and constantly evolving in response to the shifting landscape and to assessment data. If the initial draft of the curriculum doesn't work as well as anticipated, middle leaders must be allowed the breathing space of a no-blame culture to learn from their mistakes and to improve their curriculum.

2. The pupil and student culture

Once we've built a staff culture on the foundations of commitment, no-blame and trust, we need all staff to foster the right pupil and student culture and one of the best ways to do this is to define a set of social norms for what constitutes good behaviour, and this is much more than the reduction or elimination of poor behaviour.

The Bennett Report (2017), written for the DfE, argues that school leaders – not just teachers - have a crucial role to play in creating cultures that optimise pupil behaviour.

In 'Promoting the conditions for positive behaviour' (2012), meanwhile, Phillip Garner says that "It remains clear that successful outcomes for students in school, including the promotion of good behaviour and learning, can be firmly linked to effective leadership."

Senior leaders have a crucial role to play here in terms of consulting on, agreeing and articulating their school's or college's social norms for behaviour and then ensuring that these are established and enforced by every adult working there. See again what I said in Chapter One about the importance of the hidden and unplanned curriculums.

Bennett, in his 2017 report, says that an effective student culture occurs when there are:

- committed, highly visible school leaders, with ambitious goals, supported by a strong leadership team
- effectively communicated, realistic, detailed expectations understood clearly by all members of the school
- highly consistent working practices throughout the school
- a clear understanding of what the school culture is 'this is how we do things around here, and these are the values we hold'
- high levels of staff and parental commitment to the school vision and strategies
- high levels of support between leadership and staff, for example, staff training
- attention to detail and thoroughness in the execution of school policies and strategies
- high expectations of all students and staff, and a belief that all students matter equally

When the student culture fails, it is likely because there is:

- A lack of clarity of vision, or poor communication of that vision to staff or students
- A lack of sufficient in-school classroom management skills
- Poorly calibrated, or low expectations
- Inadequate orientation for new staff or students
- A burdensome workload for staff, who are therefore unable to direct behaviour effectively
- Unsuitably skilled staff in charge of pivotal behaviour roles
- Remote, unavailable, or over-occupied leadership
- Inconsistency between staff and departments

The Bennett report argues that the right culture is best created in three stages, by:

1. *Designing* the culture,
2. *Building* the culture, and
3. *Maintaining* the culture.

Let's explore each stage in turn…

Designing the culture:

A key role for senior leaders is to design a detailed vision of what the culture should look like for their school or college, focusing on social and academic conduct. Expectations must be as high as possible, for all.

Designing the school or college culture is about agreeing social norms that you'd want to see reproduced throughout the whole community. Here, senior leaders must ask, 'What would I like all students to do, routinely?' 'What do I want them to believe about themselves, their achievements, each other, the school/college?' Once these questions have been answered, senior leaders can then translate these aspirations into expectations.

Social norms are found most clearly in the routines of the school or college. Any aspect of behaviour that can be standardised because it is expected from all students at all times should be, for example walking on the left or right of the corridor, entering the class, entering assembly, clearing tables at lunch. These routines should be communicated to, and practiced by, staff and pupils until they become automatic. This then frees up time, mental effort and energy towards more useful areas, such as study.

Building the culture:

Next, senior leaders need to build the culture in practice with as much detail and clarity as possible. Staff and students need to know how to achieve this, and what the culture looks like in practice from behaviour on buses, to corridor and canteen conduct, and behaviour in the workplace when on work placements or engaging in work-based learning. This means demonstrating it, communicating it thoroughly, and ensuring that every aspect of school life feeds into and reinforces that culture.

One way to build the culture is to design routines that students and staff should follow. Any behaviour that should be performed identically, most or all of the time, should be made into a routine, for example, which side of the corridor to walk down, how to queue for lunch.

The school or college must have well-established and universally-known and understood systems of behaviour, for example, student removal, consequences, and sanctions, corridor and classroom expectations, behaviour on trips, arrival, transition and departure behaviour and so on. Any area of general behaviour that can be sensibly translated into a routine should be done so explicitly. This removes uncertainty about school expectations from mundane areas of school life, which reduces anxiety, creates a framework of social norms, and reduces the need for reflection and reinvention of what is and is not acceptable conduct. This in turn saves time and effort that would otherwise be expended in repetitive instruction. These routines should be seen as the aspiration of all members of the school community whenever possible.

Maintaining the culture:

Once built, school and college systems require regular maintenance. This is often where good cultures break down. Bennett argues that it is reasonably straightforward to identify what a good culture might look like, but like a diet, the difficulty lies in embedding and maintaining it. This includes staff training, effective use of consequences, data monitoring, staff and student surveys and maintaining standards.

3. The learning culture

As well as creating the right pupil and student culture and using rewards and sanctions, senior leaders need to build the right learning culture and – amongst other means - this can be done through the use of assemblies, displays, expectations around punctuality and appearance, and what happens if pupils and students do not come to class with the right equipment…

Assemblies

In several of the schools visited for the Bennett report, assemblies were regarded as important cultural markers. Here, core school values were reinforced, both implicitly (through speaker and topic choice, rewards and reminders) and explicitly (direct reference to school rules). Time spent in assemblies was seen as a valuable adjunct and scaffold of the whole school life, rather than a bolt on or buffer between registration and first lessons.

Additionally, assemblies frequently followed clear routines with rigour, timings, music played upon entrance, songs, prayers made if required, entrance and exit procedures. In this way, the day begins with calm, a sense of structure, and a valuable reminder to students and staff within the school premises that expectations began long before the classroom.

Wall displays

Display work can send a powerful message to pupils, students and staff. Bennett found that of particular importance was the celebration of achievement. Work of the highest standard was celebrated, as was recent as well as historic achievements of the school. Letters of praise from parents and community leaders were seen in several schools.

Timekeeping

Perhaps unsurprisingly, successful schools pay close attention to, and make good use of, time, and regard it as a precious commodity. Particular emphasis is placed on lesson transitions and scheduled breaks.

Uniforms

Some schools use uniform to help instil a sense of communal identity, by making their neat execution a way of communicating a sense of self-pride, pride in their institutional membership, and how they convey themselves to the world. If uniform rules do not need to be followed, why follow any other rule?

Stationery/equipment

A lack of appropriate materials is an impediment to learning. The best habit is to have all items to hand whenever needed. Habituating students to this routine prevents many misbehaviours and conflicts before they occur. Bennett argues that it is school leaders' responsibility to filter every aspect of their school's culture through the lens of their expectations and decide for themselves how they can use every opportunity available to convey the school's expectations, beliefs and values.

Attendance and punctuality

Attendance and punctuality are an important part of good behaviour and, therefore, of the student culture. Students who miss valuable time in classrooms fall further behind and become more disengaged from the work of the class, which in turn encourages misbehaviour.

Positive learning environment

A positive learning environment is one in which pupils' senses are stimulated so that they pay attention to the right things and are made to think hard but efficiently about curriculum content.

A positive learning environment is also one in which pupils are challenged by hard work but know that they are safe to take risks and make mistakes.

To my mind, amongst other things, a positive learning environment is one in which all pupils:

- Feel welcomed,
- Feel valued,
- Are enthusiastic about learning,
- Are engaged in their learning,
- Are eager to experiment, and
- Feel rewarded for their hard work.

Behind all these characteristics - and any more we care to mention - is a simple, albeit oxymoronic, aim: to ensure pupils are comfortable with discomfort.

In other words, we want our pupils to know that the work they'll be asked to do in our classrooms will be tough, that they will be challenged with hard work and made to think. We want our pupils to know that there will be no hiding place in our classrooms; they must ask and answer questions and attempt everything we ask of them.

However, in so doing, we want them to feel safe and protected, we want them to be eager for challenge, and to willingly attempt hard work because they know that we've strung a safety net beneath them: yes, they might falter but we will catch them if they fall.

We also want our pupils to know that taking risks and making mistakes is not just accepted in our classrooms but is positively and proactively welcomed as an essential part of the learning process. Indeed, the only people who don't make mistakes either never get any better at anything or have reached the point of automaticity - they have fully mastered something and so can now do it through habit.

Our pupils are not at the point of automaticity and so must make mistakes if they are to get better in our subject. If they don't make mistakes, they cannot receive feedback; if they don't receive feedback, they will not know how to improve; if they don't know how to improve, then they are unlikely to do so.

There are many ways of achieving a positive learning environment in which pupils are comfortable with discomfort: some are simple common sense; some are more complex...

Let's take each of the hallmarks I list above in turn and discuss some tangible ways of achieving them – but with an important caveat: although these hallmarks rely on teachers developing good habits in their classrooms, it is the responsibility of senior leaders (as part of their senior curriculum leadership responsibilities) to create the whole-school or college culture in which these are the norm and in which consistency is key.

Firstly, I said a positive learning environment is one in which pupils feel welcomed. The best - and simplest - way of achieving this is to physically welcome them into our classrooms. For example, we could establish a habit of greeting pupils at the classroom door at the start of every lesson, and then do so with a smile and by greeting some pupils by name. For some pupils in some contexts, that might be the first time someone - an adult, at least - has acknowledged their existence. If we can't show our pupils that we are pleased to see them and eager to teach them, then can we really expect them to be pleased to be in our lesson?

Secondly, I said a positive learning environment is one in which pupils feel valued. We can achieve this by making sure we're on time and have a lesson planned and ready to go. We can also do this by creating a culture whereby everyone's contributions are welcomed and given the time and attention they deserve. This might involve explicitly teaching and repeatedly reinforcing, not to mention modelling, debating skills such as active listening. Valuing each pupil's contribution is not the same as agreeing with everything they say. Indeed, if a pupil gives a wrong answer then they need to know it's wrong and why it's wrong. But a pupil's response doesn't have to be right for it to be useful.

Thirdly, I said that we want pupils to be enthusiastic about learning. This is, in part, achieved by developing pupils' intrinsic motivation but this isn't always possible and is rarely easy. So, another tangible, teacher-led strategy for enthusing pupils is to model that enthusiasm by constantly articulating - through our words and actions - our joy at teaching our pupils and at teaching our subject. In this regard, sometimes a little over-acting goes a long way. It's better to be considered the kooky, eccentric teacher who's truly, madly, deeply in love with science, say, than the boring, staid one who never cracks a smile and only perseveres for the pension.

Fourthly, we want our pupils to be engaged in their learning. But what is 'engagement' and why does it matter? Let me return to the point with which I started this chapter: fun is never our goal as teachers; we don't need pupils to enjoy our lessons in order to learn. We need them to think about the right things. If they happen to enjoy what they do, then that's an added bonus. But 'fun activities' are not our guiding star; rather, thinking hard but efficiently about curriculum content is.

So, when I talk about pupils being engaged in their learning I do not mean - or do not solely mean - that they are enjoying what they're doing. Instead, I mean that they are actively paying attention to the right things and are thinking hard. It's about being engaged (as in 'meaningfully occupied by or connected to') as distinct from enjoying (as in 'taking pleasure from').

It's understandable that we should want our pupils to enjoy our lessons and to be busy, but the emphasis should not be on enjoyment and it's not desirable to employ a strategy in which pupils are engaged by something that appears interesting but leads to little substantive learning or, at any rate, slows down the process of learning because this will prove ultimately demotivating. In other words, their initial interest and their investment of time and energy will gradually fade then disappear altogether because motivation can only be maintained if it is accompanied by positive results. Without positive results, demotivation - and indeed amotivation - quickly develops.

Our goal as teachers should therefore be to ensure our pupils learn in an effective, efficient, and enjoyable way (in that order).

Yes, we want pupils to be motivated and engaged but motivation and engagement are no substitutes for learning, nor can they be a proxy for learning.

In a paper in July 2017, Paul Kirschner said that he'd "long thought that one of the weakest proxy indicators of effective learning [was] engagement, and yet it's a term persistently used by school leaders (and some researchers) as one of the most important measures of quality. In fact, many of the things we've traditionally associated with effective teachers may not be indicative of students actually learning anything at all."

Kirschner urged "fellow researchers, teachers, trainers, instructional designers, and all other learning professionals" to "agree that motivation, engagement, fun, and many other positive emotions during learning are great to strive for but let's first go for learning."

After all, without learning, what's the point of pupils being motivated and engaged?

Fifthly, I said a positive learning environment was one in which pupils are eager to experiment. Taking risks and making mistakes is an essential part of the learning process; it should not simply be accepted, rather we must positively and proactively encourage it. But why is taking risks and making mistakes so desirable?

Allow me to explain...

Matthew Syed is three-time Commonwealth table-tennis champion. In 1995 at the tender age of 25, he became the British number one. To put that into some kind of perspective, there are 2.4 million players in Britain, 30,000 paid up members of the governing body and thousands of teams. So, what marked Syed out for excellence? Was it his speed, guile, mental strength, agility and reflexes? There was certainly no silver spoon, no nepotism. He came from an ordinary family in an ordinary suburb of an ordinary town in south-east England.

In his book, 'Bounce' (2010), Syed argues that "we like to think that sport is a meritocracy - where achievement is driven by ability and hard work - but it is nothing of the sort". He goes on to say that, "Practically every man and woman who triumphs against the odds is, on closer inspection, a beneficiary of unusual circumstances. The delusion lies in focusing on the individuality of their triumph without perceiving - or bothering to look for - the powerful opportunities stacked in their favour."

Syed says his was not a triumph of individuality, a personal odyssey of success, or a triumph against the odds; it was the result of a fortunate set of circumstances. His parents bought him a table-tennis table and they were lucky enough to have a garage big enough to house it. He had a brother who loved table-tennis as much as he did and with whom he could practice daily. He had a teacher who just happened to be the nation's top coach and a senior figure in the Table Tennis Association. His local club, Omega, was open 24 hours a day and gave out keys to its select group of members so that they could practice endlessly at any time of day and night.

As a result of these circumstances, the local area produced a number of top players not just Syed. His brother won three national titles; one of the top female players of her generation lived in the house opposite and won countless junior titles and a national senior title; in-between their two houses lived another successful player who went on to win a series of doubles titles. There were other outstanding players in the neighbourhood, too, which meant that this one ordinary street in Reading produced more outstanding table tennis players than the rest of the country put together.

This supports the famous claim made by Malcolm Gladwell in his book, 'Outliers' (2008), that outstanding performance is not about 'who you are' but rather 'what you do' and 'where you come from'.

What, then, is talent? Anders Ericsson, a psychologist at Florida State University, conducted an investigation into the causes of outstanding performance. His subjects were violinists from the Music Academy of West Berlin. He divided his subjects into three groups: the first group were the outstanding violinists who were expected to become soloists; the second group were very good (though not as accomplished as the first group) and were expected to join the world's top orchestras; the third group were good but the least able and were expected to become music teachers (no offence to any music teachers reading this). The 'setting' of the three groups was based on assessment conducted by the academy's professors and on the level of success the pupils had enjoyed in open competitions.

The biographical details of all the pupils were very similar with no systematic differences: they each began playing the violin when they were aged 8; they each decided to become musicians when they were 14; they each had the same number of music teachers and had studied the same number of musical instruments beyond the violin. In fact, there was only one difference, but it was quite a striking one: the number of hours they had devoted to practice.

By the age of twenty, the pupils in the first group had practised an average of ten thousand hours which is over two thousand hours more than the second group and over six thousand hours more than the third group. Ericsson found that there were no exceptions to this pattern: nobody in the first group who had reached the top of their game had done so without copious amounts of practice; and nobody who had worked so hard had failed to excel. The only distinguishing feature between the best and the rest was purposeful practice: the best were eager to experiment; the best took risks and made mistakes.

Jack Nicklaus, the most successful golfer of all time, has said the same thing: "Nobody - but nobody - has ever become really proficient at golf without practice, without doing a lot of thinking and then hitting a lot of shots. It isn't so much a lack of talent; it's a lack of being able to repeat good shots consistently that frustrates most players. And the only answer to that is practice."

Syed quantifies the amount of 'purposeful practice' that is required in order to achieve excellence. He points out that extensive research has come up with a specific answer: "from art to science and from board games to tennis, it has been found that a minimum of ten years is required to reach world-class status in any complex task". Malcolm Gladwell, meanwhile, asserts that most top performers practise for around one thousand hours per year.

There is a logic here: if someone believes that attaining excellence relies solely on talent, they are more likely to give up if they do not show early promise. However, if they believe that talent is not a (or is not the only) factor in achieving excellence then they are more likely to persevere.

Anders Ericsson calls talent the 'iceberg illusion'. In other words, when we witness excellence, we are witnessing the end product of a process that took years to realise. The countless hours of practice that have gone into this end result of excellence are invisible to us - they are submerged beneath the icy waters leaving only the tip of excellence visible.

Syed says that "world class performance comes by striving for a target just out of reach, but with a vivid awareness of how the gap might be breached". This is why great teachers do not 'dumb down' but provide real challenge for their pupils.

Syed says that "ten thousand hours of purposeful practice" is required to achieve excellence. By 'purposeful' he means "concentration and dedication" but also having "access to the right training system, and that sometimes means living in the right town or having the right coach".

When we transfer the idea of excellence to schools and colleges, having the right training system or method is easier to realise and less concerned with good fortune. It is about teachers creating the right conditions in their classrooms for learning to take place. It is about providing challenge for all through an ambitious curriculum, not 'dumbing down' or reducing our offer; it is about providing a safe and secure atmosphere in which it is not only acceptable to make mistakes but it is positively encouraged because to make mistakes is to learn.

Syed cites the Olympic figure-skater Shizuka Arakawa as an example of the importance of making mistakes. Arakawa fell down more than twenty thousand times in her pursuit of excellence. Syed says, "When examining [Shizuka's] story, the one question...to ask was: Why would anyone endure all that? Why would she keep striving in the teeth of constant failure? Why not give up and try something else?... It is because she did not interpret falling down as failure. Armed with a growth mindset, she interpreted falling down not merely as a means of improving, but as evidence that she was improving. Failure was not something that sapped her energy and vitality, but something that provided her with an opportunity to learn, develop, and adapt."

If this seems odd, Syed reminds us that in an advert for Nike, Michael Jordan declared: "I've missed more than nine thousand shots. I've lost almost three hundred games. Twenty-six times I've been trusted to take the game-winning shot and missed." In other words, in order to become the greatest basketball player of all time, Jordan had first to embrace failure. Jordan has said that "mental toughness and heart are a lot stronger than some of the physical advantages you might have." Thomas Edison said the same thing: "If I find 10,000 ways something won't work, I haven't failed. I am not discouraged, because every wrong attempt discarded is another step forward."

In 'Bounce', Syed asks us to think of life having two paths: one leading to mediocrity, the other to excellence. The path to mediocrity, he says, is "flat and straight [and] it is possible to cruise along on autopilot with a nice, smooth, steady, almost effortless progression [and] you can reach your destination without stumbling and falling over". The path to excellence, meanwhile, "could not be more different...it is steep, gruelling, and arduous. It is inordinately lengthy, requiring a minimum of ten thousand hours of lung-busting effort to get to the summit [and] it forces voyagers to stumble and fall on every single stretch of the journey."

Excellence, after all, is about "striving for what is just out of reach and not quite making it; it is about grappling with tasks beyond current limitations and falling short again and again." In short, excellence is about experimenting, taking risks and making mistakes, and learning from those mistakes in order to move, incrementally, towards automaticity.

A recap: so far, we have explored the importance of pupils feeling welcomed and valued, enthusiastic and engaged, and eager to experiment. The final feature of our positive learning environment, I said, was that pupils feel rewarded for their hard work…

Rewarding hard work and effort not only creates a level playing field on which every pupil has equal chance of scoring a goal (because everyone can try hard, after all), it also makes explicit the progress each pupil is making from their individual starting point. Not every pupil can achieve a grade 9 but every pupil can improve to beat their previous score.

One way to reward hard work is to cease comparing pupils with each other for that is a meaningless comparison (they are not the same person). Rather, we should compare each pupil with their earlier self and show them how far they've already come and where they need to go next.

All of the above features of the learning culture – and indeed the staff and student cultures – are ways in which senior leaders can help their school or college curriculum to flourish by affording an ambitious curriculum to all, creating a safe environment in which pupils willingly accept challenge and hard work, and in which good learning habits become the norm, consistently followed and reinforced by all.

CHAPTER SEVEN
IMPROVING PROFESSIONAL DEVELOPMENT

Another of the key aspects of senior curriculum leadership I outlined in Chapter Five was providing appropriate training to staff to ensure they are skilled at curriculum thinking. Teacher continuing professional development (CPD) is crucial if our curriculum is to be successful and it features prominently in the new EIF...

Under Ofsted's new 'quality of education' judgment, consideration is given to how school leaders align continuing professional development for teachers and staff with the curriculum, and the extent to which they develop teachers' knowledge over time.

Teacher professional development is also placed up-front and centre in 'leadership and management'; specifically, the twofold nature of CPD: developing subject knowledge *and* developing pedagogical content knowledge – the *what* and the *how* of teaching, if you like.

'Dual professionalism' is crucial to effective curriculum design and delivery because teachers need to deepen their understanding of their discipline *and* deepen their understanding of how to teach that discipline in a way that makes sense to pupils - seeing their expertise through the eyes of the novice pupil and pre-empting their likely misunderstandings, misconceptions and questions – if they are to have the knowledge and skills required of curriculum experts. Subject knowledge without pedagogical content knowledge is not enough; and vice versa.

Therefore, it is incumbent upon senior leaders to plan opportunities for their teachers to engage in professional development that aims to achieve these dual functions. Often, schools are good at providing staff with generic CPD such as a training course on feedback or metacognition. But they are less effective at helping their staff to update and upskill their subject knowledge, including through engagement with subject associations and by attending subject-specific training or reading academic research in their specialism.

Why CPD matters

With this in mind, let us start with this important - yet oft forgotten - truth about education: teachers - and what happens in their classrooms - are the main drivers of positive change in our schools. The only way to improve the quality of teaching, therefore, is to improve the quality of our teachers. And the only way to improve the quality of our teachers is to treat them fairly and with respect, and to train them well and continue to develop them throughout their careers.

Improving the quality of teachers requires systems of collaboration so that professional development becomes an everyday, collaborative exercise not an end of year 'sheep-dip' activity 'done to' teachers by school leaders.

Improving the quality of teachers requires professional development to be personalised, tailored to meet individual needs, so that it is made meaningful and encompasses all aspects of self-improvement activity - such as reading research, watching colleagues teach, working with a coach, and engaging in lesson study - not just attending a generic, formal training course.

Improving the quality of teachers also requires professional development to recognise hard work in all its forms - even the quiet, 'just doing my job' kind - and to encourage rather than stifle team-work, and to favour collaboration over competition.

In short, improving the quality of teachers is about building a mature, adult culture in which teachers and school leaders work together in the best interests of their pupils to improve the quality of teaching in their schools and to do so without fear or favour.

So how can schools and colleges ensure that they provide high quality professional development for their staff in order to support the process of curriculum development, and do so without drilling a big hole in their diminishing budgets?

The Standard for Teacher Professional Development (2016) - together with the ETF Professional Standards (FE colleges) and the DfE Teachers' Standards (schools) - may just hold the key. The five strands of the Standard are as follows:

1. Professional development should have a focus on improving and evaluating pupil outcomes.
2. Professional development should be underpinned by robust evidence and expertise.
3. Professional development should include collaboration and expert challenge.
4. Professional development programmes should be sustained over time.
5. Professional development must be prioritised by senior leadership.

So, what does this look like in practice and how can schools and colleges deliver it?

As the Standard suggests, the most effective professional development is collaborative and driven by teachers. Professional development, therefore, should involve responding to advice and feedback from colleagues, and reflecting systematically on the effectiveness of lessons and approaches to teaching. This might take the form of peer-observations and feedback, of peer-coaching, or of more formal lesson study activities. It might also take the form of peer-to-peer work scrutiny, both of pupils' marked work and assessment records, and of medium- and long-term planning documentation.

Whatever form it takes, the best professional development gives ownership to staff and creates the time and space needed for them to work together, sharing best practice and learning from each other's mistakes.

Another way to ensure that professional development is effective is to make it an unmissable event, tailored to meet the differing needs of departments and teachers. Every member of staff should recognise the importance of professional development as a mandatory part of their jobs – not as a voluntary extra. But they'll only do that when professional development is worth engaging in and it will only be worth engaging in when it is relevant, timely, keenly focused on real classroom practice, and genuinely and tangibly impactful.

In order to ensure relevance and focus, professional development should be influenced by research evidence but informed by context. In other words, it should take its lead from what research indicates works but be mindful of the unique circumstances of each school and college, subject, teacher and cohort of pupils.

As well as being unmissable, professional development should be regular, embedded and joined-up. Professional development should be seen as a collaborative enterprise involving all staff working together, rather than something which is 'done to' them by senior leaders.

Professional development also works best when it performs the twin functions of innovation and mastery. In other words, professional development should not just be about learning new ways of working – professional development for innovation - although this is undoubtedly important. Rather, it should also be about helping teachers to get better at something they already do – professional development for mastery. Professional development for mastery is about recognising what already works well and what should therefore be embedded, consolidated, built upon, and shared.

I'd like to share two approaches to professional development which I think may help teachers to improve their curriculum knowledge and work more collaboratively on curriculum planning: lesson study and professional learning communities…

Lesson study

According to Vivianne Robinson (2009), "Taking part in collaborative enquiries into improving teaching and learning is the single most impactful action a school leader can take to improve educational outcomes for pupils."

Lesson Study is one way of achieving this and it can be used as an alternative to the high stakes lesson observation. Lesson Study is a planned programme of teacher enquiry which originated in Japan. It enables teachers to work collaboratively in order to explore and improve their own practice. However, it requires a strong commitment from staff and is time-consuming. As such, school leaders must be serious about setting time aside for teachers to meet, observe each other, and give feedback. This might involve getting cover for some lessons.

Lesson Study usually involves a group of between two and four teachers (most often it's three called a triad or four called a quad) working collaboratively to plan a lesson, predict pupil reactions to that lesson, observe the reality, interview pupils, and then reflect and repeat the process. The group works best when there is a range of teaching experience and when one member is a more senior member of staff.

When observing each other and interviewing pupils, the triad focuses on three "case study students" rather than the whole class. This allows a more detailed exploration of the effects of their teaching on pupils' learning.

Here's the process:

Firstly, perhaps with the help of a coach or subject leader, the triad/quad identifies a research question – using data collected from their assessments of pupils – such as 'What impact will peer-assessment have on the quality of the written work of Year 11 grade 3/4 borderline pupils in the response to non-fiction unit of GCSE English?'

The research question, like the one above, should be focused and specific; it should identify the learning outcome which the Lesson Study seeks to improve (e.g. the quality of written work); the pupils who will be involved in the study (Year 11 3/4 borderline English pupils); the teaching and learning strategy which is to be tested (peer-assessment); and the unit or scheme of work (GCSE English 'response to non-fiction').

It's also important at the planning stage that the teachers in the triad identify the means by which they will evaluate the impact of their project. For example, the triad might want to create a test for pupils to complete before and after the project and agree a set of interview questions for pupils to answer.

Secondly, the lesson is planned collaboratively and is then taught and observed. The observation is focused on the case study pupils' learning and progress; it is not a general observation of the quality of teaching and learning. The process may be repeated, and the activities refined over time. Not all the lessons in the study need to be observed.

One alternative to 'live' peer-observation – and a potential solution to the problem of cover – is to use video technology to record lessons for later viewing. Whatever method is used to observe lessons, it should be made clear that observations are not high stakes. Indeed, because the lessons have been co-planned, there should be less fear and more trust built into the process. Also, the foci of observation are the case study pupils rather than the teacher.

Thirdly, the case study pupils are interviewed in order to gain an insight into their responses to the activity. A discussion is held with the research group to analyse how pupils have responded to the teaching strategy, what progress they have made, what they found difficult and what can be learned about how to develop the teaching strategy further.

Finally, the outcomes are shared with a wider audience (perhaps the whole department or staff).

Here's the process again in summary form:

1. Three or four teachers plan a lesson together
2. The activity they plan addresses a specific learning outcome
3. Teachers predict how pupils will react to the activity
4. A case study of three pupils is selected, perhaps based on prior assessment
5. The lesson is taught and observed, particular attention is given to the case study pupils
6. An assessment is carried out and pupils are interviewed
7. The teachers reflect on their findings (in relation to their predictions) and plan their response

Lesson Study blends the features of professional learning that Cordingley (2004) identified as having the biggest impact on teaching and learning. Namely:

• the professional learning takes place over time (it is not a one-off event)
• the research takes place in classrooms with real pupils
• there is an element of collaborative enquiry between teachers trying to solve a problem

David Hargreaves (2011) calls this kind of approach 'joint professional development' (JPD as opposed to CPD).

In his paper on the subject of teaching schools (a concept which was introduced in 2011 based on the existing model of teaching hospitals), David Hargreaves argued that, "It will not be enough for teaching schools to continue [with the traditional model] of professional development. Their challenging task is to raise professional development to a new level through the exemplary use and dissemination of joint practice development [which] "captures a process that is truly collaborative, not one-way; the practice is being improved, not just moved from one person or place to another".

Joint practice development gives birth to innovation and grounds it in the routines of what teachers naturally do. Innovation is fused with and grows out of practice, and when the new practice is demonstrably superior, escape from the poorer practice is expedited.

If joint practice development replaced sharing good practice in the professional vocabulary of teachers, we would, I believe, see much more effective practice transfer in the spirit of innovation that is at the heart of a self-improving system.

"Mentoring and coaching between schools," Hargreaves says, "are at the heart of this effective practice transfer. A school that has not developed a strong mentoring and coaching culture is not likely to be successful either at moving professional knowledge and skills to partners or at rising to the level of joint practice development." He says effective use of coaching and mentoring is a means of nurturing talent and is of particular importance in leadership development "since leaders learn best with and from outstanding leaders."

Dudley (2013) says JPD helps teachers to:

- observe pupils' learning in much sharper detail than is usually possible
- observe the gaps between what they'd assumed was happening when pupils learned and what really happens
- discover how to plan learning which is better matched to the pupils' needs
- learn in a supportive community committed to helping pupils learn

Here are some useful rules for the triad to observe:

- All members of the group should be treated as equals because they are all pupils irrespective of age, seniority, and experience.
- All members should be allowed to contribute, and their contributions should be treated positively, albeit challenged and analysed in a professional manner.
- The teacher who teaches the research lesson should be supported – observations should be focused on the case study pupils not on the teacher and their practice.
- Pupils' work and interview responses should inform the post-lesson discussion and pupil's responses to activities should be compared with the group's earlier predictions.
- All the findings should be shared with a wider audience and acted upon.

Professional learning communities

Another useful model of CPD which can help improve teachers' curriculum knowledge and engender more effective collaborative planning is the professional learning community…

In his book, 'Drive' (2009), Daniel Pink explores what motivates people at work. He argues that people tend to be motivated by autonomy – in other words, being accorded control over the way they work; mastery – being good at their jobs and getting better; and purpose – doing a job which is considered meaningful and worthy.

One way to promote autonomy, mastery, and purpose is through the establishment of professional learning communities in which teachers are provided with the time, space and – perhaps most importantly of all – the safety net they need in order to feel able and supported to take risks, to try out new teaching methods without fear or favour.

Joyce and Showers' report, 'Student achievement through staff development' (2002), explores the idea of professional learning communities further.

The authors argue that teaching has at least three times the effect on pupil achievement as any other factor and assert that teaching is best improved through experimentation. In other words, teachers need to be accorded the opportunity to try out new teaching strategies and then to candidly discuss with colleagues what worked and what did not.

Joyce and Showers suggest the following method:

Identify training needs: teachers ask themselves 'What do we feel are our most pressing needs? And 'What do our results tell us? Then a list of 10-20 ideas for improvement is drawn up, combined, compromised and prioritised into one common goal. This common goal is focused on a process designed to produce better outcomes which will directly affect pupils' experiences.

Training is devised: training is planned in the following sequence…

- Knowledge – new theories and rationale are explained
- Demonstration – new theories are modelled
- Practice – teachers try out the theories for themselves
- Peer coaching – teachers work together to solve the problems and answer the questions which arise during the 'practice' stage.

Training is delivered: the above training takes place over a period of time and is continually evaluated.

Joyce and Showers found that teachers must practice new methods 20-25 times if they are to learn how to use them as effectively as they do their usual methods.

There is a lot of research which underlines the importance of deliberate practice in achieving mastery and all insist that practice must be carried out over a long period of time. Most notably, there is the '10,000-hour rule' propounded by Malcolm Gladwell, Matthew Syed and others, which argues that in order to become an expert you must accrue 10,000 hours of practice.

Joyce and Showers also warn that the first few attempts at trying out a new teaching technique might fail but the teacher must remain positive and keep trying.

This process of experimentation works best – according to Joyce and Showers – when teachers:

- Practice the use of the new methods repeatedly over time
- Monitor the effect of the new methods on pupils
- Ask pupils their opinions on the new methods, garnering further suggestions
- Bring issues to peer coaching sessions for discussion
- Help and support others with their experimentation

It is important that leaders support experimentation by modelling what Joyce and Showers call an 'improvement and renewal' style of leadership. That is to say, they display an emphatic belief that it is always possible to get better, no matter how good you already are. And they display the belief that the factors which most affect pupil outcomes are in pupils' and teachers' control. They do not blame achievement on socio-economic factors nor suggest that ability is innate. They do not accept low standards.

What professional learning communities also do best is encourage risk-taking. Because they are about developing teaching expertise rather than judging colleagues' abilities, they encourage colleagues to try out new ways of teaching, some which will work and some which will not. Risk-taking and innovation are key to the long-term development of teaching because they help us as professionals to keep on getting better over time. And as lead learners, teachers should model the process of learning for their pupils. We need to show our pupils that we are also learning all the time and that we are unafraid of trying new things even if that means we sometimes make mistakes. Actually, not "even if that means we make mistakes" but "exactly because it means we make mistakes"! After all, to make mistakes is to learn; to learn is to increase our IQs. As Samuel Beckett wrote back in 1884, "Ever tried? Ever failed? Try again. Fail again. Fail better." Teachers need to model the "growth mindset" approach pioneered by Carol Dweck.

Professional learning communities also encourage teachers to do exactly what we want all of our pupils to do in order to achieve success: namely, to work outside their comfort zones, to try something difficult. And setting ourselves tough tasks is also to be encouraged because challenge leads to deeper learning and greater achievement. Challenge is, after all, a central feature of outstanding learning. If you think back to a time when you've felt challenged either personally or professionally, you'll probably recall feeling discomfort. But, once you'd overcome the challenge and achieved, the sense of success with which you were rewarded felt far greater than if you'd achieved something easy without even breaking into a sweat.

The workshops

Dylan Wiliam suggests a six-part structure for professional learning community workshops. He advocates following the same structure each time so that all colleagues come to know what is expected. This structure is as follows:

Introduction. Approximately five minutes to share learning intentions for the workshop.

Starter. Approximately five minutes as a warm-up or to share some recent positive and negative experiences.

Feedback. Between twenty-five and fifty minutes for colleagues to talk about what they've done since the last workshop, perhaps by talking through their professional development plan. It is important that all colleagues prepare for this session and are clear and detailed in the experiences they talk about including outlining what went well and what did not, and what they have learned from the experience.

New learning. Between twenty and forty minutes to discuss new learning, learning which can then be put into practice between this workshop and the next one. This might involve watching a video, discussing a book, and so on.

Professional development planning. Approximately fifteen minutes to update professional development plans and organise with colleagues future peer observations and acts of work scrutiny.

Review of learning. Approximately five minutes to recap on the core learning from this workshop.

Each workshop, Wiliam says, should last between seventy-five and one hundred and twenty minutes.

Garmston and Wellman share 7 Ps of effective collaboration which may be useful in setting a supportive tone at the learning community workshops:

- *Pausing* – this is about allowing all participants time to think, reflect on what's been said and develop their understanding.

- *Paraphrasing* – this is about the workshop leader reiterating key points, repeating back what others say in order that all participants can hear and understand what is being said.

- *Probing* – this is about the workshop leader asking questions and requesting participants develop their ideas further.

- *Putting ideas on the table* – this is about welcoming everybody's input and greeting ideas with respect; it is also about the workshop leader accepting that there are different points of view which need to be considered and thought-through without prejudice.

- *Paying attention to self and others* – this is about thinking through how to say something in a way that does not offend others nor incites argument.

- *Presuming positive intentions* – this is about presuming others mean well and trying to prevent argument.

- *Pursuing balance between advocacy and inquiry* – this is about striking the right balance between inquiring into others' ideas before advocating your own.

Dylan Wiliam says that the most effective learning communities run for two years, meet monthly to discuss new ideas and to share experiences, and identify dedicated time between meetings for colleagues to carry out peer observations and to plan collaboratively.

Robert Coe agrees that the best professional development is sustained over the long-term, content-focused, active and evidence-based.

Dylan Wiliam advocates starting with the content then moving on to the process. Content is about choosing the appropriate evidence, formulating the initial ideas; process is about according people with choice and flexibility, encouraging them to take small steps forward with support but also with accountability. In other words, content is about the *what?*; process is about the *how?*

Of course, engaging in professional development – as well as designing curricular – is a time-consuming task and senior leaders have a duty to protect their teachers' workloads. So, what can SLT do to balance the demands of the job with protecting staff health and wellbeing? We'll take a look in Chapter Eight…

CHAPTER EIGHT
PROTECTING TEACHER WORKLOAD

If we are to encourage teachers and middle leaders to engage in the curriculum planning process, and if we recognise that to do so requires them to participate in more professional development, then we must carefully consider the impact of this on their work life balance.

This new focus on curriculum could, if left unchecked, lead to a significant increase in teacher workload. For example, in June 2019 I heard first-hand of middle leaders and teachers being mandated by their senior colleagues to re-write all their schemes of work for the next academic year in order to incorporate Ofsted's 3I's. This is not what Ofsted intended and certainly not what I wish to advocate with this book.

Although it's inevitable that a new, sharper focus on curriculum planning will create more work in the short-term, this increase must be balanced with reductions in the workload elsewhere. In simple terms, it is about protecting or reducing the overall workload of staff but refocusing their time and energies on what matters most and on what will have the biggest impact on pupils and students.

For example, I happen to think that time spent identifying the key concepts pupils must learn and the threshold concepts that lead towards them is time well spent because this helps teachers teach and helps pupils learn. On the other hand, I happen to think that time spent on triple-marking is a waste of time. So, if you currently require teachers to do all manner of things that do not lead to demonstrable academic gains for pupils – or not significant enough gains – then tell them to stop, carve out some time and use that more wisely.

What more can senior leaders do to help protect their staff from an unnecessary workload?

Firstly, consideration should be given to the nature of the work staff are expected to complete, and not solely the volume of it. Indeed, a recent UCL Institute of Education survey of around 1,200 current and former teachers found that it was the nature rather than the quantity of workload, linked to notions of "performativity and accountability", that was a crucial factor in determining staff satisfaction.

The UCL report found there was a contradiction between expectation and reality, the practices of being a teacher impeded some teachers' abilities to actually be teachers. Many of those surveyed by UCL thought they could cope with the amount of workload they were given, but a lack of support and a targets-driven accountability system was worse than they had thought and led to many teachers leaving the profession, and yet more teachers considering it.

The general response from government is that teaching will be improved by reducing workload, removing unnecessary tasks and increasing pay. This may help, say the UCL, but their survey also indicates that part of the problem lies within the culture of teaching, the constant scrutiny, the need to perform and hyper-critical management. Reducing workload will not address these cultural issues.

The UCL findings illustrate the link between workload fears and the reality of working within what the report authors (Dr Jane Perryman and Graham Calvert) call "the accountability performativity context".

This takes me back to my initial point: that the key to improving teacher workload is to focus teachers' time on what matters most and on what will have the biggest impact on pupil academic gains. If teachers know that what they're being asked to do is important and will help their pupils, they are likely to feel motivated to do it and not regard it as a burden. If they regard a task as purely fulfilling management purposes, however, they will begrudge doing it and regard it as a distraction from their core purpose which, in turn, will lead to feelings of being burdened and stressed.

In order to ensure that a teacher's workload is manageable and meaningful, I think senior leaders should consider the impact of their demands on staff's autonomy, mastery, and purpose…

In terms of **autonomy**, school and college leaders need to better understand what motivates staff, and accept that teachers need to feel valued, rewarded, and professionally developed. In practice, rather than telling staff what to do or presenting them with a school improvement plan of actions, school leaders might invite staff to identify a problem that exists in their department or in the wider school. Then they might be afforded the time - and resources - to solve it in their own way, perhaps during twilight INSET or in staff meeting time. It is important to end this process by implementing staff's innovations in order to make it clear that their contributions are valued. As I've already argued, autonomy should certainly be afforded in the way subject specialists design their disciplinary curriculums.

In terms of **mastery**, school and college leaders might wish to improve their system of performance management. In particular, they may wish to sharper the focus on performance *improvement* and personal *development* rather than on compliance with a set of norms. They may also want to ensure that performance feedback derives from a wide range of sources, not just from observation and not just from the line manager.

School and college leaders might also introduce a means by which teachers can be recognised and rewarded for their contributions beyond exam results. This means being clear and transparent about what being a high value member of staff means, having clear and transparent processes for identifying such members of staff, and ensuring that staff know that their potential has been recognised. This might mean developing a no-blame culture of openness, offering high quality feedback that allows teachers to learn from their mistakes without fear or favour.

In terms of **purpose**, school and college leaders need to understand and articulate what their school has to offer teachers and what makes it unique. They should talk to existing staff and pupils about why it's a good place to be then communicate this clearly and frequently. They should also be clear about the school's direction of travel - about where it is headed and how it intends to get there – and this includes sharing their curriculum vision and explaining the purpose of education in their school.

Ways to reduce workload to make way for curriculum design

As well as considering teachers' autonomy, mastery and purpose, and focusing on the nature as well as the volume of work you give teachers and middle leaders to do, here are some other ways in which you might reduce workload in order to create the space for curriculum discussions and planning…

School calendar

It is, I think, helpful for senior leaders to ask themselves how the school calendar might add to a busy teacher's burden. Is there an avoidable congestion of parents' evenings and other late-night events such as open evenings, awards nights, drama productions, and so on? Are meetings and CPD events similarly congested, or do they all fall on the same night of the week which may cause difficulty for some staff?

Often, calendar congestion is the result of unintended consequences – senior leaders put together what they think is a sensible, logical plan for the year. I'm sure no one sets out to cause their colleagues difficulty! But, perhaps because they do not themselves teach a full timetable, they don't always consider the impact of their decisions on the full-time classroom teacher. This can be solved – to some extent – by either consulting on the calendar before it is finalised, by forming a working party of staff from a wide variety of job-roles to co-produce the calendar, or by simply talking to teachers and other staff. Combing charts are sometimes helpful as a way of getting staff to set out their preferences before the school calendar and timetable are written. It's impossible to please everyone all the time, of course; but without consultation, it's likely many staff will be avoidably inconvenienced.

When I was a headteacher I followed a simple maxim: before I took any decision, I asked myself: What will this feel like for a teacher with twenty-three lessons a week, teaching across all year groups and ability groups? Often the best teacher to have in mind is the one who teaches a minority subject to almost every child in the school.

This maxim proves particularly useful when writing the school timetable or scheduling reports and parents' evenings. What looks sensible on paper may be unworkable for the teacher who teaches several groups in the same year or every year group from 7 to 11.

Assessment schedule

What about the collection of data and the writing of reports? Is there a bottleneck at certain points of the year? More importantly, are the processes and systems used for data collection and reporting onerous and convoluted? Or do teachers lack the training to be able to use these systems quickly and fluently? Again, what are the implications of our scheduling decisions on the teacher who teaches right across the age and ability spectrum? Are we expecting a teacher to write hundreds of reports and meet hundreds of parents within a very short space of time?

School timetable

As well as looking again with fresh eyes at the annual calendar and assessment schedule, senior leaders may wish to consider the shape of the working week, for staff as a body and for individual teachers. For example, when timetabling, are we seeking to – wherever possible – provide a spread of PPA time and other non-teaching time or do some teachers teach several full days and then have an entire morning, afternoon or full day off-timetable?

When timetabling, have we considered the impact of the groups we have assigned to teachers? Are teachers being given too many different classes, perhaps because they teach split-classes or only one group in any year? Could we cut their planning load by giving them two or more classes from the same year group? Or could we do more to avoid split classes which in itself adds to a teacher's workload because they have to find time to liaise with their opposite number to discuss their planning and marking, and to compare notes on the progress being made by pupils. How are exam classes assigned? Do some teachers teach only exam classes and therefore have a much higher marking load not to mention the pressure applied through their accountability for outcomes?

How are we assigning teaching assistants? Could more be done to utilise TAs to support teachers? Do we take account of TAs' subject specialisms and interests to ensure they are supporting in subject disciplines about which they have knowledge?

For those teachers teaching a full day, have we also inadvertently scheduled their bus, break or lunch duty on the same day, meaning they have no downtime at all? How many duties do we expect staff to undertake and is this fair? Often it is middle leaders who suffer here because they are weighed down by duties and meetings as a perverse reward for being a member of the extended school leadership team but commonly, unlike the core-SLT, they continue to teach a heavy timetable.

Advantage of staff collaborative planning

Working memory is small and we can't make it any bigger. Whenever we think about or do anything, we use working memory and it's not just the information we are thinking about that takes up space. In fact, there is a constant battle being fought in our working memories for its limited capacity. Every task - whether it's mental or physical - requires us to balance three forms of cognitive load: intrinsic load, germane load and extraneous load.

Intrinsic load is the amount of mental activity involved in **performing a task,** to actively think about what we're doing.

Germane load is the amount of mental effort involved in **trying to understand the task** - if the task is new or unfamiliar, we have to use some working memory capacity to try make sense of it and decide how to tackle it.

Extraneous load, meanwhile, is concerned with **understanding the immediate environment** within which we are trying to perform a task. Disorganised or unfamiliar contexts contribute extraneous load to a task. For example, if I am trying to read a challenging book, such as *Ulysses* by James Joyce, I will fare better if I am sitting in a quiet, comfortable room devoid of distractions than if I am on a noisy train being buffeted back and forth whilst a baby bawls in the background.

When pupils are learning in our classrooms, there is a war being waged in their working memories. If we present them with unfamiliar tasks which contain entirely new information and which is presented in a new way, then we are placing unsustainable demands on their working memories and learning is likely to fail.

We can't - and wouldn't want to - eliminate all the cognitive load because if everything was too familiar and undemanding - in other words, too easy - then pupils wouldn't have to think at all and therefore would not encode anything into long-term memory. No, work has got to be hard so that pupils are made to actively think about it. But we want the focus of their hard work in lessons to be on curriculum content, not on having to contend with a distracting instructional style or learning environment.

Every time teachers do things differently to one another; they require pupils to use some of their working memory to process the instructional context and learning environment. In short, the extraneous load gets bigger when teachers are left to their own devices. And that leaves less space for the intrinsic load and therefore means pupils perform less well.

For this reason, I have come to recognise the importance of collective rather than individual autonomy, and now appreciate the need for greater consistency across a department and school. This means that teachers need to be afforded the time to get together as a subject team for curriculum planning and the creation of pooled resources.

And the added benefit of this approach – and crucial to the focal point of this chapter – is that teachers' workloads will also be reduced. Rather than every member of a department planning their own schemes of work and creating their own resources, the team do this collectively - and a scheme of work shared is a scheme of work halved, after all!

In order to put the above advice into practice, I'd suggest the following approach:

1. As a department, decide on the key concepts and ideas that need to be taught and for each identify a schema to help pupils process, retrieve and apply their knowledge - then work together to create that schema and ensure all the department use the same one and present it in the same way. For example, for the use of rhetorical devices, all teachers agree to use the same version of AFOREST and does so using the same PowerPoint slide

2. As a department, identify the key concepts and ideas pupils are bringing to your subject from their previous school. Identify the language they have been taught - such as the technical vocabulary they've used - and their definitions. Ensure all teachers use the same language and definitions or, if it important to increase the complexity of this, explicitly signpost the change, linking the new language to what pupils already know and use.

3. Agree a set of classroom displays that will act as schema or aide memoir and place them in every room in the department and ideally in the same location. Refer to these displays as often as possible so that pupils automatically utilise them as and when required.

4. Establish consistent rules and routines for entering classrooms, for transitions between activities, for group work, for self- and peer-assessment, and for class debate and discussion. Again, develop consistent schema to remind pupils of these rules - such as SLANT which is used by the Uncommon Schools network in America for class debates and stands for Sit up - Listen - Ask and answer questions - Nod - Track the speaker. Refer to three - using the same slide or display - whenever pupils engage in a relevant task until it becomes automated.

We have reached the end of Step 1 in our six-step curriculum design process. Now that we have agreed our vision, we must, in Step 2, set the destination…

PART TWO

SET THE DESTINATION

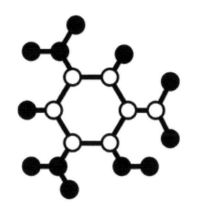

CHAPTER NINE
WHY KNOWLEDGE MATTERS

Earlier, I explained that, with its new Education Inspection Framework, Ofsted will shine a brighter light on the quality of school and college curriculums. This, I said, posed a problem because there is no agreed definition of what the curriculum is and should comprise. Whereas Ofsted believe it is "a framework for setting out the aims of the programme of education, including the knowledge and understanding to be gained at each stage," a means of "translating that framework over time into a structure and narrative, within an instructional context," and a means of "evaluating what knowledge and understanding pupils have gained against expectations," others promote a broader definition of the curriculum which comprises "everything children do, see, hear or feel in their setting, both planned and unplanned" (QCA 2000).

The notion of an unplanned curriculum – or a hidden curriculum – is important, as I explained in Chapter One, because pupils learn not solely through their experiences in the classroom, but also from other pupils, and through the accidental juxtaposition of a school's stated values and its actual practice. As John Dunford (2012) puts it, "The school curriculum is not only the subjects on the timetable; it is the whole experience of education."

The curriculum, therefore, can be found, not just in a policy statement, but in the subjects and qualifications on the timetable, in the pedagogy and behaviours teachers and other adults use, in the space between lessons when pupils interact with each other, in approaches to managing behaviour, uniform, and attendance and punctuality, in assemblies and extra-curricular activities, and in the pastoral care and support offered to pupils... in short, in the holistic experience every pupil and student is afforded in school and college.

In Chapter Two, I attempted to define what makes a curriculum 'broad and balanced'...

A broad curriculum, I said, is one in which there are enough subjects on the timetable – for all pupils - to cover all the experiences deemed important by society. Narrowing the curriculum for less able pupils or stretching GCSE study into Key Stage 3 clearly runs counter to this definition of breadth. A broad curriculum offers all pupils a wide range of subjects for as long as possible.

A balanced curriculum, meanwhile, is one in which each subject is not only taught to all pupils but is afforded enough time on the timetable to deliver its distinct contribution. The danger is that some subjects, such as art, music, and languages, are squeezed out of the timetable by English, maths and science.

Before we consider why a knowledge-rich curriculum is important and then how we might decide upon the knowledge we wish to teach our pupils, first let's return to our debate about the purpose of education because only when we are clear about this purpose can we decide *why* we need to teach knowledge and *what* knowledge to teach...

In a 2014 speech, Michael Gove – during his tenure as Secretary of State for Education - set out what he regarded as the purpose of education. He said, "I want every child to be able to go to a state school which excels, which nurtures their talents, which introduces them to the best that has been thought and written, which prepares them for the world of work and adult responsibility, which imbues them with the strength of character to withstand life's adversities and treat other humans with courtesy and dignity, which gives them the chance to appreciate art and culture, to enjoy music and drama, to participate in sport and games, which nurtures intellectual curiosity and which provides a secure grounding in the practical skills the modern world requires."

In practice, the way in which Gove implemented his education policies prevented much of his vision from being realised and rather than afford pupils the opportunity to appreciate art and culture, and enjoy music and drama, the curriculum in many schools was narrowed to the academic suite of subjects contained within the English Baccalaureate. But – and I never thought I'd say this - Gove's vision is a good place to start when considering why knowledge matters in our schools and why our curriculum has a duty to introduce pupils to the best that has been thought and written.

This last statement alludes to Matthew Arnold who, in 'Culture and Anarchy' (1869), argued that "Culture...is a study of perfection [and] seeks to do away with classes; to make the best that has been thought and known in the world current everywhere; to make all men live in an atmosphere of sweetness and light."

In the preface to 'Culture and Anarchy', Arnold argued that culture is the pursuit of "total perfection by means of getting to know, on all the matters which most concern us, the best which has been thought and said in the world, and, through this knowledge, turning a stream of fresh and free thought upon our stock notions and habits, which we now follow staunchly but mechanically, vainly imagining that there is a virtue in following them staunchly which makes up for the mischief of following them mechanically".

Arnold was therefore arguing in favour of polymathy and a resurgence of the Renaissance Man... and I think we could do worse than shape our knowledge-rich curriculum around this Renaissance ideal…

A renaissance of the Renaissance?

The Renaissance is the name given to a period of European history which provided a bridge between the Middle Ages and modern history. The intellectual foundations of the Renaissance lay in 'humanism', a concept that derived from Roman Humanitas and the rediscovery of classical Greek philosophy, such as that of Protagoras, who said that "Man is the measure of all things."

This new way of thinking came to permeate the fields of architecture, art, literature, politics, and science. As a cultural movement, the Renaissance signalled a resurgence of learning based on classical sources, which contemporaries credited to Petrarch, as well as gradual but widespread educational reform.

The Renaissance began in Italy in the 14th Century but had spread to the rest of Europe by the 16th Century. During this time, Renaissance humanists studied classical Latin and Greek, and its authors began to use vernacular languages which - combined with the introduction of printing presses - allowed many more people access to books.

The term 'Renaissance Man' was first recorded in written English in the early 20th Century to describe great thinkers living before, during, or after the Renaissance.

The Italian painter, Leonardo da Vinci - whose impressive array of interests included anatomy, architecture, and art, botany, cartography, and engineering, literature, maths, and music, and science, sculpting, and writing - is often described as the archetypal Renaissance Man.

Da Vinci and other notable polymaths who lived during the period were called Renaissance Men because they had a rounded approach to education that reflected the ideals of the humanists of the time. For example, a gentleman or courtier of the era was expected to speak several languages, play a musical instrument, write poetry and so on, thus fulfilling the Renaissance ideal.

The universal

The idea of a universal education was essential to becoming a polymath, hence the word 'university' was used to describe a seat of learning.

At this time, university students did not specialise in specific subjects as is the case today, but rather trained in science, philosophy and theology. This universal education gave them a grounding from which they could build their mastery of a specific field through subsequent apprenticeships.

Today, we use the term Renaissance Man - or 'polymath' which comes from the Greek 'having learned much' - to refer to a person whose expertise spans a significant number of different subject areas, and who is therefore able to draw on complex bodies of knowledge to solve specific problems.

If we are to provide a broad and balanced curriculum for our pupils, I believe we should return to this Renaissance ideal. Our curriculum vision should be to provide a broad and balanced curriculum which gives pupils a solid grounding from which, later, they can build their mastery in a specific field.

In terms of colleges, the Renaissance ideal can be achieved by ensuring every learner, no matter their age, level of study or qualification, is afforded a rounded study programme which includes opportunities to continue to develop their literacy and numeracy skills, their employability skills and other skills through enrichment opportunities. The 16-18 study programme already mandates this for young students, but the same broad curriculum should be afforded for every learner and it should be meaningful and relevant, not a tick-box exercise.

In short, our curriculum vision should be to produce polymaths.

Having fixed on this aim, the big question is: how do we decide what core knowledge is included in our broad and balanced curriculum? And why, in this internet age, does it matter what knowledge pupils learn? I will now attempt to answer these questions…

Just Google it?

It seems to me the world is full of education experts. The people who criticise schools for their outdated pedagogy wouldn't dream of proselytising their views on medicine or law without having first qualified in these areas, but because they've been to school or their children are at school, they think they know what works and what doesn't.

Many of the highest profile commentators are what we might call 'outliers', successful entrepreneurs who themselves failed at school. They are the exceptions who think they prove the rule that traditional schooling doesn't work, is outdated, and doesn't prepare people for the world of work.

Virgin boss Richard Branson, for example, has said that, at school, "children are taught to pass exams rather than understand concepts and expand their minds" and thus schools are failing to teach the skills that are needed in the business world. He went on to say that "many children are set up to fail by a system that only cares about exam results."

Mark Zuckerberg, the founder of Facebook, has bemoaned the fact that "every student [has to] sit in a classroom and listen to a teacher explain the same material at the same pace in the same way" and has argued that "students will perform better if they can learn at their own pace, based on their own interests, and in a style that fits them."

Every exam results day brings with it well-intentioned but ultimately unhelpful interjections from the likes of Russell Brand who once tweeted, "Good luck today – I didn't get any [A Levels] and still ended up with a job as a psychedelic bus driver", and Jeremy Clarkson who tweeted, "If your A Level results are disappointing, don't worry. I got a C and two Us, and I'm currently on a superyacht in the Med". As I say, some of these messages are, I am certain, well intentioned, reassuring young people that life is full of second chances, but they also reinforce the message that education doesn't matter.

And yet education does matter. It matters to a young person's health – well-educated people are more likely to live long, healthy lives; it matters to a young person's success in life – well-educated people are more likely to vote and contribute positively to society; it matters to a young person's success at work – well-educated people are more likely to earn more in later life. Well-educated people are also less likely to become teenage parents and go to prison.

So, despite its detractors, education does matter.

Those who claim it does not often make the mistake of thinking we live in a world where technology has replaced knowledge and we must prepare young people for jobs that haven't yet been invented, perhaps by developing 21st Century skills. And yet, as E D Hirsch said, skill *is* content, and content *is* skill. A 21st Century skill such as creativity – which, according to Sir Ken Robinson, schools kill off – isn't really a skill at all; rather, creativity is a combination of many different skills which are specific to a particular discipline and require a lot of content knowledge.

Having said this, I do believe that pupils need to be taught traits such as resilience or grit, but not as an isolated 'skill' taught out of context; rather, resilience needs to be developed as the hallmark of an effective learner who willingly grapples with difficult tasks and finds a way through the quagmire towards clarity. Resilience is best developed in context when pupils face challenges head-on and - through trial and error and learning from their mistakes - find their own light in the darkness.

These 'experts' also believe the industrial model of education – whereby pupils sit in rows and are taught facts – is dead because we live in an internet age where you can 'just Google it'. Knowledge doesn't matter, they say, because knowledge is easily accessible on the web. What matters, therefore, are workplace skills such as team-work and problem-solving.

But there's a fundamental flaw with this argument: you can't just Google it because acquiring new knowledge requires existing knowledge and we process new information within the context of what we already know. E D Hirsch argues that, "Those who repudiate a fact-filled curriculum on the grounds that kids can always look things up miss the paradox that de-emphasising factual knowledge actually disables children from looking things up effectively."

Hirsch goes on to say that, "To stress process at the expense of factual knowledge actually hinders children from learning to learn. Yes, the internet has placed a wealth of information at our fingertips. But to be able to use that information – to absorb it, to add to our knowledge – we must already possess a storehouse of knowledge."

It may sound paradoxical, but it's a theory easily tested…

The cognitive scientist George Miller, for example, conducted an experiment whereby pupils were asked to look up definitions in a dictionary and then use those words in a sentence of their own construction. Miller was given sentences such as 'Our family erodes a lot' meaning they frequently eat out, and 'Mrs Morrow stimulated the soup' meaning she stirred the broth.

Commenting on Miller's study, Hirsch said that although "Miller is in favour of dictionaries in appropriate contexts where they can be used effectively… those contexts turn out to be the somewhat rare occasions when nuances of meaning can be confidently understood."

In his book 'Why Don't Students Like School?' (2009), the cognitive scientist Daniel Willingham says that "Thinking well requires knowing facts, [and] critical thinking processes such as reasoning and problem solving are intertwined with factual knowledge stored in long-term memory."

Knowledge really is power.

As John Sweller (2011) said, "Novices need to use thinking skills. Experts use knowledge."

Knowledge in long-term memory is essential in helping make sense of new information because, amongst other things, it improves reading comprehension and critical thinking...

Knowledge in long-term memory is essential for reading comprehension because, although the ability to decode words is transferable to different texts, pupils are more likely to understand a text if they have prior knowledge about the topic. Put simply, the more you know about a topic, the more effectively you can read a text on that topic and understand it. If I asked you to read a text on, say, nuclear physics or macroeconomics, you'd probably struggle to make full sense of it because some of the words would be unfamiliar and many of the concepts certainly would be. However, if I asked you to read an article on teaching strategies, you'd probably fare well, bringing your prior knowledge to bear on the words and meanings contained within the text.

Knowledge in long-term memory is also essential for critical thinking. Critical thinking – often regarded as a transferable skill that can be taught in isolation – cannot occur if a pupil does not have sufficient foundational knowledge on the topic being discussed. In history, for example, in order for pupils to be able to reason effectively about chronology and cause and effect, they must know enough curriculum content. Teaching pupils about history in an abstract way doesn't work as well as arming them with lots of knowledge with which to better understand the way the world works. In maths, pupils need to be taught through worked examples rather than unstructured problems. And in science, pupils need to be taught the knowledge gained through scientific discovery not necessarily *how* science discovered that knowledge. Facts matter. Put simply, you cannot be critical about something of which you are ignorant (although, admittedly, that doesn't stop Nigel Farage from trying).

But not only is factual knowledge essential to reading comprehension and critical thinking, it's also a means of closing the gap between the attainment of disadvantaged learners and their non-disadvantaged peers, and this is the reason our curriculum should promote challenge for all not just the most able…

Building cultural capital

I mentioned cultural capital earlier when providing the Ofsted context because the new inspection framework explicitly mentions the importance of teaching pupils the knowledge and cultural capital they need to succeed in life. I will return to cultural capital again in more detail in Chapter Twenty-Three. But I'd like us to consider it here as a means of closing the gap between disadvantaged pupils and their more advantaged peers…

Educational disadvantage starts early - certainly before a child enters formal education. One of the reasons for this is that children born into families who read books, newspapers and magazines, visit museums, art galleries, zoos, and stately homes and gardens, take regular holidays, watch the nightly news and documentaries, and talk - around the dinner table, on weekend walks, in the car - about current affairs and about what they're reading or doing or watching - develop what's called 'cultural capital'…

In other words, they acquire an awareness of the world around them, an understanding of how life works, and - crucially - a language with which to explain it... all of which provides a solid foundation on which these children can build further knowledge, skills and understanding.

Those children not born and raised in such knowledge-rich environments don't do as well in school because new knowledge and skills have nothing to 'stick' to or build upon. Put simply, the more you know, the easier it is to know more and so the culturally rich will always stay ahead of the impoverished, and the gap between rich and poor will continue to grow as children travel through our education system.

One of the aims of our broad and balanced school or college curriculum, therefore, must be to help the disadvantaged build their cultural capital and this takes one tangible form: vocabulary.

The size of a pupil's vocabulary in their early years of schooling is a significant predictor of academic attainment in later schooling and of success in life. Most children are experienced speakers of the language when they begin school but reading the language requires more complex, abstract vocabulary than that used in everyday conversation.

Young people who develop reading skills early in their lives by reading frequently add to their vocabularies exponentially over time. Department for Education research suggests that, by the age of seven, the gap in the vocabulary known by children in the top and bottom quartiles is something like 4,000 words (children in the top quartile know around 7,000 words).

For this reason, when designing our curriculum, we must recognise the importance of vocabulary and support its development across the curriculum – in lessons and in the space between lessons - so that pupils who do not develop this foundational knowledge before they start school are helped to catch up. Literacy – or 'the language of learning' – should permeate our curriculum plan.

Of course, diminishing disadvantage is not as simple as building word power – disadvantage takes many forms and is a complex subject. The solutions are, by necessity, complex too. We will explore other means of building knowledge and cultural capital later but, for now, let us remember the centrality of vocabulary to our curriculum.

Now let us return to the subject of polymathy...

CHAPTER TEN
WHAT KNOWLEDGE MATTERS

Among the many slurs directed at the playwright William Shakespeare, it is claimed he was a plagiarist. *The Tempest*, we are told, is his only truly original play. Robert Greene famously called Shakespeare "an upstart crow, beautified with our feathers". Plagiarism software has recently been used to analyse Shakespeare's texts and has found, amongst other things, that he 'borrowed' liberally from a book called *A Brief Discourse of Rebellion and Rebels* by George North. "Shakespeare not only uses the same words as North, but often uses them in scenes about similar themes, and even the same historical characters," explains the New York Times.

Geoffrey Bullough's eight-volume *Narrative and Dramatic Sources of Shakespeare* lifts the lid on some of the source texts from which Shakespeare shamelessly stole. He was inspired by Plutarch's *Lives* and Hollinshed's *Chronicles*, as well as Montaigne's *Essays* and of course by Ovid, Seneca and Plautus. But his plays were not merely carbon copies, Shakespeare combined them in unconventional ways, subverted them, and made substantial changes to them.

For example, Bullough shows us how Shakespeare entwined two separate tales to make *The Merchant of Venice* and decided to kill Lear and Cordelia at the end of *King Lear* when in his chronicle source both characters survived with Lear restored to the throne. Bullough also shows us how Shakespeare had Othello murder Desdemona, when in Cinthio's original Italian story, Iago did the devilish deed. He also added an extra set of twins to *The Comedy of Errors*.

Therefore, to call Shakespeare a plagiarist is unfair: his originality was his ability to transform what he had read, heard recited, or remembered from his school days and make something new and startling from them. Indeed, I'm reminded of T S Eliot's aphorism: "Immature poets imitate; mature poets steal; bad poets deface what they take, and good poets make it into something better or at least something different."

What's more, Shakespeare inhabited a literary culture in which imitation of earlier models was applauded rather than derided. In Renaissance creative writing - or 'rhetoric' as it was called - invention was highly regarded.

In *Shakespeare's Originality* by John Kerrigan, there's a chapter devoted to *Much Ado About Nothing* which reveals a play that is "pieced and patched and recycled" out of various Italian tales. It's "radical novelty" was a matter of the "piecemeal superflux" of reused materials.

As such, Shakespeare's gift, it could be argued, is the breadth and depth of the foundational knowledge – his cultural capital - upon which he was able to draw to create his original works. It is therefore worthwhile, as we seek to set the parameters of our own broad and balanced curriculum, exploring the curriculum to which Shakespeare was exposed whilst at school in Stratford…

In *Teaching Shakespeare*, Rex Gibson says that "Shakespeare's schooling provided an excellent resource for the future playwright. Everything Shakespeare learned at school he used in some way in his plays." For example, Gibson tells us, "Having mastered the rules of language, he was able to break and transform them."

We believe Shakespeare attended King Edward VI Grammar School in Stratford although there is no record of Shakespeare's name on the register. His father's position on the council (by the time Shakespeare was of school age, his father John was an alderman) brought with it free education for his sons so it's inconceivable to think he wouldn't have taken advantage of the opportunity.

Grammar schools like King Edward VI were part of the Tudor educational revolution of which the chief beneficiaries were middle class boys like Shakespeare, who were being groomed to be lawyers and clerks, Church of England ministers, and secretaries to politicians or indeed politicians themselves.

Grammar school pupils didn't study history or maths, and they didn't study geography, or indeed science. However, they did study grammar (hence 'grammar school') and did so from dawn to dusk, six days a week, all year round. They translated from Latin into English and from English into Latin. At school, ordinary conversation was in Latin and any boy caught speaking English would have been flogged.

The boys also mastered the tropes of rhetoric, from antimetabole (where words are repeated in inverse order) to zeugma (where one verb looks after two nouns). Rhetoric was - and still is - the language of power and politics; it was - and is - the language of law and government.

Shakespeare would have started school at six in the morning in the summer months and at seven o'clock in winter. In his seven years at King Edward VI, Shakespeare is likely to have spent in excess of 2,000 hours studying which is more than double what a pupil today would spend in school, meaning he accessed the equivalent of fourteen years' education.

The Renaissance was the driving force behind the curriculum. Shakespeare would have memorised entire textbooks by heart, and would have studied Aesop's fables, Cicero, the Geneva Bible, Ovid, Plutarch, Seneca and Virgil among many others.

In short, Shakespeare studied the best that had been thought and said.

In tackling the design of our curriculum, therefore, I think we can learn a lot from Shakespeare's experience of school life.

Curriculum planning backwards

We may no longer regard learning Latin as essential to success, but much of the knowledge Shakespeare learnt is still relevant. The best means of identifying what knowledge should underpin our curriculum, I think, is to start at the end and work backwards…

I will model the process by exploring the foundational concepts – the knowledge and skills – that pupils need to have mastered by the end of key stage 4 in order to succeed at GCSE in English. I will then consider how we might use these foundations to build a secondary English curriculum, starting in Year 7 and moving progressively through key stages 3 and 4.

Next, I will consider how to bridge the gap between the primary and secondary English curriculums, ensuring that Year 7 builds upon the knowledge and skills pupils bring with them from Year 6. In other words, the curriculum needs to make sure the transitions between years, key stages and phases of education are smooth and progressive, and that the knowledge and skills pupils bring with them from primary school are consolidated and extended, not disregarded or repeated.

Finally, weaving its way through all of this, and across the curriculum, I will look at how we might make provision for the development of pupils' language *for* learning and language *of* learning.

The above model comes with an important caveat, though: it is merely a model for illustrative purposes, and I'd advise you look beyond exam specifications when deciding *what* knowledge matters to your curriculum. One way to think more ambitiously than this, and thus to future-proof your curriculum against awarding body and Ofqual changes, is to ask yourselves: what do we want our pupils to know and be able to do in our subject in ten years' time? What will success look like when our pupils are at the next stages of their education, employment and lives?

This model comes with another caveat: although I am modelling the process using the example of GCSE English and therefore relating it to the secondary school curriculum, the same principles and approaches apply to the primary and FE curriculums, too, and indeed to all subject disciplines.

CHAPTER ELEVEN
IDENTIFYING KEY CONCEPTS

Lawton (1975) argued that the curriculum is "a selection from the culture of a society" and, as such, each school's and college's local curriculum will be different; it will reflect the community it serves and prepare its pupils for the particular society in which they will live and work. That's why I said your school and college's curriculum vision should be unique. However, there is clearly a bank of knowledge – perhaps dictated by national curriculum and qualifications – that all pupils in the UK should acquire in order to succeed in school, in work and in life.

I will model selecting content for this foundational curriculum using English language as an example. I will start at the end of key stage 4 by examining what pupils need to know in order to do well at GCSE.

First, though, a healthy warning about tracking GCSE outcomes into key stage 3...

I am going to advocate identifying the knowledge and skills required at GCSE and to begin teaching them in Year 7. However, this is not synonymous with stretching the GCSE programme of study down into key stage 3, thus squeezing or narrowing the key stage 3 curriculum. Rather, it is about providing the skills and foundations required for GCSE success as early as possible and ensuring we teach a progressive, joined-up curriculum. If we do not start secondary schooling with the end in mind, how can we be certain we are best preparing our pupils for success? How can we be sure we're teaching them what they will need to know and do? And how can we be confident we are planning sufficient opportunities to repeat and reinforce – through deliberate practice – the knowledge and skills that matter most?

Mapping from the beginning of Year 7 the foundational concepts required for success at GCSE is not the same as teaching GCSEs in key stage 3 - schools which extend GCSEs into key stage 3 risk narrowing their curriculum and are in danger of teaching the GCSE specification too early. I believe that key stage 3 should provide as broad and balanced a curriculum as possible and should be different to that which proceeds and succeeds it, but at the same time it should provide a bridge from primary to secondary and from key stage 3 to key stage 4 and beyond. Mapping foundational concepts from Year 7 is about teaching a logical, ever-expanding and developing curriculum that best prepares pupils for their current and future schooling and indeed later life.

Some might argue that tracking GCSE outcomes back to Year 7 is asking too much of younger pupils and that we cannot possibly expect the same of Year 7 pupils as we do of Year 11. But this is similar, to my mind, as arguing that we cannot expect children to talk at eighteen months' old because we also expect them to do so as adults. We teach children to talk from an early age and continually improve their ability to do so - both in terms of the biological function of articulating meaning through sound, and their vocabulary and syntax - throughout their childhood and indeed throughout life.

Tracking foundational concepts back through the years, key stages and phases of education means we begin the process of teaching pupils the knowledge and skills that are essential for academic success as early as possible *in order to* afford us the time to repeat learning several times and deepen pupils' understanding of that knowledge over time. In short, we expect the same basic content knowledge but for the depth of that knowledge and the connections between different pieces of knowledge (thus improving transferability) to increase as the pupil gets older.

A cognitive balancing act

As I explained in Chapter Eight when advocating collaborative planning as a means of reducing teachers' workloads, the working memory is always trying to balance intrinsic cognitive load (the space in working memory dedicated to performing a task), germane cognitive load (the space in working memory dedicated to trying to understand the task), and extraneous cognitive load (the space in working memory dedicated to understanding and responding to the instructional context).

John Sweller suggests that in order to minimise extraneous cognitive load, instructional design (the way we teach the curriculum) should address the needs of three broad groups of expertise:

1. Novice level– "detailed, direct instructional support... preferably in integrated or dual-modality formats",
2. Intermediate level– "a mix of direct instruction and problem-solving practice with reduced support", and
3. Advanced level– "minimally guided problem-solving tasks... provide cognitively optimal instructional methods".

In other words, we need to design a curriculum that affords sufficient repetition of content knowledge and to return to prior learning with increasing complexity. In Year 7 we might begin by teaching our 'novices' through detailed direct instruction and introduce new content knowledge at a basic – though not superficial – level. As pupils return to this learning in Years 8 and 9, we might teach our 'intermediates' through a combination of direct instruction and problem-solving activities. And then, at GCSE, we might teach the same content knowledge at an advanced level through minimally guided, problem-solving activities. In short, the way we teach the same content knowledge as pupils get older necessarily changes as pupils move from novices to experts. The scaffolds fall away, and pupils become increasingly independent.

But we also return to the content knowledge we taught previously and add more and more layers of meaning in order to develop schemata. In so doing, we encourage pupils to practice, not until they solve a problem correctly, but until they can no longer get it wrong.

The end is also the beginning

Above, I explained that Ofsted's new Education Inspection Framework - which evaluates the intent, implementation and impact of the school curriculum – was, at least in part, a response to HMCI Amanda Spielman's call to arms that education "should be about broadening minds, enriching communities and advancing civilisation" and "ultimately, about leaving the world a better place than we found it."

I also explained that there are at least four distinct elements to a curriculum: the national curriculum which is prescribed by statute and consists of the core and foundation subjects, the basic curriculum which comprises the requirements in current legislation for the teaching of RE, sex education, careers education, and opportunities for work-related learning, the local curriculum which is one that schools are free to adopt in order to complement the national and basic curriculums with content that is relevant to their community and its people, and the hidden curriculum which consists of the behaviours, values and attitudes that adults (and the learning environment) transmit to pupils through their own – often unintentional – behaviours, i.e. the learning that takes place outside of the taught timetable, in the 'hidden' spaces between lessons.

However, I also argued that the curriculum is even more than this: it is, as the QCA put it in 2000: "Everything children do, see, hear or feel in their setting, both planned and unplanned."

The unplanned curriculum, I said, is learning that takes place outside the classroom such as from other pupils as well as learning that arises from an accidental juxtaposition of the school's stated values and its actual practice.

I said that, although the curriculum can be found, not just in a policy statement, but in the subjects and qualifications on the timetable, in the pedagogy and behaviours teachers and other adults use, in the space between lessons when pupils interact with each other, in approaches to managing behaviour, uniform, and attendance and punctuality, in assemblies and extra-curricular activities, and in the pastoral care and support offered to pupils, it is nevertheless important to start the process of curriculum design by articulating a clear vision of what the curriculum seeks to do in your school – and a good place to begin is by defining what is meant by a 'broad and balanced' curriculum…

A broad curriculum, I argued above, is one in which there are enough subjects on the timetable to provide, say, linguistic, mathematical, scientific, technological, human and social, physical, and aesthetic and creative, and spiritual, moral, social and cultural development. A balanced curriculum, meanwhile, is one in which each subject is not only taught to all pupils but is afforded enough time on the timetable to deliver its distinct contribution.

In short, I've argued that we should consider the curriculum in its widest sense – it takes place in and between lessons, in subjects and in extra-curricular activities, and it develops pupils' skills in a range of areas including in the arts and sport, and – although important – is not solely concerned with the pursuit of academic outcomes. We should ensure our curriculum prepares pupils, not only for the next stage of their education and training, but also for their lives as active citizens and for success in the world of work, developing employability skills and attitudes, and educating pupils on their career options. And we should think carefully about how, once we've designed the curriculum, we will implement and evaluate it in order to ensure it delivers its stated aims and continues to be relevant.

I explained above that establishing a vision for your curriculum will provide the benchmark against which all subsequent decisions about its content, structure, sequence, monitoring, evaluation and review can be tested. A good place to start is to consider what the school regards as the purpose of education. One answer, I said, was to produce polymaths – pupils with a well-rounded knowledge in a range of subjects so that they leave school with a solid grounding from which they can build their mastery of a specific field.

Having fixed on this vision, I said, the big question is: how do we decide what core knowledge is included in our broad and balanced curriculum? And why, in this internet age, does it matter what knowledge pupils learn?

In Chapter Nine, I attempted to answer this question...

Knowledge is power, I said, because information held in long-term memory is essential in helping make sense of new information. Knowledge is essential for reading comprehension, critical thinking and for closing the gap... Children not born and raised in knowledge-rich environments don't do as well in school because new knowledge and skills have nothing to 'stick' to or build upon. Put simply, the more you know, the easier it is to know more and so the culturally rich will always stay ahead of the impoverished, and the gap between rich and poor will continue to grow as children travel through our education system. One of the aims of our broad and balanced school curriculum, therefore, must be to help the disadvantaged build their cultural capital and this takes one tangible form: vocabulary.

I argued in Chapter Ten that Shakespeare's gift is the breadth and depth of the foundational knowledge upon which he was able to draw in order to create his original works. I said that, as such, we could learn by exploring the curriculum to which Shakespeare was exposed whilst at school in Stratford...

In *Teaching Shakespeare*, Rex Gibson says that "Shakespeare's schooling provided an excellent resource for the future playwright. Everything Shakespeare learned at school he used in some way in his plays." For example, Gibson tells us, "Having mastered the rules of language, he was able to break and transform them." The Renaissance, I said, was the driving force behind the curriculum Shakespeare studied. He would have memorised entire textbooks by heart, and would have studied Aesop's fables, Cicero, the Geneva Bible, Ovid, Plutarch, Seneca and Virgil among many others. In short, Shakespeare studied the best that had been thought and said.

In tackling the design of our curriculum, therefore, I think we can learn a lot from Shakespeare's experience of school life and the best way to do this is to plan our curriculum content backwards… in other words, as I explained last week, we should begin by exploring the foundational concepts – the knowledge and skills – that pupils will need to have mastered by the end of key stage 4 in order to succeed at GCSE and then consider how we might use these foundations to build our secondary curriculum, starting in Year 7 and moving progressively through key stages 3 and 4.

Let me now model this process using the example of English language…

My starting point in determining the key concepts pupils must acquire if our curriculum is to be successful is to look at the assessment objectives and learning outcomes and to identify the key concepts upon which success is contingent.

For example, one of the outcomes required for success in GCSE English language is for pupils to be able to "identify and interpret *explicit* and *implicit* information and ideas". I therefore need to ensure that the concept of explicit and implicit meanings form a part of my curriculum from Year 7 onwards. We might start in Year 7 by teaching pupils what is meant by the words 'explicit' and 'implicit'. We might introduce these words, once we've assessed their prior knowledge from primary school, by following Isobel Beck's advice (see 'Bringing Words to Life', 2002) and:

- Read a sentence in which the word appears
- Show pupils the word and get them to say it out loud
- Discuss possible meanings of the word
- Identify any parts of the word that may be familiar (e.g. Greek or Latinate roots, common prefixes and suffixes)
- Re-read the sentence with the word in it to detect any contextual clues
- Explicitly explain the meaning of the word through definition and the use of synonyms
- Provide several other examples of the word being used in context
- Ask pupils to use the word in sentences of their own.

Thus, in Year 7, pupils will be expected to know that 'explicit' means stated clearly, leaving no room for doubt or confusion, whereas 'implicit' means suggested though not directly stated or expressed. This will form part of our assessment of the curriculum.

But knowing what the words mean isn't enough. As pupils travel through our curriculum we need to return to these concepts and teach pupils how to identify explicit and implicit meanings in a range of different texts. Then we need to teach them how to interpret both explicit and implicit meanings, and comment on why the writer used either explicit or implicit language and what effect their choice has on the reader.

Our end goal is for pupils to be able to comment on what a text overtly says - its literal, stated meaning - and also discern what is implied or suggested by the text; for example, what the writer might have been trying to say. To arrive at this destination, we begin teaching explicit and implicit meanings from Year 7 but do so at different levels of complexity and skill as we return to it, in different contexts and tied to different content knowledge, throughout the curriculum.

We do the same for all the other outcomes in GCSE English language including, for reading:

- What language features to identify and comment on
- What structural features to identify and comment on
- How to compare two or more texts
- How to make references to a text, using quotations
- What tone, style and register mean and how to identify them in texts as well as how to use them to influence writing
- What form, purpose and audience mean and how to identify them in texts as well as how to use them to influence writing
- What is meant by grammatical features and how to use various grammatical features for effect
- What is meant by sentence structure and how to use different types of sentence for effect

We've reached the end of Step 2 in our six-step curriculum design process – set the destination – and can now embark upon the third step which is to assess the starting points…

PART THREE

ASSESS THE STARTING POINTS

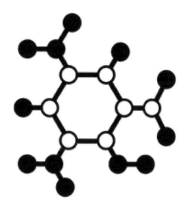

CHAPTER TWELVE
THE IMPORTANCE OF CURRICULUM CONTINUITY

In Chapters Ten and Eleven I modelled how to use GCSE outcomes (in the form of assessment objectives) to determine some of the foundational concepts (or content knowledge) that should underpin our secondary curriculum. For example, I said that, to succeed at GCSE English language, pupils need to be able to identify and explain explicit and implicit meanings and, as such, we should introduce pupils to the words 'explicit' and 'implicit' in Year 7 (perhaps using the teaching sequence suggested by Beck) and revisit these concepts throughout key stages 3 and 4, albeit with increasing complexity each time. In other words, I said we should teach the same concepts throughout key stages 3 and 4 – building in time for repetition and reinforcement as retrieval practice – but develop pupils' knowledge and understanding of these concepts as they travel through the school curriculum.

First, pupils might learn to define the word 'implicit' then learn how to identify implicit meanings in a range of texts. Next, they might learn to explain why a writer wanted to imply rather than explicitly state something, and then articulate the effect this has on the reader.

Think of our progressive curriculum as peeling back the layers of an onion, deepening pupils' understanding of content but also enabling them, as they acquire more and more content knowledge, to make connections and develop schemata in long-term memory that permits thinking – including thinking about any new content they encounter – to become more efficient and accurate. As I said earlier, the more we know, the easier it is to know more because we process new information in the context of what we already know. We can't think critically about something of which we are ignorant.

In this section of the book, I want to look backwards rather than forwards. In other words, rather than look at the end goal – GCSE outcomes or what we want pupils to remember about our subject in ten years' time – I want us to investigate pupils' pasts and identify what they have been taught before they embark on their curriculum journey with us, because a truly joined-up and progressive curriculum bridges the gaps between years, key stages and phases of education and this includes the gap between primary and secondary school, and between secondary school and college.

If you want to find directions on Google Maps, first it will ask you 'where to?' then it will ask you 'where from?'. In other words, first it needs to know the destination then it needs to know the starting point. And curriculum design is no different. First, we need to know what the intended outcomes of our curriculum are – what we want pupils to know and be able to do at the end; then we need to know from where pupils are starting their journeys towards these clear end-points. With these two pins stuck in our map, we can begin to plot a course between the two.

In this section of the book we will look at assessing starting points. First we will explore the importance of curriculum continuity, then we will look at ways of improving transition to help pupils journey through our curriculum, next we will consider the advantages of adopting a consistent language *of* and *for* learning, and finally we will look at ways of identifying pupils' individual starting points through assessment.

But first a note on the thorny subject of skills…

What are skills?

You can't go near Twitter without becoming entangled in a heated debate about knowledge versus skills. Put simply, traditionalist teachers (or 'trads') don't believe in skills and so fight against the notion of thematic curricular and project-based learning. They don't believe in teaching transferable skills such as critical thinking because they believe skills are actually a form of knowledge and must be developed within context. The progressive teachers (or 'progs'), meanwhile, think knowledge can be found on Google and so believe in the importance of skills development instead. They think that pupils will be better served by being taught transferable skills – sometimes referred to as 21st Century skills – which they can apply to any field. Progs don't believe in teaching facts by rote and kick against a knowledge-led curriculum and direct instruction.

Of course, I've simplified the two positions and most of the teachers debating trad v prog approaches take a much more nuanced stand.

I don't think knowledge is in battle with skills but rather that pupils need both knowledge *and* skills to be able to complete any task. Skills might more helpfully be referred to as procedural knowledge because it is the know-how; whereas knowledge might better be called declarative knowledge because it is the know-what.

Pupils need to know-how and know-what if they are to be successful. For example, I might know how to construct an essay but if I don't know what I'm writing about, no matter how well written it is, the essay will be useless. Likewise, if I knew everything there was to know about a topic but didn't know how to write a logical argument on that topic, I wouldn't perform particularly well either. What I do know about procedural knowledge is that most of it is indeed best taught in context to give it meaning. I also know that some procedural knowledge is domain-specific – for example, as I argued in Chapter Seven, you cannot think critically about a subject on which you have no knowledge – but I do not think all of it is. In short, I think there are some transferable and some non-transferable skills we need to teach our pupils, but that all knowledge is best taught in context rather than in isolation. For example, I would argue that the concept of 'explicit and implicit meanings' should be taught through the study of great literature.

Our curriculum should, therefore, identify, not just the key concepts, but also the skills that our pupils must acquire in order to succeed. Then we must identify which of these skills is domain-specific and should only be taught alongside the knowledge it relates to, and which of these skills are transferable and should be taught repeatedly in different contexts to aid their transferability. For example, essay-writing is a transferable skill which should be taught and reinforced each time it is required in different contexts. Likewise, note-taking and internet research are skills which pupils will need to call upon in different topics within a subject discipline and in different subject disciplines, and we therefore need to ensure our curriculum explicitly teaches these skills in different contexts and explicitly draws the links between contexts – activating prior knowledge each time pupils are required to use them again in a different situation.

Let's take a closer look…

Transferable and non-transferable skills

It is helpful, I find, once we have determined the concepts that provide the foundations of our curriculum – the content knowledge upon which success at GCSE is dependent - to differentiate between the transferable concepts that a particular programme of study will introduce and embed, and those concepts which are indivisible from their context. Allow me to elaborate…

When teaching Romeo and Juliet, for example, pupils will need to learn about how playscripts work and about stagecraft; they'll need to understand the language used, including blank verse; they'll need to learn about themes such as conflict, romance, and tragedy; and so on. These concepts are all transferable because they can - and should - be applied to different texts and indeed to life. The narrative shape of an Elizabethan tragedy is almost the same for every tragic play – certainly a contemporary audience would know to expect mass bloodshed in the fifth act, whereas they'd expect a romance to end in marriage. Knowing this can help pupils to understand a range of different texts and different playwrights and compare one with another. (By the same token, when teaching prose fiction, it's helpful to teach pupils Freytag's Pyramid or the six-part story structure and get them to comment on how the author builds towards a climax.)

But, in order to study Romeo and Juliet, pupils will also need to learn the names of characters and details about the plot, as well as contextual information about when and where the play is set, and when and where it was written and first performed. These concepts are not transferable because they are specific to this play.

Both transferable and non-transferable concepts are important, but the transferable concepts must be mapped across the curriculum and repeated and reinforced regularly. We must make the explicit link between the study of these concepts in the context of Romeo and Juliet and how these concepts apply in other parts of the curriculum. So long as we teach the non-transferable concepts well when taught in context, there is no need to repeat them beyond the bounds of normal exam revision. For example, we do not – knowing we will teach Romeo and Juliet in Year 11 – need to start introducing the play in Year 7. It is enough to introduce the transferable concepts that will aid pupils' understanding of the play.

The poor relations

If our new curriculum is to be joined-up and well-taught, then no key stage must be regarded as a poor relation to the exam years for this will only prove to be a vicious cycle. For example, in secondary schools we need to avoid the temptation to timetable key stages 4 and 5 first then fill in the gaps with key stage 3 lessons, thus increasing the chances of key stage 3 classes being split between two or more teachers. And we need to avoid timetabling non-specialist, underperforming and/or inexperienced teachers for key stage 3 lessons. Rather, we should utilise our best teachers because this will pay dividends in later years and limit the need of remedial interventions to help pupils catch up for lost time.

In addition to being appropriately staffed, the key stage 3 curriculum should strike the right balance between providing pupils with a grounding for GCSE and being different enough to key stage 4 so as to be engaging. We need to ensure key stage 3 provides a springboard for GCSE. But key stage 3 also needs to flow naturally from key stage 2…

Ofsted's 2015 report, 'The Wasted Years', argued that too many secondary schools do not work effectively with partner primary schools in order to understand pupils' prior learning and therefore ensure that they build on this during key stage 3. Indeed, some secondary leaders simply accept that pupils will repeat what they have already done in primary school. This problem, sadly, has only worsened since the government implemented the last iteration of the national curriculum…

Richard Hudson, emeritus professor of linguistics at University College, London, who was part of an expert group advising the government on the primary curriculum, admitted that the process - overseen by then Education Secretary, Michael Gove - was "chaotic". Hudson says that, as a result, the new curriculum and assessments are not based on good research evidence and many primary teachers are not equipped to teach it.

Hudson is not alone in criticising the new primary curriculum he helped to write. Indeed, all four members of the expert panel have spoken publicly about their concerns. The government's key curriculum adviser, Tim Oates, has also warned that the spelling, punctuation and grammar (SPaG) tests "need a rethink [because there is a] genuine problem about [the] undue complexity of demand [of the] "language about language" that pupils are now expected to know.

David Crystal, one of Britain's leading English language experts, has argued that the SPaG test, and its underlying view of language, "turns the clock back half a century" because it places too much emphasis on simply spotting and labelling linguistic features and regards this as an end in itself rather than as a starting point that enables discussions about effective writing.

Hudson, in an interview with *The Guardian* in May 2017, recalled the disorganised process of writing the curriculum: "To give you an idea of how chaotic things were, when [the expert panel] was originally put together, we had about four meetings and were supposed to be devising a grammar curriculum to cover the whole of compulsory education: primary and secondary. We started off with the primary curriculum, which we were a bit unconfident about as none of us had much experience of primary education and were looking forward to getting stuck into the real thing: secondary. Then the DfE pulled the plug by saying: 'We are not going to do any secondary curriculum.' So [the primary curriculum that] was published was meant to be about building the foundations for the real thing. But that's all there is."

Hudson went on to say that the result is "terribly worrying, because it means that all the work children do in primary is wasted, as they probably won't take it on in secondary."

The government did eventually produce a new secondary curriculum, but it was a slimmed down, less prescriptive version of what had gone before, and therefore did not build upon the foundations laid down by the primary curriculum.

So, in short, at the time of writing we have a primary national curriculum which is much more prescriptive than that which preceded it. However, because it proved so problematic to write and implement, the government abandoned its plan to follow it with a progressive secondary curriculum. The secondary curriculum the government did eventually introduce was less prescriptive. As a result, the current primary curriculum does not flow naturally into the secondary curriculum and the knowledge and skills taught at key stage 3 do not build upon that which is taught in key stage 2.

The problem seems to be that curriculum reforms at the national level have been implemented in isolation, and primary and secondary schools don't have enough time to talk to each other about what and how they teach. What's more, the government hasn't provided - or equipped schools with the funding for - staff training on the new curriculum and so many teachers are stumbling in the dark.

Another consequence of this lack of joined up thinking on the curriculum is that the primary curriculum now better prepares pupils for the new, more demanding GCSEs but renders near-pointless the three years of key stage 3 sandwiched in between.

This poses an additional challenge to secondary schools than those outlined in 'The Wasted Years' report: what can we cover in the Years 7, 8 and 9 curriculums to ensure that pupils are challenged, engaged and making progress? One answer, I think, in English at least, is to put into context the technical terminology now taught at primary. This involves reading and writing increasingly complex texts, developing a love of reading for reading's sake, and developing pupils' ability to write in a range of contexts, for a variety of purposes, and in different styles.

Another solution is to ensure that pupils are fed a rich diet of subjects from across the arts, humanities, languages and sciences, and are afforded experiences outside the classroom by visiting museums and art galleries, theatres and monuments. In short, schools should do as Amanda Spielman advised in her Festival of Education speech in 2017 and ensure that the key stage 3 curriculum broadens minds, enriches communities, and advances civilisation.

And all of the above applies to primary education and further education, too. Often in primary schools, Year 6 is the focus because it is in this year that pupils sit the all-important key stage 2 SATs. As such, not only do pupils spend most of their time in Year 6 learning English and maths at the expense of other subjects, pupils in other years tend to be given a raw deal when it comes to time, money and expertise. At the least, there is little consideration given to how well pupils will be prepared for the next stage of their education and how each year, stage and phase of education connects to what went before and what comes next.

Bridging the gap

As I say above, the primary curriculum provides pupils with an impressive knowledge of, say, grammatical terms. Indeed, the terminology and concepts now being taught in key stage 2 would not, ordinarily, be introduced until A Level. However, the primary national curriculum encourages schools to teach concepts and skills in isolation. One job for our joined up, progressive secondary curriculum, therefore, is to place these concepts and skills into some sort of context, for example by studying the best that has been thought and said.

In fact, I would advise a teaching sequence that begins with the development of spoken language, then develops reading comprehension, before moving onto writing composition. Once this sequence has been followed, we can zigzag back and forth so that writing composition can inform reading comprehension and spoken language, and so on.

We need pupils in key stage 3 to enjoy whole texts - and, yes, reading and writing in silence for a full lesson. Studying extracts is valuable, too, of course, in allowing pupils to apply their skills and knowledge, particularly to unseen texts as they will need to in the exam. But there is no substitute for reading a book from cover to cover, understanding and appreciating the plot arc and the detailed, sustained development of character, setting and theme. What's more, in this digital age of instant gratification, pupils rely on schools to teach them the art of concentration and attention.

CHAPTER THIRTEEN
IMPROVING TRANSITION ARRANGEMENTS

One way in which we can achieve greater curriculum continuity is to improve the transition arrangements for pupils and students as they transfer between the various years, key stages and phases of education, including when they change schools or college.

In this chapter, by way of illustration, I will focus on the primary to secondary transition as pupils move from Year 6 into Year 7 but my advice holds for any type of transition because at each stage we need to ensure we do all we can to mitigate the social and emotional effects of change and think more carefully – and collaboratively – about how we can ensure each year's curriculum builds on and extends the previous whilst preparing pupils for the next.

In short, we need to avoid pupils going backwards whenever they experience a change, either finding the next stage too easy because it needlessly repeats what they've already done, or too hard because pupils have not been properly prepared for the increased challenge and complexity.

Why do we need to improve transition?

According to Galton (1999), almost forty per cent of children fail to make expected progress during the year immediately following a change of schools and DfE data from 2011 shows that average progress drops between key stage 2 and key stage 3 for reading, writing and maths. Moreover, the effects of transition are amplified by risk factors such as poverty and ethnicity.

And why should this be? Primarily, I believe, it's because there is insufficient or ineffective communication between primary and secondary schools, and this has a number of harmful consequences...

Firstly, secondary school teachers have a weak understanding of the curriculum content that precedes what they personally teach whilst primary school teachers have a weak understanding of the curriculum that succeeds their own. In practice, this means that the curriculum is not joined up and that pupils are taught content and skills more than once or are taught the same concepts in contradictory ways.

Secondly, assessment practices in the two phases are inconsistent and therefore there is little correlation between Year 6 and 7 data. This leads to a lack of trust on both sides of the 'divide' in terms of the validity of assessment data and to pupils being re-tested at the start of Year 7 just weeks after sitting stressful, high stakes key stage 2 SATs. It also generates confusion and even animosity amongst parents who perceive that their sons and daughters are regressing when in fact the data may mask their progress or, at any rate, exaggerate the decline.

Thirdly, and in part a further consequence of the first two points above but also the result of pedagogical differences between the two phases, there is often a weak understanding in Year 7 of what pupils can achieve and therefore insufficient challenge in the curriculum.

How can we improve transition?

There are five broad categories of school life - sometimes referred to as 'bridges' - in which the transition process can be improved:

1. Administrative
2. Social and personal
3. Curricular
4. Pedagogic
5. Managing learning

The administrative 'bridge' is concerned with the general management of the transition process such as the formal liaison between a secondary school and its feeder primaries, usually at a senior leadership level. In practice, this might take the form of the transfer of pupil records and achievement data, meetings with pupils and parents, and visits from headteachers, senior leaders and teachers.

The social and personal 'bridge' is concerned with forging links between pupils/parents and their new school prior to and immediately after transfer. It is also concerned with the pupil induction process into their new school and might take the form of induction days, open evenings, school orientation activities, team-building days, taster classes, the production and issuing of prospectuses and booklets, and so on.

The curricular 'bridge' is concerned with improving curriculum continuity between the primary and secondary phases of education by sharing plans that show what content is taught on either side of the transition. This involves teachers rather than senior leaders and might take the form of cross-phase teaching, the teaching of bridging units at the end of Year 6 and start of Year 7, summer schools, joint CPD networks and INSET days, the sharing of good practice and shared planning, and teacher exchanges.

Whereas the curricular bridge is concerned with what pupils are taught, the pedagogic 'bridge' is concerned with establishing a shared understanding of how pupils are taught - as well as how they learn - in order to achieve a greater continuity in classroom practice and teaching. This is achieved by understanding differing teaching styles and skills, by engaging in shared CPD and teacher exchanges, and by primary and secondary teachers observing each other in practice.

The managing learning 'bridge' is about ensuring that pupils are active participants, rather than passive observers, in the transition process. This is achieved by empowering pupils and their parents with information about achievement and empowering them with the confidence to articulate their learning needs in a new environment. This might take the form of giving information to parents/pupils, providing pupils with learning portfolios and samples of achievements, and raising pupils' awareness of their needs and talents by sharing and explaining data.

What would an effective transition look like?

There are, I believe, three main measures of an effective transition process.

1. Social adjustment
2. Institutional adjustment
3. Curriculum interest and continuity

Social adjustment is about pupils successfully making new friends and reporting higher self-esteem.

Institutional adjustment is about pupils settling in well at their new school and getting used to their new school's routines, systems and structures.

Curriculum interest and continuity is about pupils being prepared for the level and style of work they encounter at secondary school, as well as being appropriately challenged and engaged, and building on the progress they made at primary school.

Putting it into practice...

So, we need to span the river that flows between primary and secondary schools (and indeed any educational waterway!) with five transition 'bridges' so that we can safely reach our destination: the shores of social adjustment, institutional adjustment, and curriculum interest and continuity.

But what does this look like in practice? What do we need to do in order to improve our transition arrangements? Here are some suggested actions...

We can arrange regular visits from secondary school teachers to Year 6 to talk about life in 'big school' and, perhaps an even more impactful strategy, we can arrange for regular visits from Year 7 pupils to talk to Year 6 and share their experiences of the transition process and of life after transition. Pupils are more likely to listen to their peers than they are to their teachers and will be relieved to hear from pupils in the year above them that life in 'big school' isn't quite as daunting as they think.

Feeder primary schools can operate an open-door policy for parents to air any concerns and questions. Secondary schools, meanwhile, can hold a parents' evening in the summer term to welcome new parents and answer questions about the transition and induction process, and a further parents' evening in the autumn term for 'settling in' discussions and to talk to their child's form tutor.

We can make sure that all staff have clear roles and responsibilities that make explicit the part they play in securing a smooth and successful transition for pupils.

We can make sure each year and each department have a 'transition expert' who is afforded the time (and possibly remunerated) to become the go-to person for all aspects of transition. For example, a transition expert within the English department of a secondary school could make it their mission to know as much as possible about the primary English curriculum and could map what is taught at primary, including the glossary of grammatical terms pupils must know by the end of Year 6, to the key stage 3 curriculum. They could ensure that what is taught in Year 7 represents a natural progression from what is taught in Year 6, and that it consolidates and extends prior learning. They could also ensure that the language of learning used in Years and 7 is consistent - both in terms of the technical language pupils know and use (for example, using the word 'conjunction' rather than 'connective' to describe 'and'), and also the language teachers use to describe aspects of pedagogy and practice (for example, WAGOLL and WABOLL). This expert could be the main liaison with primary feeder schools, too. They might, for example, work with primary colleagues on developing a bridging unit and on teaching a summer school.

As well as recruiting transition experts in each year and/or department, we can make sure that every teacher in each phase and stage develops a deeper knowledge of the curriculum content and means of assessment from the preceding and succeeding phases and stages to that which they teach. This means Year 6 teachers reading the secondary curriculum and familiarising themselves with the way in which their pupils will be assessed when they move into Year 7 (which, with 'assessment without levels' may be different in each of the secondary schools to which pupils transfer). It also means those Year 6 teachers speaking to and observing Year 7 teachers to understand how the curriculum is taught and what is expected of pupils. Likewise, it means Year 7 teachers reading the primary curriculum and familiarising themselves with the KS2 SATs and other forms of teacher assessment in Year 6. It means talking to and observing Year 6 teachers.

Of course, observing teaching in the phase before or after that which you teach is time-consuming and may require lessons to be covered. But, in my view, it is one of the most impactful forms of CPD in which a teacher can engage and time and money well-spent. What's more, I would recommend senior leaders provide class cover to enable their teachers to visit and observe other teachers. Not only are school leaders often better placed to cover lessons because they know the pupils and are less likely to encounter behavioural problems, teaching cover lessons is a great way to 'lead by example' as well as - for those leaders without timetabled lessons - 'keep their hand in' and feel the impact of the decisions they make in the classroom.

We can run joint social events between Year 6 and Year 7, such as a disco in the summer term. This would more naturally take place in the secondary school to enable Year 6 pupils to experience secondary school life and become familiar with the buildings.

We can ensure that transition days, whereby Year 6s visit their new school in the summer term prior to transfer, strike the right balance between enthusing pupils about what delights await them in September (and allaying their fears) AND not over-selling the secondary experience. We want the day to be fun and engaging, to make pupils excited about starting their new school, but we don't want to give the false impression that every science lesson, say, is a veritable firework display or that every day is full of fun, because the reality will only prove disappointing by contrast and pupils will feel cheated.

We can ask Year 6 pupils to produce a Pupil Passport or portfolio which contains examples of their best work and information about how they like to learn and about what motivates them. This puts some ownership of the transition process into pupils' hands, thus engaging them as active participants in the process rather just passive recipients whereby transition is done to them by others.

Year 6 teachers need to help pupils become increasingly 'secondary ready' as they travel towards transition. For example, they need to help pupils to understand their strengths and areas for improvement, and to develop their ability to talk confidently to their teachers. This necessitates primary teachers observing and working with their secondary colleagues to understand what a secondary classroom looks and sounds like, then starting to emulate it. Of course, this is a two-way process and secondary teachers also need to observe and work with their primary colleagues to ensure the beginning of Year 7 more closely resembles the end of primary school and slowly bridges the gap between primary and secondary ways of working. In short, both sides of the divide need to make adjustments in order to ensure pupils are eased through transition.

Another strategy to help bridge the gap between the primary and secondary curriculum is to use a mixed model of curriculum delivery in Year 7. For example, there might be some project-based learning whereby several subject areas (say, all the humanities, all the sciences, all the arts) combine to create one cross-curricular project. This not only helps pupils to see the natural links between subjects (and helps improve their ability to 'transfer' knowledge and skills from one context to another), it also helps to reduce the number of different teachers and subjects to which a new Year 7 pupil - used to working with one or two teachers all year in primary school) will be exposed.

As well as project-based learning, pupils in Year 7 may have some subjects taught by their form tutor in their form room. Again, this helps limit the number of teachers and classrooms - and therefore the logistical transition along busy corridors - pupils have to encounter and it helps foster a sense of belonging and emotional stability. The Year 7 timetable can also be blocked creatively - for example, in a two-week timetable by mirroring weeks 1 and 2 so pupils have less information to remember, and by scheduling double lessons - to reduce the number of transitions pupils have to make and to facilitate the creation of nurture groups for the most vulnerable pupils.

We can have a staggered start to the new academic year so that new Year 7 pupils can acclimatise to their new environment and navigate around the site without the looming presence of older, bigger students. This might extend into staggered breaks and lunches for the first week so that new Year 7 pupils can experience lunch in the canteen without vying for position with older pupils and can enjoy the playgrounds, and make new friends, without fear.

We can make sure that transiti   ements are not confined to the transfer of pupils from Year 6 int   ut also cover the other transitions that pupils encounter. In other   nsition should not just be about pupils' transfer from one phase o   ory schooling to another, but also about the transition pupils expe   ween the key stages and years of school life. For example, we c   place transition arrangements to support pupils as they move fro   nto Year 8, from Year 8 and into Year 9, and from key stage 3 int   e 4, bridging the gap between key stage 3 and GCSE study. At ea   ransition arrangements should be put in place for pupils but also t   ts/carers…

One simple strategy to employ is to require pupils to start a new book or folder in the final half-term of every year which they will take with them into the next year. Not only does this focus their attentions on producing their best work, it provides the next teacher with ready examples of what pupils are capable of achieving when outside of test conditions and in their comfort zones. This simple act can aid target-setting and lesson planning - pitching work in pupils' 'struggle zones' - better than end of year tests.

Another strategy to help pupils transition from one year to the next is to start the new timetable before the summer. Often, once Year 11 pupils have concluded their studies, there is flexibility to start the next year's timetable so that pupils and teachers get to know each other in the final few weeks of term. This enables teachers to set the tone and make clear their expectations, and also affords the opportunity to set homework to be completed over the summer holiday, better preparing pupils for the start of September. If this wholesale adoption of the new timetable is not logistically possible, then the same goals can be achieved on a smaller scale by pupils attending 'taster classes' with their new teachers once or twice in the last couple of weeks and by work being set for the summer holidays.

Another means of improving the transfer of pupils at every stage of their education - not just from primary to secondary school - is to establish peer mentoring schemes. Although research recommends that a reading mentor be at least two years older (and have a reading age at least two years greater) than the mentee, there is much to be said for enlisting Year 8 pupils as mentors for new Year 7s. Year 8s have more recently experienced transition and settling in arrangements, and thus are better placed to offer relevant advice and guidance. Being closer in age and experience, they are also better placed to communicate and understand how a Year 7 pupil is feeling.

What's more, Year 8 is often regarded as the most wasted of the so-called 'wasted years', sandwiched between the exciting newness of Year 7 and the more meaningful curriculum of Year 9 with its elective subjects and end-of-key stage tests. As such, Year 8 pupils would likely benefit from being given leadership opportunities, and a sense of responsibility and purpose. The mentoring could start whilst the mentees are in Year 6 and the mentors in Year 7 (on transition days, for example) and continue after the summer of transfer.

We can ensure we secure more and earlier parental engagement including via telephone calls, emails, texts, and face-to-face visits. As well as engaging the parents of current Year 6 pupils before and during transition, we could make good use of their experiences after transition has concluded. For example, we could elicit parental feedback on their - and their child's - experience of the transition process, finding out what worked and what did not. Indeed, schools in both phases need to evaluate and adapt their transition plans in order to take account of pupil, parent and teacher feedback. And, in order to do this, both primary and secondary schools need to collect feedback at every available opportunity.

There is much to be gained by Year 6 and Year 7 teachers working collaboratively on their curriculum planning, too. This is no more important than in the final half-term of Year 6 and the first half-term of Year 7 where curriculum content and pedagogy need to meld. In so doing, Year 6 and 7 teachers can establish a shared language of learning and establish common processes for, for example, how they run self- and peer-assessment and group work. Cross-phase partnerships might include joint primary and secondary CPD events and INSET days and peer observation schemes.

Another useful product of this cross-phase partnership working is to create a 'bridging unit' which pupils begin working on at the end of Year 6 (perhaps after they have sat their SATs), continue working on over the summer holidays and complete at the start of Year 7. Bridging units enable pupils to produce good work to take with them to secondary school which shows their new teachers what they're capable of achieving. They also allay some of pupils' natural apprehensions about the kind of work they'll be expected to do in secondary school. And bridging units help pupils to see the natural links between the primary and secondary curricula, and to understand that secondary education is about progression not about starting again.

Of course, extra consideration will be needed for those pupils who do not have supportive homes and who will therefore be placed at a disadvantage when continuing their work over the summer holidays. To resolve this, it may be advisable to run a 'summer school' which enables pupils to access help and support in school. Although discrete summer schools funding has been scrapped, it is a good use of Pupil Premium funding and the literacy and numeracy catch-up funding.

Another consideration to take if running bridging units is whether or not, as a secondary school, you have access to and support from every feeder primary school. If not, working with some pupils but not all could lead to an academic attainment gap. If you do not have access to all feeders, it doesn't mean the strategy should be abandoned, however. Bridging units are hugely beneficial, after all. Rather, it means taking mitigating action to support those pupils who study at primary schools to which you cannot liaise. For example, pupils who are not going to start the unit in Year 6 lessons could do some of the work at home or after-hours at the secondary school.

Cloud services and other technological means of communicating and sharing information can also be used to engage the parents of pupils in primary schools with which there is little contact or collaboration (as well as hard-to-reach parents). For example, it may be possible to send the Year 6 unit and any work that's required over the summer break directly to parents using Google Drive or OneDrive. Work can also be submitted by parents or pupils in this way, ensuring no one is unduly disadvantaged by being in a primary school which, for whatever reason, does not engage in the teaching of bridging units.

Whilst we're on the subject of cross-phase working, another useful strategy for primary and secondary teachers to employ when working together to improve transition, is to map the curriculum content covered - and the skills required of pupils - in Years 6 and 7, and then to audit which skills are explicitly taught and when, thus identifying any gaps whereby pupils are expected to know or be able to do something which they haven't been taught. These gaps then need to be filled so the process comes full circle as teachers plan where to teach these skills. Of course, once a skill has been taught for the first time, say in Year 6, we need to decide if it needs to be re-taught again when it is needed next (and, if so, whether we need to completely re-teach it or just recap and practice).

Transition days

One tangible form that transition takes is the 'transition day' or week, usually scheduled for June or July after Year 6 pupils have taken their SATs and Year 11 have finished their GCSEs. Let's take a look at how we might better use this time to ensure curriculum continuity and to be better prepare pupils for secondary school education...

Let's start with a thought experiment:

Imagine you've taught in the same school since you qualified. Now, after many happy years, you're on the move. You've secured a promotion in the school down the road and start in September. You've already met your new boss a couple of times and have read the school prospectus and staff handbook cover-to-cover, over and over. Now, your new headteacher has invited you into her school for a day before the summer holidays in order to help you acclimatise.

What would you need to have accomplished by the end of the day in order to consider your visit a success, do you think? What would help you make the move?

Of course, it's not all about you! A workplace visit is a two-way process. There are some things your new school will need you to do – such as have your photo taken for your staff badge and read and sign the school's IT policy before setting you up on the school network. And there are some things you will need to do in order to better prepare yourself and alleviate some of your natural anxieties – such as familiarising yourself with the school's expectations of lesson planning, getting to grips with their assessment policy, and feeling the shape of the school day.

I believe that, in the balance of school and staff needs, the scales should always tilt towards the new member of staff. Indeed, as a headteacher, I would always ensure new staff were put before bureaucracy – their 'getting to know you' visits were specifically designed to make them feel at ease and to enthuse them about the future, not as a means of ticking some boxes off the induction process

But I digress...

Imagine how you're feeling on the morning of your visit. Excited? Almost certainly. It's a new job and a promotion at that. You can't wait to get started. A little apprehensive, perhaps? It's a big change, there will be lots of new systems and structures to get used to. You've only known the inner workings of one school before. It will be a steep learning curve, that's for sure.

Now imagine how you'd feel if, upon arrival, rather than a coffee in the staff room and a friendly chat with the head, you are shepherded into a windowless room and made to sit a number of exams.

It would feel pretty soul-destroying, wouldn't it? You'd feel under intense pressure, determined to do well and make a good first impression, but nervous about what would happen if you failed the tests – would it mean you'd lose the job before you'd even started it? Whatever the consequences, you'd certainly be embarrassed if the results were not good.

And what does this testing regime say about your new school? Is that what it's going to be like in your new job? No tea and comfort, no supportive chats, no arm round the shoulders and reassurance?

Whatever your anxiety, imagine how much worse it would be if you were only eleven years old and therefore less socially and emotionally developed, less used to life changes.

Now think about what your school does on its transition day in July.

Many schools do exactly what I've described above: they use the opportunity to test pupils in English and maths in order to get baseline data for setting classes and writing targets. Personally, I feel this is misguided and potentially harmful.

Other schools, in contrast, strap their pupils into a rollercoaster and give their new pupils an exciting, high octane ride through the very best that secondary school has to offer. Every 'taster' lesson is a veritable firework display – literally in the case of science. Teachers are funny and self-effacing, relaxed and patient, and lessons are fun-packed and short, punctuated by lots of 'down time' to socialise. I feel this is – though perhaps not quite as misguided as testing pupils – potentially harmful, too, because it proffers a false promise upon which reality inevitably fails to deliver.

My advice? Ensure your transition days strike the right balance between enthusing pupils about what delights await them in September (whilst also allaying their fears) and giving them a realistic vision of the future.

In short, don't test and don't over-sell the secondary experience.

You want the day to be fun and engaging, to make pupils excited about starting their new school, but you don't want to give the false impression that every day is full of fun and social time, because the reality will not only prove disappointing by contrast but pupils will also feel mis-sold and cheated. This may then demotivate them in September.

What you definitely should avoid on transition days – which often fall hot on the heels of high-stakes, high-pressure key stage 2 SATs – is testing…

Some schools understandably want to re-test pupils to help determine which sets they will be in. Personally, I would argue that, in an ideal world where SATs results and Year 6 teacher assessments are trusted and where primary and secondary colleagues work more collaboratively, re-testing should not be necessary. After all, what message does it send to pupils if they are re-tested prior to or immediately after starting Year 7? That their SATs were pointless? That everything they've achieved to date was for nothing? And to what extent does further testing punish pupils and pile on more emotional pressure?

No, I don't much like re-testing. But…. I understand and accept that some schools feel re-testing is necessary and therefore use CATs tests or other diagnostics assessments. So, re-test if you feel you have to but please don't do it on a transition day.

I happen to agree that the best time to do it is not at the start of September immediately following transfer – it's not the best start for pupils who are already feeling nervous, discomforted and unconfident. And September is too late if the test results are to be used to inform setting and targets. Tests should, therefore, be carried out before the summer when pupils are more confident and comfortable – the big fishes in the little pond – and when the results of the tests can be used to set pupils from the start of September and help with target-setting, rather than after pupils have been organised into sets and may then need to be moved up or down.

However, the July transition day is not – in my view – the time or the place for this. Transition days are precious, you should value them and use them wisely to help your new pupils adjust to secondary life and to make friends. You should use transition days to help pupils grow in confidence and self-esteem and become accustomed to the systems and structures they'll have to work within from September.

If you really want to know what to do on these days, then ask your current Year 7s and their parents. What would have helped them make the move more smoothly? What did they enjoy about their transition day last year and what, conversely, made them feel more anxious?

Transitions within a school

We've examined why improving the transition between the different phases of school – such as from primary to secondary - is so important. Now let's turn our attention to transition in its wider sense because transition is not just about the move from, say, Year 6 into Year 7, from one key stage or phase to another. Indeed, it is about the various movements within a school or college, too.

I will exemplify this by looking at the transition from Year 7 to Year 8 because this is often regarded as a stop-gap year but, again, the principles apply to any in-school or in-college move.

The dip year

Year 7 is new and exciting, if not a little daunting; Year 9 assumes a higher status because its curriculum often includes elective subjects, it comes at the end of a key stage and carries with it national tests (albeit now optional) and GCSE options or, in some schools, signals the start of a three-year key stage 4. Year 8, however, which is awkwardly sandwiched between them, is often seen as a stopgap, wandering alone and confused in the wilderness.

In Year 8 there are no tests of any great import, no big decisions to make, and nothing is particularly new or exciting anymore. New school is now old hat. What's more, it's often the year in which pupils' hormones begin to rage. As a result, towards the end of Year 7 and during Year 8, pupils begin to get demotivated and their progress slows or stalls.

If you Google 'Year 8 dip' you'll find plenty of frustrated patter in parents' forums as mums and dads, ask if it's normal for their son or daughter to be so demotivated at school and to be stalling in their studies. The responses they garner are invariably reassuring: yes, it's perfectly normal and a perennial problem in schools. But aside from the chatroom chatter, there is precious little research or advice on how to tackle this phenomenon. So how can we avoid this 'dip'?

Well, as is often the case, I find the solution lies in the problem. If the problem is that Year 8 isn't regarded as new or exciting, then we need to make it feel new and exciting. If the problem is that Year 8 is the year in which pupils usually start puberty and their hormones kick in with a vengeance as they begin the journey towards maturity, then we need to recognise this increasing maturity. If the problem is that Year 8, without tests and options, is regarded as meaningless, as a stopgap, then we need to make it feel meaningful and use assessment and feedback to motivate pupils to make better progress.

So, here are my top tips for avoiding the Year 8 'dip' and ensuring that the transition from Year 7 into Year 8 is just as smooth and effective as we hope the transition from primary to secondary proved to be...

Make each year special and have a curriculum that ensures progression and continuity. We need to ensure that Year 8 is different to Year 7 and Year 9, that it offers something unique, challenging and engaging. This might be in the form of cross-curricular project-based learning but whatever approach to the curriculum we take we must make sure that Year 8 represents a significant step-change in terms of difficulty and complexity.

Notwithstanding the importance of spaced practice (of repeating learning several times and leaving increasingly long gaps before returning to re-test), what Year 8 must not do is unnecessarily repeat curriculum content from primary school and Year 7. In order to ensure Year 8 offers something new, Year 7 and Year 8 teachers, if they are different, must closely liaise on their curriculum planning to achieve continuity.

Another way to make Year 8 feel special is to take advantage of the freedom afforded by its lack of formal testing and qualifications and pack it full of extra-curricular opportunities such as educational visits, residential trips, and so on. Serve a rich diet of culture - in or out of school - with theatre productions and museum visits, healthy eating expos and sporting events, science fairs and art and design competitions and exhibitions. Really bring learning to life.

Of course, money is always a consideration, but we must take Ofsted's advice and make better use of the Pupil Premium funding in key stage 3 rather than stockpile it for key stage 4 interventions. If we use more of it in Year 8 (and therefore less at GCSE) - in conjunction with other funding streams - in order to ensure that all pupils get fair access to enrichment opportunities, then they will be motivated and make better progress, hence they will commence their GCSEs from a more advantageous starting point and far fewer remedial interventions will be needed in Years 10 and 11.

Recognise the increasing maturity of pupils. We need to ensure that pupils - who are starting to experience puberty and grow into young adults - feel that their increasing maturity is being recognised and appreciated.

To do this, we need to make Year 8 pupils feel set apart from Year 7 but only in the best sense. Rather than setting Year 8 in opposition to Year 7 we should utilise their maturity and experience to support, advise and mentor the new cohort of pupils. Year 8 pupils could be trained as reading mentors, for example, or as break and lunchtime 'buddies' and guides. They could play a big role during the Year 7 induction.

We tend to favour much older pupils in these roles - and not without good reason as sixth form students are mature, more accomplished readers, and in need of supporting evidence for their UCAS applications - but older students are also busy with important exams whereas Year 8 have the time to spare and need to feel valued. They are also more able to empathise with their Year 7 peers, being closer in age and having more recently experienced transition and induction.

We could also recognise the increasing maturity of Year 8 pupils by tweaking our rewards and sanctions policy, ensuring that rewards remain age-appropriate and motivational, and that sanctions continue to be suitably punitive but not demeaning. Ideally, we should involve Year 8 pupils in this process by consulting them on what the rewards and sanctions should be - the very process of consultation, whatever the outcome, will make them feel valued and mature.

Have systems that recognise and correct disaffection early and provide opportunities for a fresh start. As well as ensuring our rewards and sanctions policy remains relevant as pupils grow in maturity, we need to make sure that low-level disruption and general disaffection - which are prevalent in Year 8 - are spotted early and tackled effectively. Those systems need to be positive and motivating, giving pupils a reason to reassert themselves and work hard. The key, again, is in an effective rewards policy but also in the use of intrinsic rewards, the reward of learning itself not extrinsic rewards such as prizes.

In order for pupils to feel rewarded by learning and achieving, we need them to believe that their work has a genuine audience and purpose. Pupils also need to feel that they have some ownership of the work - both in terms of the content and format, and in terms of how it will be assessed.

Perhaps most importantly, any system that seeks to recognise and correct disaffection and low-level disruption must make clear that there is a way back. Pupils need to be afforded a fresh start. This applies to pupils who may have misbehaved or underachieved in Year 7 who now need to know - explicitly and implicitly - that Year 8 represents a new start for them and an opportunity to make amends, and to pupils who let themselves down during Year 8 but need a way back before they start Year 9.

Have pastoral systems that support pupils in their learning as well as their behaviour. We need to make sure that our pastoral systems do not focus solely on pupils' behaviour and wellbeing - as is often the case in the early years of key stage 3. We must not neglect pupils' academic needs. In practice, this means providing support for pupils whose behaviour is good but who need support either over the long-term or at key waypoints on their learning journey. This might be in the form of in-class support or extra sessions, or it might be in the form of differentiated learning such as differentiated questioning, a choice of outcomes or the application of mastery learning approaches.

Regularly evaluate progress and have effective intervention plans. We need to ensure that Year 8 isn't a wasted year filled with 'fluff' assignments and meaningless assessments. We need to set meaningful work that will stretch and challenge pupils and then assess their progress regularly and accurately so that they can be given detailed formative feedback on which they can act and improve. In short, we should ensure that we put in place the same robust assessment, monitoring and tracking systems in Year 8 that we use for our GCSE and A Level students.

In practice, this means that pupil progress is regularly observed and analysed and that the data is shared with all interested parties - parents, staff and governors. This means that the data is used in a number of ways including to identify underperforming groups, to direct the appropriate deployment of staff and resources, to inform target-setting, to monitor the impact of strategies and interventions, and to challenge the aspirations and assumptions of pupils, parents and staff. This also means having in place a well-developed pupil tracking system to capture a wider range of data in addition to attainment levels and using external data and self-evaluation in order to focus on gaps and progress, not just average attainment. And it means that attainment data, as well as informing staff on pupil progress, is used to provide pupils with regular feedback on their progress.

Cross-phase partnerships

Making a pupil's transition from a year, key stage or phase of education to the next as smooth as possible – thus ensuring greater curriculum continuity – takes more than just a little teamwork at the end of one year and the beginning of the next.

Indeed, even starting the process a year earlier is not really sufficient. Rather, what is needed is long-term, genuine and sustainable collaboration between teachers of different years, key stages and phases, which of course means different schools. We need early years, primary, secondary and FE staff to work in close partnership on all aspects of a child's and young person's education, sharing information and resources, in order to ensure that each child is well-protected and experiences a continuity of service and support.

Why do we need better collaboration? Because projects that link up pupils, teachers and schools across early years, primary, secondary and FE phases can have a positive impact on pupils and teachers by supporting pupils to experience a smoother transition and make continuous academic progress, and by enabling teachers and schools to learn from best practice across different stages of the system.

So, what might this collaboration look like in practice? It might involve all phases of compulsory education establishing family links, sharing services such as family liaison officers, education welfare officers, SENCOs, EAL teachers and other specialists. It might involve all phases jointly planning and running projects and events such as summer schools or careers fairs. It might – indeed should - take the form of joint curriculum planning. It might take the form of joint CPD networks and INSET days, and teacher visits and exchanges. It might also involve cross-phase mentoring and tutoring.

Whatever form it takes in practice - and I will explore more examples in a moment - it is important, as much as is possible, to see the two phases as one, particularly to see Years 5 through to 8 as a single phase when it comes to planning the curriculum because this will help to bridge the primary/secondary divide. Planning a unique 'middle years' curriculum will also help to combat the problem of key stage 3 particularly Year 8 - being seen as 'wasted years' and a poor relation to GCSE. Indeed, it will give it identify and purpose.

Whilst we're on this topic, what will also help to bridge the divide - and one of the desired outcomes of an effective cross-phase partnership - is encouraging pupils to bring in their best work from each subject in one year when they start the next, including the best work from primary school when they start secondary. This work can then be affixed to the front of pupils' exercise books to remind them and their teachers what they're capable of producing. Such a tactic will help combat the common complaint that secondary teachers underestimate pupils' abilities and that pupils' standards slide following transition.

Another desired outcome of an effective cross-phase partnership is to ensure that all Year 6 and 7 teachers, for example, work together to familiarise each other with the national curriculum of the phase they teach as well as the secondary school's own curriculum and the school curriculum for the main feeder primaries.

Cross-phase partnerships can also be fruitfully employed designing 'settling-in' sessions and summer schools for pupils but these should have an academic rather than pastoral flavour. Primary and secondary colleagues could also work together to design formative and summative assessment strategies which make it easier for teachers to track pupils' progress as they move out of one phase and into the next.

Where possible, cross-phase partnerships could enable teachers to work across the different phases in order to introduce more subject-specialist teaching to the later years of primary school as well as encourage a more holistic approach to pupils' development at the beginning of key stage 3.

Primary school leaders play a crucial role in making cross-phase partnerships work. Firstly, they need to set clear expectations for their staff about the importance of sharing and communicating with their secondary colleagues by encouraging teachers to help pupils produce transition 'passports' which showcase both their academic and their broader achievements at primary school. Secondary school leaders play an equally important role. For example, they need to encourage Year 7 teachers who are struggling to understand a particular pupil's needs to consider contacting their old Year 6 teacher for a conversation.

Multi-academy trusts that encompass secondaries and some of their feeder primaries have an advantage when it comes to cross-phase partnerships and many are already ahead of the curve. Their shared HR and payroll structures and systems enable greater and easier collaboration. For example, in cross-phase MATs it is possible to employ teachers who work across the primary and secondary phases. This might mean that Year 6 teachers move up with their classes and teach them in Year 7, thus making the transition much less daunting.

It is also possible to have cross-phase subject leaders so that, for example, a

Director of English oversees the MAT's English provision from Reception right through to A Level and perhaps has a Subject Leader for each phase but the phases do not follow the traditional pattern but straddle the key stage divide such as the 'middle years' of Years 5 to 8. The same could be said of pastoral leaders, too, with a Pastoral Leader of Years 5, 6 and 7 rather than the traditional key stage 3. And senior leader roles could also be designed to ensure that assessment, for example, as well as, say, the curriculum and pedagogy, are joined up and continuous across all phases.

In Wales, an experiment in cross-phase partnerships has led to improvements in pupil outcomes and the raising of standards of educational practice and attainment. NFER researchers analysed twenty schools – four matched pairs of secondary schools and six of primary schools - who were involved in the experiments in 2016 and found that most of the schools believed their partnerships had improved standards of teaching and learning, and had raised pupil performance in maths and numeracy.

The NFER also found evidence that leadership at both senior and middle levels had been enhanced as a result of cross-phase partnerships and that schools' data tracking and assessment systems had been strengthened.

Most of the staff who were interviewed noted the positive impact of the partnerships, and particularly praised the "mutual trust, willingness and respect between the schools which had facilitated effective collaboration". However, they also admitted that there were some factors which might have constrained the relationships, including proximity and differences in pupils, cohorts and characteristics.

One headteacher involved in the project told NFER researchers: "The key for us in the beginning was trust and we are now in the situation where we are very open with each other, friendly ... it was about developing relationships, going slowly, getting to know each other and having the confidence to be open and honest."

Teachers who were involved in the project reported that they had refined approaches to teaching and learning, which had had a big impact on the work done. Teachers felt more confident to try different approaches and to experiment with techniques that they may not have used previously. As a result, lessons become more dynamic and interactive, inviting pupils to become active participants. The quality of feedback improved, and teachers changed the way they asked questions, allowing them to elicit answers which delved into how well learners understood concepts and issues.

Some schools had also used the partnerships to look at how they might deliver the curriculum more effectively, including focusing on literacy and numeracy. Teachers told the NFER that being involved in a partnership had made them more reflective of their own practice, and that they had looked at different ways of learning. This included examining how they used data as part of teaching and learning to suit the individual needs of classes of individual pupils.

In secondary schools, most heads and teachers said that participation in the partnership had had a positive effect on teaching, with one senior leader describing it as a "journey of improvement". Teachers said that they had more opportunities to self-evaluate their own classroom practice and were developing an "extended repertoire of teaching, assessment and tracking skills". This was achieved by discussing different methods and approaches, sharing schemes of work and methods of tracking and using data, as well as lesson observations. Teachers also said they had gained the skills to teach smaller classes and of working with individual pupils.

The NFER report said: "Most senior leaders and teachers considered that classroom practice was improving as a result of the increased interaction between staff within and between schools, which had raised staff awareness of alternative approaches when planning, teaching and assessing."

At the whole-school level, one primary or secondary school in the partnership often influenced how things were done in the other. Headteachers became more reflective of their own leadership styles and in some cases, leadership teams were restructured as a result of the partnership. There were also changes among some middle leadership teams, with some middle leaders taking on new responsibilities.

The use of data was also strengthened, with schools changing how they collected data and how they then used this to support teaching and learning, in particular in supporting individual pupils. NFER researchers noted that in some partnerships staff raised their expectations of what learners could achieve. At the same time, pupils were made more aware of their targets and the level at which they should be working. This had the knock-on effect of making them reflect on their own needs, even setting down their own success criteria. Partnership schools used pupils' work from both settings to standardise judgments for assessment and moderation. In some cases, work from one school was adapted for use in the other.

However, what did not work was an approach based on transferring practice directly from one school to another, or where school leaders assumed that what worked in their school would be effective practice elsewhere. As a result of all this, the NFER found that: "Learners' motivation improved and they were more engaged with teachers and the learning process. All of these changes were related to work to strengthen learners' voices, through formal processes for them to make their views known about their own learning and other work to nurture their independence and their enjoyment of their work."

The most lasting changes, researchers found, came about when there was a shift in attitude and culture, and this was needed alongside structural and procedural changes if reforms were to work.

The partnerships appear to have helped schools to make sustained improvements. The study concluded that the partnerships had been effective in supporting and speeding up changes in participating schools. This was achieved partly through matching up schools effectively, the support that was given by the government, and the 'emotional intelligence' shown by senior leaders in getting their staff on board with the project while being mindful of their emotions and sensibilities.

CHAPTER FOURTEEN
THE LANGUAGE *OF* AND *FOR* LEARNING

Weaving its way through the curriculum like a golden thread, is the importance of language, both as a means of accessing and understanding the curriculum and as a means of demonstrating learning.

Without good spoken and written language capabilities, pupils and students cannot meet the language demands of an academic curriculum and make progress. Literacy, therefore, is not about teachers teaching their subject or vocation in addition to teaching English; rather, it is about teaching their subject better by teaching pupils and students how to speak, read and write like a subject specialist. For example, in Science, teachers need to teach their pupils how to speak like a scientist, using the correct terminology, formality and register, how to read, interpret and understand scientific texts, including how to follow a detailed and technical argument and how to skim and scan for key facts, and how to write like a scientist by adopting the conventions, structure, syntax and vocabulary of good scientific writing.

When we engage in the curriculum design process, therefore, we must consider how we will make provision for the development of pupils' language skills.

We will explore the wider aspects of cross-curricular literacy development in Chapter Twenty-Five but here, for the purposes of assessing the starting points of our curriculum and providing curriculum continuity, I would like to focus on the language *of* learning and language *for* learning…

One way in which we can bridge the gap between the primary and secondary curriculums, and the secondary and FE curriculums, is to ensure that teachers on either side of the transition 'divide' use the same, or at least similar, language *of* - and language *for* - learning.

By 'language *of* learning' I mean the technical vocabulary that pupils are required to learn as part of the curriculum content knowledge. For example, if teachers in primary schools (as stated in the primary curriculum) refer to the words 'and' and 'but' as 'conjunctions' but their secondary school colleagues are wedded to the term 'connective', it may prove confusing for pupils and their Year 7 teachers may assume they haven't been taught, or at least haven't learnt, what a connective is when their use of the term is greeted with a wall of blank faces, whereas pupils may know connectives inside out but by another name. Likewise, in Science, secondary teachers might refer to independent variable, dependent variable and controlled variables when conducting an experiment whereas primary teachers might simply ask 'how do you make it a fair test?' without introducing the technical vocabulary. The concepts are familiar but the language is not.

Of course, there will always be differences in the language used in primary and secondary and FE – some terms will be too difficult or complex for younger pupils to say and use knowingly. However, primary and secondary schools and FE colleges could work together more closely to identify the avoidable differences in the language of learning they use – the unnecessarily confusing and contradictory – and explicitly signpost to new language when it is introduced.

By 'learning *for* learning' I mean the vocabulary we, as teachers, use to describe teaching and learning methods and activities. For example, in primary schools teachers routinely talk about WAGOLLs which stands for 'What a good one looks like'. Pupils become confident using this term and certainly know what it means. However, when they transfer to secondary school, they're unlikely to hear it uttered again and may, instead, be confronted with the Latinate term 'exemplar'. Some pupils may make the link with 'example' and understand its meaning but many – particularly the word poor who, more than anyone else, need the social and emotional effects of transition to be mitigated – may not be familiar with the word family and may miss its meaning.

Our teaching is littered – often unknowingly – with pedagogic jargon and the teaching terms we use in secondary are often different to those used in primary. Again, primary, secondary and FE teachers need to work more closely to ensure what they teach and the way in which they teach it –

including the language they use and how they operate their classrooms (e.g. what they expect of pupils, what roles pupils are given, how they manage behaviour and use rewards and sanctions, and how they plan transitions between tasks) - is consistent. Of course, just as content knowledge needs to grow in complexity as is it retaught throughout the curriculum; the language teachers use should also develop. But more needs to be done to smooth the transition and to draw links between the end of one year and the beginning of the next.

CHAPTER FIFTEEN
IDENTIFYING CURRICULUM STARTING POINTS

So far in this section of the book on 'assessing starting points' I've explored ways of assessing the taught curriculum – in other words, ways of understanding what has been taught before the curriculum we teach so that we can ensure there is greater curriculum continuity.

But the *taught* curriculum is only part of the picture, we also need to understand the *learnt* curriculum – what have individual pupils actually learnt so far, what do they know and what can they do, and what are their misconceptions and misunderstandings? In other words, we need to understand individual pupils' starting points and identify the gaps in their knowledge and skills.

This can be achieved in part by ensuring there is better data sharing at the point of transition so that teachers of, say, Year 6 provide detailed information – in addition to the key stages 2 SATs results in the form of scaled scores, and in each subject discipline – about what the pupil was capable of outside of test conditions and constraints, what they enjoyed and did not enjoy, what they could do and could not do, what motivated them and demotivated them, and what they mastered and what they have only tentatively grasped but require further reinforcement on, and so on and so forth.

But better data sharing is still only half the battle won… we also need to assess pupils 'on the go' as they begin their curriculum journey with us, and we need to continue to assess them as they travel through our curriculum.

One method of doing just this is to activate prior knowledge. For example, if I wanted my pupils early in Year 7 to conduct some internet research into, say, Shakespeare's life story in order to inform their analysis of the authorial context for a study of Macbeth, I should not assume that they have conducted internet research before or that, even if they have, they can remember how to do it or be able to transfer their prior experience of this skill (or procedural knowledge) into a new context or domain. I need to activate their prior knowledge of this skill by asking them questions about what they've done before, what they remember of this, how they went about it, what decisions they had to make and what they had to think about.

By so doing, I can retrieve from long-term memory the procedural knowledge pupils previously encoded and bring it into their working memories so they can think about it. Then, because activating prior knowledge is a form of retrieval practice, through repetition, we can begin to automate the decisions pupils have to make in order to free up space in their working memories for them to actively think about the context and task in hand. Put simply, because pupils have done internet research before, they do not need to use as much of their limited working memory capacity to do it again as they would if performing the task for the very first time. If I had not taken time to activate their prior knowledge and instead had assumed all pupils were starting from scratch, they might not have made the link (and developed schema) and would have found the task harder.

Activating prior knowledge in this way also enables me to uncover and unpack any gaps in pupils' knowledge of internet research as well as any misconceptions they may have. I can then ensure all the class are 'on the same page' and are following the same steps.

What's more, activating prior knowledge helps join-up the curriculum in pupils' minds because they can see how they use and expand the knowledge and skills they learnt previously as they progress through school, and this provides intrinsic motivation because they can see the purpose of what they learn and can begin to understand the usefulness of curriculum content.

Further, as pupils activate prior knowledge, they can add increasing complexity to it, progressively developing their knowledge and applying it to different contexts. Think of it like putting a Russian Doll inside a slightly bigger version of that doll, and then another and another, and so on. In the example above, we might start with some basic rules of internet research such as how to use a search engine. Next, we might put that knowledge inside a slightly bigger doll by teaching the skills of using at least three sources and identifying trustworthy sources. Next, we might add the skill of skimming and scanning webpages for key facts, etc. Each time, the doll gets bigger, but pupils are helped to make active connections between all the interrelated knowledge and skills they are learning, and as such create ever-more complex schema in long-term memory.

There are several ways in which we can assess pupils' starting points and continue to assess their prior knowledge as they travel through our curriculum. For example, we could begin each new topic with a KWL chart…

The KWL chart

One common diagnostic technique and a means of acquiring data on pupils' starting points is asking pupils at the beginning of a lesson or new topic to identify what they already know (or think they know) about what they are about to study. Their responses can then be listed in a table or on a graphic organiser. The contents of the first column provide us with a sense of pupils' prior knowledge, while also unmasking any misconceptions that may exist and therefore may need to be addressed.

Next, we should ask pupils to identify "what I want to learn" about the topic and ask them to raise any questions they may have at this early stage. These responses can be recorded in the second column to serve as indicators of areas of interest.

As the unit unfolds, the knowledge and skills that pupils begin to acquire should be recorded in the third column of the table, providing a record for pupils of "what I have learned".

An alternative to this is to begin a topic with an initial assessment, perhaps a low-stakes multiple-choice quiz. The results of these pre-tests can yield invaluable evidence about pupils' prior knowledge and misconceptions and, when repeated at various stages of the teaching sequence, can provide evidence of pupils' growing knowledge and understanding.

Regardless of the approach taken, information from diagnostic assessments can guide us in our ongoing curriculum planning so that lessons are more responsive to pupils' needs and their existing knowledge-base, and so that knowledge builds upon knowledge.

An important practical implication, of course, is that we must remember to plan opportunities for assessments and allow sufficient 'wriggle room' to make adjustments based on the feedback garnered by the assessments.

In-built flexibility like this is not just advisable, it is a key aspect of effective curriculum design and differentiation because it enables learning to be personalised to match the needs and pace of pupils' learning. It also ensures that gaps in pupils' learning are identified and filled, which in turn will avoid an off-the-peg, one-size-fits-all approach to lesson-planning and enable good progress to be made by all pupils, irrespective of their additional and different needs.

Exit tickets

Another way to assess pupils' starting points is through the use of exit tickets...

Exit tickets are slips of paper carrying questions to which pupils provide responses. Exit tickets act as quick, informal assessments of learning that enable teachers to rapidly evaluate their pupils' understanding of the lesson content. They also help pupils to reflect on what they have understood and not understood, and they enable pupils to express what or how they are thinking about new information and, by so doing, they encourage pupils to think more critically.

According to Fisher and Frey (2004), there are three categories of exit slips:

1. Prompts that document learning:
E.g. Write one thing you learned today; Discuss how today's lesson could be used in the real world; etc.

2. Prompts that emphasise the process of learning:
E.g. I didn't understand...; Write one question you have about today's lesson; etc.

3. Prompts to evaluate the effectiveness of instruction:
E.g. Did you enjoy working in small groups today?; Did you find peer-assessment helpful?; etc.

Other useful exit ticket prompts might include:

• I would like to learn more about...
• Next lesson, I'd like you to explain more about...
• The thing I found easiest today was...
• The thing I found hardest today was...

I would go further than Fisher and Frey and suggest that the most effective exit tickets pose questions specific to the curriculum content of the lesson and require pupils to explicitly demonstrate their grasp of that content. For example, if I'd taught pupils how to use an apostrophe correctly, rather than ask them to vaguely comment on something they thought they'd learnt, my exit ticket might require pupils to add an apostrophe to three sentences whereby one would be an apostrophe for possession, one for omission and at least one would require a decision to be made about whether to use -s' or -s's. I could see at a glance if pupils had understood how to use apostrophes by assessing the three sentences.

Doug Lemov, in his book 'Teach Like a Champion' (2010), says that exit tickets allow teachers to "know how effective [their] lesson was, as measured by how well [pupils] learned it, not how well [they] thought [they] taught it."

A good exit ticket, therefore, must be closely aligned to the lesson's objectives. A good exit ticket must also:

- Assess pupils' understanding in all aspects of the lesson
- Differentiate accurately between levels of understanding
- Be quick to answer and assess

Limiting the amount of space available for pupils to respond ensures the task is kept focused and, by the same token, writing a single question which incorporates the whole lesson helps to make assessing exit tickets more manageable.

Talking of which… when assessing the exit tickets pupils have handed in on their way out of the room, we are likely to find that:

- All pupils got the right answer – in which case we can move on to the next topic, or…
- All pupils got the wrong answer – in which case we can re-teach the topic next lesson before moving on, or most likely….
- Some pupils got the right answer but some got it wrong – in which case we can briefly recap on the topic next lesson (perhaps as a starter activity), get a pupil who 'got it' to peer-teach the topic or share their work as an exemplar to deconstruct (or group pupils to do this in pairs), and/or sit down with the pupils who didn't get it when there's a suitable opportunity next lesson and re-teach them whilst the others move on to the next topic.

A caveat: learning is not always observable in the lesson. We can assess pupils' performances - the immediate regurgitation of what they've just seen or heard - but learning only becomes evident at a later time. What's more, performance is often a poor proxy for learning – those pupils who appear to struggle initially often learn better long-term. Exit tickets, because they review pupils' understanding at the end of the lesson not days or weeks later, are in danger of assessing performance rather than learning so some caution should be applied, but they remain a helpful means of reviewing the success of the lesson and can provide a useful focus for the next lesson's starter activity.

To mitigate the limitations of exit tickets, however, it is worthwhile repeating the task in a later lesson and comparing responses – do pupils still claim to understand what they said they'd learnt last time? Do we need to recap or reteach a topic in light of their long-term retrieval ability?

Hinge questions

Another useful strategy – though one that's often harder to get right – is the use of hinge questions...

Hinge questions are multiple choice questions so, before we go any further, let's explain and defend the humble multiple-choice question which, although once a staple of schooling, has become unfashionable in recent years...

With open questions, the rubric defines the rigour. With multiple choice questions, however, the options define the rigour. This is particularly true of hinge questions which can be used just as effectively with the most able pupils as with the less able. The trick to making multiple choice questions effective is to create several wrong options which are nevertheless plausible and closely related to the right answer.

The best 'wrong' options also uncover common misconceptions or false assumptions. As such, the best way to create the wrong options in a way which makes them plausible is to mine a class's work - or look back to a previous year when the topic was last taught - for pupils' common misconceptions, misunderstandings and mistakes. If nothing else, trawling through pupils' work to discover what they tend to get wrong and what tends to stump them, helps inform the lesson planning process, allowing the teacher to dedicate more time to those elements with which pupils most often struggle.

This act of mining pupils' work for misconceptions and then applying the findings in a way that helps anticipate pupils' difficulties and questions, is the difference between content knowledge and pedagogical content knowledge, between knowing your subject and knowing how to teach your subject in a way which makes sense to pupils. Analysing misconceptions also helps an expert teacher to view a topic through the lens of the novice pupil, to narrow the knowledge gap between them and improve the lesson planning process.

A 'hinge' is a point in a lesson when a teacher needs to check whether or not pupils have grasped a key concept and are ready to move on to study another. Usually, pupils' mastery of the concept that has just been taught is contingent on them being able to understand the next concept. It's important, therefore, that the teacher assesses pupils' levels of mastery before moving on… and this is exactly what a hinge question can do…

A hinge question is a diagnostic tool which a teacher employs when their pupils reach the 'hinge' point. Pupils' responses provide the teacher with valuable evidence about what their pupils know, don't know and need to do next. A class's response to a hinge question should inform the teacher whether to completely re-teach the topic, recap the main points, or move on to the next topic.

A hinge question, then, is a multiple-choice question which provides an immediate check of pupils' understanding. Crucially, a hinge question provides a check of understanding for every pupil in a class. A hinge question informs the teacher if pupils have understood what they've taught and, if not, what they have misunderstood. As I say above, a hinge question should be asked at the end of an activity as the teacher moves from teaching one key concept to another, when the teaching of the second concept is reliant on understanding the first.

Every pupil must respond within a set timeframe, ideally one to two minutes. A hinge question is a quick assessment - a line in the sand - and, therefore, responses should be instinctive and almost immediate. All pupils must participate in the process. As such, it's best to avoid a 'hands up' approach and instead employ a tactic that ensures every pupil shows the teacher their answer at the same time. This enables the teacher to assess every pupil and prevents pupils from being unduly influenced by their peers.

Simultaneous, all-class responses can be achieved by using mini-whiteboards on which pupils write their answers then hold them up when instructed. Alternatively, voting buttons could be used, perhaps on iPads, with the responses - anonymised, of course; perhaps reported as a percentage response against each option - displayed on the interactive whiteboard. Or, perhaps more simply, pupils could hold up lettered, numbered, or coloured cards to indicate their answer. A set of four cards could be kept on desks or given to pupils to retain in their books or planners in order to reduce the logistical strain and permit hinge questions to become a quick, simple, everyday feature of lessons.

The teacher must be able to interpret pupils' responses quickly, ideally within a minute, so that the flow of the lesson isn't stunted. Before pupils show their responses, the teacher - as I say above - needs to set a pass rate for what they consider to be an acceptable level of 'mastery'. For example, the teacher might decide that they'll move on to the next topic if more than eighty per cent of pupils answer the hinge question correctly. They'll then need to consider what they'll do to support the twenty per cent who got the question wrong.

The teacher could set a task for the eighty per cent to do whist working with the twenty per cent, scaffolding their learning, recapping on key points, and so on. Or perhaps the teacher could enlist some of the eighty per cent as peer-teachers to explain the topic to the twenty per cent.

Whatever method you choose, it's important that the means of assessing pupils' starting points is not bureaucratic or burdensome for the teacher and that it provides useful information that can be acted upon. As I discussed earlier and will do again in Book Three of this series, you should always consider the purpose, process and validity of any assessment you carry out, and ensure that it is meaningful, manageable and motivating.

We've reached the end of Step 3 in our six-step curriculum design process – assess the starting points – and can now embark upon the fourth step which is to identify the way-points...

PART FOUR

IDENTIFY THE WAYPOINTS

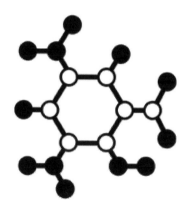

CHAPTER SIXTEEN
PLOTTING A COURSE THROUGH THE CURRICULUM

Once you have set the destination and assessed the starting points of your curriculum, you must plot a course between the two...

As I said at the start of Chapter Twelve, if you wanted to find directions using Google Maps (other maps are available!), you would need to input the destination first then your current location. In other words, Google would ask 'where to?' and then 'where from?'

Once these two pins have been dropped onto the map, Google can begin to find the right path.

In terms of curriculum design, the destination, as we discovered in Part One of this book, is the intended outcomes of our curriculum, or to use Ofsted's parlance 'the clear end-points' or 'body of knowledge' to be learnt. These end points articulate what we expect our pupils and students to have acquired by the time they have finished their curriculum journey with us. The destination can be positioned at the end of a topic or module, at the end of a year, key stage or phase of education, or indeed many years into the future – say ten years – when pupils are applying their knowledge to life and work.

We can think of the starting points, meanwhile, in two ways: the starting points of the *taught* curriculum; and the starting points of the *learnt* curriculum. Put another way, the taught curriculum is what is in the written curriculum plans for the stage or phase immediately preceding that which we teach. This might be the national curriculum or the local curriculum of the schools our pupils come from. We can think of this as the intended curriculum (written down) and the enacted curriculum (actually taught in the classroom).

The learnt curriculum, meanwhile, is what pupils actually know and can do. We can think of this as the real curriculum (what pupils encoded into and can now retrieve from long-term memory). The real curriculum must be assessed on a pupil-by-pupil basis in order to understand what each pupil actually knows and can do, and what gaps remain in their knowledge and skills.

Once we know the destination and starting points, we must carve a path from one to the other. This path is what populates curriculum plans, assessment schedules, and schemes of work.

The shape of the path taken in each subject discipline will be different. Some curriculums are linear, following a neat line between the starting point and the destination as pupils build on prior knowledge and make progress. But many curriculums are neither linear nor neat. They may be spiral or helical in shape; they may zigzag.

But, irrespective of their shape, most subjects will find it useful to identify threshold concepts or waypoints that provide a useful checkpoint on the way towards the destination. Checkpoints have several advantages: firstly, they provide manageable and achievable stepping stones for pupils to aim for along the way rather than setting pupils a goal they cannot hope to hit; secondly, they provide a useful pitstop – a means of assessing, recognising and celebrating pupils' progress to date.

When these threshold concepts are used well, they can also become the means of assessment as I described in Chapter Three.

So, without further ado, let us consider how to identify threshold concepts or waypoints before we look at ways to ensure these waypoints provide for an increasingly complex curriculum…

Identifying threshold concepts

In Chapter Eleven I explained the importance of identifying key concepts – the clear end points of our curriculum. I said that these concepts are the foundations on which our curriculum is built and the destination to which our pupils are headed. I modelled one way of identifying these concepts – albeit with caveats – by using GCSE assessment objectives and learning outcomes. The caveats concerned the importance of looking beyond exam specifications and considering the longer-term goals of studying any given subject. For example, though awarding bodies change their specifications, there are some concepts our pupils must know in order for a study of our subject to prove useful to them once they've left school. To help, I suggested we ask ourselves: what do you expect pupils to know and be able to do in our subject in ten years' time?

However, for now we will continue to model the process using GCSE assessment objectives and learning outcomes. So far, I have homed in on the concept of 'explicit and implicit meanings'. I have said that our pupils must acquire this knowledge if they are to succeed in English Language at secondary school.

I have said that we need to repeatedly return to these concepts all the way through pupils' schooling and, each time, do so with increasing complexity and anchored in different contexts in order to create more schemata – or mental maps.

As we return to these foundational concepts at increasingly complex levels, we could make use of 'threshold assessments' which encourage pupils to move up the reading comprehension 'ladder' from:

Identifies – whereby a pupil shows a simple awareness of language, identifies and gives a simple explanation, identifies literal meanings, and shows some understanding of what is going on...

To:

Explains – whereby a pupil understands language and how it works – for example, they can talk about effects on the reader and use appropriate quotations...

To:

Analyses – whereby a pupil explains the effects of language, goes beyond the literal, analyses words and sentences, and shows an awareness of different meanings, both implicit and explicit...

And, finally, to:

Evaluates – whereby a pupil evaluates the writer's choice of language or impact on the reader and offers their own opinion which is supported by appropriate evidence.

Or, more simply, we could write a sequence of 'can do' statements such as these:

- I can define the words explicit and implicit
- I can identify an explicit and implicit meaning in a non-fiction text
- I can identify both explicit and implicit meanings in a range of different text types
- I can explain why a writer has implied rather than explicitly stated something
- I can comment on the effect of both explicit and implicit meanings on the reader
- I can analyse a writer's use of explicit and implicit meanings

...and so on

There are several advantages to this approach, including – in no particular order:

- The statements make sense to pupils – they're concrete not abstract, simple not lofty
- Pupils can be assessed easily against each statement with a 'yes/no'
- The assessment will inform us what each pupil knows and can do, and what they do not yet know and cannot yet do
- The individual assessment outcomes can be aggregated to provide a percentage of 'mastery' for any given cohort (e.g. 80% of pupils in this class can define both explicit and implicit meanings)
- Both the individual and aggregated assessment outcomes can be used to inform our teaching, notifying us if we need to re-teach or re-cap a concept or concepts, or if can we move on
- Pupils' journeys through this hierarchy of statements can provide tangible evidence of progress – to pupils, parents and schools
- The statements can also be used as learning objectives to provide a clear focus to a lesson or sequence of lessons which can be revisited in the plenary or used on an exit ticket

Of course, as I've already admitted, learning is neither easy nor neat. Pupils do not often make linear progress and our curriculum is not often linear in shape. Rather, learning is messy; learners can go backwards as well as forwards, and not all assessments can be used to extrapolate progress over time because what is being assessed at various points through the year may be very different.

As such, 'can do' statements may work for some curriculum content in some subjects but may not – indeed, probably will not – work for everything. Sometimes, the key concepts and their various layers of accomplishment may take the form of questions, factual statements, key features, schools of thought, or exemplars.

Accordingly, and as I argued in Chapter Five, it is crucial that subject specialists are afforded autonomy in deciding what their key concepts look like and how these might be planned and sequenced over time and used as a form of assessment.

Breaking all the rules

Earlier, in my defence of Shakespeare's 'inventive borrowing', I quoted T S Eliot who claimed that "Immature poets imitate; mature poets steal." The same can be said of pupils: they need to learn the rules before they can break them. For example, to help pupils know how to write a textual analysis, we need to teach them a framework such as PEE (point, evidence, explanation/or exploration) or SQI (statement, quote, inference) or indeed 'What? Where? How? And Why?', so that they can learn how to analyse a text and practice doing so until the process becomes automatic – until they cannot fail.

Once they have ingrained this useful framework, they can develop the confidence to deviate from it and to find their own 'voice'. As an English examiner I quickly recognise the classes who've been drilled on PEE and use it effectively if somewhat mechanically. They pick up the marks and certainly achieve a grade 5 or higher but offer formulaic responses. I also recognise the highest performing pupils who achieve grades 8 and 9 because they retain the depth of analysis that PEE promotes but lose the formulaic structure and write in a distinctive manner, offering their own considered opinions.

I make no apology, therefore, for recommending our joined-up, progressive curriculum teaches pupils a series of useful frameworks and formula – other forms of schemata - to help them cheat the limitations of working memory by providing them with cues to knowledge in long-term memory which, in turn, allows them to automate certain processes.

Certainly in English (and indeed other essay-based subjects), the PEE paragraph is a useful starting point and should be taught from Year 7 onwards so that pupils are afforded sufficient time before they sit their GCSEs to practice using it in a range of contexts until they can automate it (thus, it becomes second nature and releases space in working memory for thinking about content). Once they've automated it, they can learn to deviate from it (in order to develop a voice of their own).

We can teach useful frameworks – or schema – for writing, too. For example, when teaching pupils how to write for different purposes, we could begin by drilling pupils on the types of text they need to write, what conventions they need to be aware of for each text type (teaching them first to obey those conventions before knowing when and how – and having the confidence - to ignore them or subvert them for effect.

For each of these conventions, we should explain how it works, model using it, construct a model with the class, then allow pupils to practice using the convention themselves. Practice is made easier if pupils have mnemonics to rely on…

Mnemonics – yet another type of schemata – help cheat the limitations of working memory by shortcutting to knowledge stored in long-term memory. For example, the acronym AFOREST – commonly used in schools – is an easy way for pupils to remember what to include in a piece of persuasive writing. AFOREST takes up little space in working memory but each letter stands for a feature that is stored in long-term memory because we have taught it from Year 7 onwards and allowed pupils to repeat their prior learning in order to improve both the storage and retrieval strength of that information in long-term memory. AFOREST, at least in my version, stands for: Amazing opening, Facts, Rhetorical questions, Emotive language, Statistics, and a Thought-provoking ending.

CHAPTER SEVENTEEN
USING WAYPOINTS AS THE PROGRESSION MODEL

I've already set out my approach to identifying threshold concepts and explained why I think it is helpful and indeed advisable to use these as a means of assessment. I modelled this earlier using one 'clear end-point' of the secondary school English language curriculum: explicit and implicit meanings. I said that we could carve a path between the starting point and the destination by writing a series of 'can do' statements such as those which follow:

- I can define the words explicit and implicit
- I can identify an explicit and implicit meaning in a non-fiction text
- I can identify both explicit and implicit meanings in a range of different text types
- I can explain why a writer has implied rather than explicitly stated something
- I can comment on the effect of both explicit and implicit meanings on the reader
- I can analyse a writer's use of explicit and implicit meanings

…and so on

I then said that such a series of statements could be used as a progression model, a means of assessing pupils' knowledge and skills. I'd now like to share a suggested process for this and will focus on assessment in key stage 3 because the abolition of national curriculum levels has afforded schools a golden opportunity to design a more effective system of assessment that is wedded to the curriculum.

Assessment without levels

The Commission for Assessment Without Levels, in their 2015 report, claimed that the use of national curriculum levels led to a curriculum driven by targets which, in turn, came to dominate all forms of in-school assessment and had a profoundly negative impact on teaching and learning.

As a result, progress - they said - became synonymous with moving up to the next 'level' or 'sub-level'. But this posed a problem: progress - in real terms - involves developing a deeper and broader understanding of subject matter, not simply moving on to work that affords a greater level of difficulty. As I have already argued, learning and progress are not always neat and linear.

The Commission also said that, as a consequence of national curriculum levels becoming synonymous with assessment, the more informal, everyday formative assessment that should always have been an integral part of effective teaching at key stage 3 was largely abandoned. Instead, teachers were simply tracking pupils' progress towards target levels rather than engaging in genuine dialogue with pupils about what they had mastered and what they still needed to practice.

One of the other problems with this approach was that the language of levels did not lend itself to assessing the underpinning knowledge and understanding of a concept. Level descriptors offered pseudo-scientific and ostensibly precise measurements which, when analysed, offer little help to pupils in their quest to know how to improve.

Removing the 'label' of levels, the Commission suggested, could help to improve pupils' mindsets about their own ability...

Once levels have been removed, teachers - in reviewing their teaching and assessment strategies - could then aim to ensure that they used methods that allowed all pupils full access to the curriculum.

The Commission also claimed that the expectation placed on teachers to collect data in order to track pupils' progress towards target levels and sub-levels considerably increases teachers' workloads. Without levels, the Commission said, teachers would gradually increase their confidence in using a wider range of formative assessment strategies without the burden of unnecessary recording and tracking.

Removing levels would also shine a brighter spotlight on high quality formative assessment, thereby improving the quality of teaching, as well as contributing to raising standards and reinforcing schools' freedoms to deliver a quality education in the way that best suits the needs of their pupils and the strengths and skills of their staff.

The Commission therefore recommended that schools developed an alternative to levels that marked a definitive departure from the prevailing culture rather than replicated the existing system in all but name. They strongly hinted that schools should base their new assessment systems on the mastery learning approach developed by Benjamin Bloom in the 1960s. This makes sense because the new national curriculum also has mastery learning at its core.

In Bloom's version of 'mastery', learning is broken down into discrete units and is presented in a logical order. Pupils are required to demonstrate a comprehensive knowledge of each unit before being allowed to move on to the next unit, the assumption being that all pupils will achieve this level of mastery if they are appropriately supported: some may take longer and need more help, but all will get there in the end.

Designing a new system

In a moment we will explore how a school might build a new assessment system to replace national curriculum levels and measure progress through our new curriculum based on the concept of mastery learning but first we must take a step back...

Before a school can agree a new assessment system - whether it designs one in-house or purchases one 'off the peg' so to speak - it should make sure it has written, consulted upon and agreed a whole-school assessment policy. From this point forwards, the assessment policy should be the school's guiding light; everything the school does to develop an alternative to levels should support the delivery of this policy. Ofsted have made clear that they will not comment on how and how often teachers assess pupils, only whether or not they do in line with the school's assessment policy so it's important to get the policy right.

Once a new assessment policy is in place, a school needs to decide what unit of measurement will replace national curriculum levels. In other words, how will the school describe pupils' learning and progress? Whatever measure a school decides to use, it must successfully quantify learning and progress and must do so in a more meaningful way than levels and sub-levels did, or else why change?

So where should a school start?

Some schools I've worked with or spoken to have made the mistake of developing a new assessment system that has been a system of 'levels' in all but name.

Rather, as I explained in Chapter Three, schools should start by engaging in a process of detailed curriculum planning before they set about designing a system of assessment. Assessment should be the servant and not the master; the curriculum should be king. After all, how can you decide on your assessment criteria before you know what it is you're assessing? How we teach our curriculum and how pupils respond to it should form the basis of any new assessment system.

What's more, assessment systems which simply recreate grading similar to levels and sub-levels are, to my mind, missing the point.

The national curriculum is a description of the content that must be taught in each subject and might, therefore, prove a useful starting point in deciding upon the units of measurement a school will use to quantify learning and progress.

A school's first task, therefore, should be to design a curriculum with clear end-points or bodies of knowledge which describes what will be taught and when, and what learning will result. This kind of detailed curriculum planning is necessary if a school is to successfully develop assessment criteria. Schools should not make the mistake of rushing into designing a new assessment system before they've considered how their curriculum will be taught in practice.

A school's second task, then, is to understand how a pupil's knowledge and skills in those parts of the subject covered in a particular module or scheme of work will accumulate over the course of a term, year or key stage into an holistic understanding of the concepts, key ideas, and capabilities learnt in the subject. As such, curriculum plans need to be progressive in nature, developing gradually over time.

Only once everyone is clear about how pupils' knowledge and skills will develop over the course of time, can a school move on to the third and final task: to develop a means of describing and quantifying what pupils are learning as they move through the curriculum.

Let's now turn our attentions to how this will work in practice and to how we might quantify pupils' learning...

Putting it into practice

The Commission for Assessment Without Levels were clear in their report that 'life after levels' should be less bureaucratic for teachers. Teachers should spend more time engaged in formative classroom assessments with pupils and less time tracking and recording data. As such, a majority of the assessments that take place should be informal, leading to diagnostic feedback given to pupils and students either in writing in their books or verbally in lessons. Naturally, this data will either be unrecorded or held locally in teachers' mark-books.

Diagnostic feedback should be comment-only and be specific about what pupils need to do in order to improve. The best feedback addresses faulty interpretations and comments on rather than grades work. The best feedback also provides cues or prompts for further work, is timely, specific and clear, and is focused on task and process rather than on praise. Feedback also works best when it is explicit about the marking criteria, offers suggestions for improvement, and is focused on how pupils can close the gap between their current and their desired performance; it does not focus on presentation or quantity of work.

Occasionally, however, it will be necessary for teachers to reflect on how well their pupils are responding to what is being taught and to share this information more formally with their subject leaders, senior leaders, and other colleagues who teach the same class. This more formal assessment will need to take the form of progress against or towards targets - or perhaps age-related expectations - so what should it look like in practice?

The use of levels and sub-levels assumed that pupils scaled the mountain of progress in a uniform manner in response to teaching, and that we could measure each step with accuracy then categorise and label each pupil accordingly.

Mastery learning replaces this rush to hike up the mountainside with the belief that all pupils will comprehensively know and understand the learning from each topic or module before moving on to the next. Progress, therefore, tends to be non-linear and tailored to meet the needs of each pupil.

'Progress' is a complex concept - a dotted line used to summarise the overall path taken along the mountainside, snaking towards the peak, which may go up as well as down as pupils find the right terrain and get a solid foothold in the rock. But, statistically-speaking, we can estimate the average grade that a pupil is capable of achieving based on their prior performance and this information can be used to notify us if pupils fall below expectations.

Intended learning outcomes or objectives provide a good starting start - a foundation, if you like - for tracking pupil progress because they summarise what is taught in each lesson or unit and they are already widely used in lesson planning and delivery. Teachers routinely write and share objectives with pupils at the start of lessons and use them to measure progress in lesson plenaries.

As long as intended learning outcomes cover all the key concepts (end points) that must be learnt, then tracking and recording pupils' acquisition of them should provide a cumulative assessment log which will quantify their progress at any given point.

We've reached the end of Step 4 in our six-step curriculum design process – identify the way-points – and can now embark upon the fifth step which is to define excellence…

PART FIVE

DEFINE EXCELLENCE

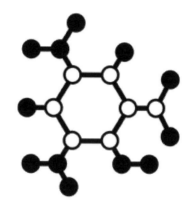

CHAPTER EIGHTEEN
ENSURING EQUAL ACCESS TO THE
CURRICULUM

Once we have designed a curriculum that is ambitious, we need to ensure it is accessible to all our pupils and students and that all have a fair – if not equal – chance of success, which means ensuring all pupils can understand the curriculum content to be learnt and the language in which it is expressed, and that all pupils have the prior knowledge and schema (or mental maps) to reach, incrementally, the destinations we set for them.

Accordingly, in Chapter Nineteen we will explore the importance of teaching to the top – of giving all pupils work that is hard but achievable – and examine what this means in practice. In Chapter Twenty we will consider the importance of having high expectations of all our pupils, of expecting the best and accepting nothing less. And in Chapter Twenty-One we will talk about getting the pitch right because if the work is not hard, pupils will not think and if pupils do not think they will not learn. But first let's drag that pesky elephant out of the shadows…

Not all pupils are equal. There, I've said it. We can now stare down the elephant in the room. Whatever your belief in genetics, we know that pupils will come to our curriculum knowing different things, being able to do different things, and with differing capacities to know and do more.

One popular argument against the notion of 'teaching to the top' is the heritability of intelligence. Some people believe that nature, not nurture, has the biggest impact on pupil outcomes and no matter what teachers do, some pupils will always fail. So, before we 'define excellence', let us explore the thorny subject of genetics and, to do this, let's take a trip back in time...

Gene genius

At the time of writing, though probably not by the time of publication, Dominic Cummings is serving as chief advisor to the prime minister, Boris Johnson. He is widely regarded as the power behind the throne, orchestrating from the shadows the political crisis that has beset the UK. It is, for example, assumed that Cummings made the decision to prorogue parliament and suggested calling for a general election, all in an attempt to force the country into leaving the European Union without a deal.

But, before he entered the national consciousness and was portrayed on television by Benedict Cumberbatch, he engaged in an email exchange with me about genetics...

It was 2014 and Cummings had just stepped down as special advisor to Education Secretary Michael Gove and, as his parting shot, issued a 250-page thesis in which he argued that "the education of the majority... is between awful and mediocre".

In England, he argued, "few [students] are well trained in the basics of extended writing or mathematical and scientific modelling and problem-solving". Among teachers, he said, "real talent is rare, and mediocrity is ubiquitous."

He didn't just train his weapons on schools, though. He said that "in many third-rate higher education institutions there is a large amount of 'social science' work in economics, anthropology, sociology, literary theory and so on of questionable value".

Not that he seemed to lose sleep over third-rate education systems. Rather, Cummings said he believed that genetics - not teaching - was the real cause of academic success or failure...

"There is a strong resistance across the politician spectrum," he said, "to accepting scientific evidence on genetics. Most of those that now dominate discussions on issues such as social mobility entirely ignores genetics and therefore their arguments are at best misleading and often worthless."

Cummings is a fan of Professor Plomin who – Cummings argues – believes that as much as 70% of a person's abilities are down to genes and are therefore fixed. It would be easy to ignore Cummings's report (which, in fairness, is slightly more nuanced than my synopsis suggests) if it were not for the fact that his was not a lone voice within the DfE: in 2013, Michael Gove invited Professor Plomin to address various ministers at the DfE.

It seems that – at least under Gove's leadership if not so much now - there was a growing interest at the DfE in the belief that children largely inherit their intellect and that there is little they or educationalists can do to improve it.

The debate about genes versus environment, nature versus nurture, is not new, of course…

In 'Outliers' (2008), Malcolm Gladwell recounts an experiment carried out by Lewis Terman, a young professor of psychology at Stanford University. Terman's speciality was intelligence testing and he created the widely-used Stanford-Binet IQ test.

In 1921 Terman decided to study gifted children, 'gifted' being another way of saying genetically intelligent or born clever. He went into California's elementary schools and, following a series of tests, identified 1,470 children (out of around 250,000) whose IQs averaged over 140 and ranged as high as 200. That group of children became known as the 'Termites' and Terman's study of them became one of the world's most famous psychological experiments to which he dedicated the rest of his life. He tracked and tested the 'Termites', measured and analysed them; he noted their academic attainment, social successes, illnesses, jobs… you name it he tested it and recorded it.

Terman once said that there was "nothing about an individual as important as his IQ" and those with very high IQs must be regarded as our future leaders who would "advance science, art, government, education, and social welfare".

So, what were his findings?

By the time the 'Termites' had reached adulthood, some had grown up to publish scholarly articles and books and to thrive in business. Some had run for public office. But few were nationally-known figures – they were good but not that good. There were no Nobel winners – although, importantly, two of the elementary students Terman tested and rejected for not having high enough IQs did go on to become Nobel laureates.

So disappointing were Terman's findings that the sociologist Pitirm Sorokin said that if Terman had simply selected his subjects at random – or used family background rather than IQ – he would have achieved the same outcome. "By no stretch of the imagination or of standards of genius is the gifted group as a whole gifted," Sorokin said.

Terman himself eventually conceded – albeit reluctantly – that "intellect and achievement are far from perfectly correlated".

Gladwell also tells the story of Chris Langan who has a one-in-a-million mind but has experienced failure all his life. Why? In short, because he hasn't had the kind of luck in life most successful people have had. Langan was the eldest of four brothers whose father disappeared before Langan was born. Langan's mother's second husband was murdered; her third committed suicide; her fourth, Jack, was a failed journalist.

Langan was poor. His step-father Jack was an alcoholic who beat his sons. The family moved around a lot and Langan – despite being exceptionally 'gifted' – struggled to fit in at school and was largely ignored by his teachers. He lost a scholarship because his mother forgot to fill out a form. His personal circumstances meant he couldn't attend classes on time and had to drop out of college. Without a degree his academic aspirations floundered, and he began working a series of unskilled, low-paid jobs.

Gladwell contrasts Langan's life story with that of Robert Oppenheimer, the physicist who was in charge of America's effort to develop a nuclear bomb during World War Two. As a child, Oppenheimer was similar to Langan: he was doing lab experiments by Third Grade and studying physics and chemistry by Fifth Grade. By age nine, he was able to answer in Greek a question which was asked of him in Latin.

Oppenheimer's life was not all rosy: he suffered depression and once tried to poison his university tutor (yes, really). Unlike Langan who wasn't given any second chances, however, Oppenheimer was sent to a psychiatrist and allowed to stay at university.

The real difference was upbringing. Langan didn't have the kind of start in life that enables a child to deal with setbacks and rejection. When he was told he'd lost his scholarship he was angry and inarticulate; when he was told his classes couldn't be moved to accommodate his travel arrangements, he grew despondent.

Oppenheimer, meanwhile, was able to plead his case.

The psychologist Robert Sternberg calls what Oppenheimer had "practical intelligence" which includes such qualities as "knowing what to say to whom, knowing when to say it, and knowing how to say it for maximum effect".

Gladwell explains that general intelligence and practical intelligence (what we might call IQ and common sense or indeed EQ) are 'orthogonal'. In other words, the presence of one doesn't imply the presence of the other. Langan was brimming full of general intelligence but had not been afforded the opportunities he needed in order to develop sufficient practical intelligence to be successful. Oppenheimer – by gift of this family background – was lucky enough to have had both.

And now we're getting to the crux of the matter... whereas most people accept that – as Cummings says – to some extent general intelligence is genetic (Langan, for example, started talking at six months old), practical intelligence – which as we've just seen is actually more crucial to our success – is not genetic.

Practical intelligence is not something we are born with; it is a combination of knowledge and skills which have to be learned and which are hugely influenced by our social and economic background.

In other words, Cummings is right to suggest that we are not all born equal: some people are born with higher IQs than others; some people are indeed 'gifted' with a greater aptitude in some areas. But what Cummings did not acknowledge is that we are not constrained by our general intelligences. Our starting IQ is just that: a starting point not a fixed point.

Cummings's thesis would have us believe that some of us are doomed, that there is nothing we can do to overcome our genetics. But I happen to believe he is wrong and if I did not believe so I would probably not work in education and dedicate so much of my time to issues of social justice and to tackling academic disadvantage. What's more, if others did not believe it too, then I would probably not be here for I was born into disadvantage and had it existed then, I would probably have been eligible for the Pupil Premium.

To prove that we are not constrained by our general intelligences, I'd like to cite the sociologist Annette Lareau who conducted an experiment on twelve families in America: some were rich, some were poor. Rather than finding, as you might expect, twelve ways of parenting children, Lareau found – broadly speaking – just two.

One style involved parents playing an active part in their children's free time, encouraging them to take part in activities such as swimming then taking them to the pool, asking them about their days at school, and generally involving them in the adult world of conversation. These parents didn't just issue commands, they'd negotiate, and their children would question them.

Lareau called this style of parenting "concerted cultivation" which, she said, was an attempt to actively "foster and assess a child's talents, opinions, and skills".

The other style involved parents allowing "natural growth". In other words, the children – albeit taken care of – were expected to grow and develop on their own.

Lareau argued that one style wasn't preferable to the other. The "natural growth" children were often better behaved, more creative in making use of their time, and were independent. But, she argued, "concerted cultivation" had enormous advantages in terms of a child's future success. The "concerted cultivation" children learnt team-work and knew how to cope in structured environments; they could interact confidently with adults and speak up for themselves.

In short, and to quote Lareau, the "concerted cultivation" children learnt a sense of "entitlement".

Lareau doesn't use the word 'entitlement' in a negative sense that we might associate with the landed gentry in England who think they are born to rule. She uses it to explain that children "acted as though they had a right to pursue their own individual preferences and to actively manage interactions in institutional settings" and were "comfortable in those settings…open to sharing information and asking for attention". They "acted on their own behalf to gain advantages [and] to accommodate their desires". We have already seen that Oppenheimer succeeded where Langan failed because he was a "concerted cultivation" child.

It will not surprise you to learn that the "concerted cultivation" children were from affluent middle-class families whereas the "natural growth" children were from poorer working-class families.

Returning to Malcolm Gladwell, he says that such differences in upbringing explain where mastery comes from. It's not genetic. The wealthier children didn't inherit their knowledge and skills; they were gained through cultural advantage. The wealthier children developed their skills over the course of their young lives because their parents and others taught them and provided them with the right opportunities.

Gladwell argues that the most successful people are successful, not because it's in their genes, but because they have been taught "a sense of entitlement [that's]... perfectly suited to succeeding in the modern world".

Let's return to Terman and his Termites for a moment...we've already learnt that his proteges disappointed him because they didn't achieve in line with their IQs. But why did some do better than others?

Terman later returned to study 730 of his original 'Termites' who'd been picked because they had extraordinarily high IQs. Terman divided those 730 into three groups. The A group consisted of the top 20%: they were the success stories, the lawyers and doctors and engineers and academics. 90% of the A group graduated from college. The B group consisted of the middle 60%: they had achieved "satisfactorily". The C group consisted of the bottom 20%: they were postal workers, book-keepers or jobless. A third of the C group were college drop-outs and only eight of the 150 Cs earned a degree.

What was the difference between the As and the Cs? After much testing and research in which Terman analysed IQ scores even more precisely and looked into health and interests, Terman found only one difference: family background. The As overwhelmingly came from the middle and upper classes; the Cs were from disadvantaged backgrounds.

The damning fact is this: almost none of the exceptionally gifted children from the lowest social and economic class achieved anything of note professionally. Gladwell says that the Cs didn't lack something "encoded in DNA", they "lacked something that could have been given to them... a community around them that prepared them properly for the world".

Again, I make the point that we are not all born equal, we begin life at different stages – Gladwell himself says that the heritability of IQ is probably about 50% – but as I say above our starting points are exactly that: starting points from which we can all progress. With hard work and deliberate practice, everyone can get better at everything.

Anyway, back to Dominic Cummings...

It seems that the natural conclusion to his thesis is this: abandon hope all ye who enter here – your destiny is preordained. It is nature rather than nurture, genetics rather than environment that determines your success. Plomin's research – as Cummings would have us understand it – is depressing reading for teachers. Well, perhaps not...

A somewhat reassuring rebuttal of this thinking comes from Professor Steve Jones, the University College London geneticist, who was quoted in The Guardian as saying that Cummings "fundamentally misunderstands" how biology works and the 70% that Plomin cites is "a statement about populations, not individuals".

"It certainly does not mean that seven-tenths of every child's talents reside in the double helix," Jones continues.

The curriculum, and teachers, become more, not less, important, Jones argues, when examining the close interaction of environment and genes. Moving to affluence, for example, increases a working-class child's IQ by 15 points.

"The more we learn about genes, the more important the environment appears to be."

Jones seems to be drawing the same conclusions as Gladwell: that practical intelligence - the result of nurture – not general intelligence – the result of nature – is the key to our success.

If moving to affluence can increase a child's IQ by 15 points, just imagine what an ambitious curriculum taught by great teachers could do...

If environment is more important than genetics, then the teacher's role is vital in helping every pupil to make progress from their different starting points. It is the teacher's responsibility to ensure that every pupil in their class believes he or she can get better with hard work and deliberate practice. And the first step towards achieving this is to have the highest of expectations of every pupil in your class and to teach to the top.

For teachers, the distinction between general intelligence and practical intelligence – or nature and nurture, genetics and environment – is an important distinction to make for one reason: we can't change a pupil's genetics, but we can do much to help a pupil overcome their socio-economic background.

And how do teachers help pupils overcome their social and economic background? How do they convince pupils that, regardless of their general intelligence or starting points, they can succeed? For me, it's the difference between having a fixed mindset approach and a growth mindset one…

In my book 'The IQ Myth' (2012), I wrote in detail about growth mindset teaching. At that time the idea of deliberate practice was not very well known in education circles. Thankfully, advocates of deliberate practice are now ubiquitous so I imagine I'm probably preaching to the converted when I say that I think it's important to teach students to believe in themselves and to use our ambitious curriculum to help them to reach for the stars.

So, by way of conclusion to this particular polemic, I'd like to share with you an extract from 'The IQ Myth' in which I introduce the idea of the growth mindset and argue that IQs are not fixed entities but can improved with hard work and deliberate practice:

> I suppose the most common measure of someone's intelligence is the IQ test. And yet this test was devised by the Parisian Alfred Binet at the start of the twentieth century – not as a measure of innate intellect or ability, nor as a number which could be used to determine what someone was and was not capable of – but as a way of identifying children who were not profiting from the Paris public school system. Binet used the IQ test to help him design new – by which is meant 'more effective' – educational programmes to help get Parisian schoolchildren back on track.
>
> Let's take a moment to think about that… the IQ test was devised in order to identify students who needed help to improve. The IQ test was devised in order to identify a better school system for these children. It was a snapshot of what these students could do at that moment in time – a measure of current performance, if you like – designed to identify students who were being failed by the school system. In other words, it did not show someone's intellect, it showed whether or not the school system was working for them.
>
> So Binet (without explicitly denying that there were differences in children's intellects) believed that education and practice could bring about fundamental changes in intelligence. Binet said, in his book 'Major Ideas About Children', that "a few modern philosophers assert that an individual's intelligence is a fixed quantity, a quantity which cannot be increased. We must protest and react against this brutal pessimism…with practice, training, and above all, method, we manage to increase our attention, our memory, our judgment and literally to become more intelligent than we were before."

Practice, training, and above all, method – Binet's words. These three things – uttered over a hundred years ago – are still a perfect summary of what the best teachers provide for their students. The best teachers do not sit in judgment; the best teachers provide a safe and secure environment in which all students can learn without fear of failure and in which all students can increase their intelligence with practice.

The Stanford University psychologist, Dr Carol S. Dweck, said in her book, 'Mindset': "Today most experts agree that it's not either-or. It's not nature or nurture, genes or environment. From conception on, there's a constant give and take between the two…. People may start with different temperaments and different aptitudes, but it is clear that experience, training and personal effort take them the rest of the way".

Their choice of words may differ slightly, but their sentiment is the same – Dweck and Binet agree that everyone can improve with practice; they agree that effort is more important than 'talent' or 'innate ability'. This is an important lesson for every teacher to learn. Teachers must challenge their students to be the best, they should not teach to the 'lowest common denominator'. They must have high expectations of all their students, and they must encourage their students to take a leap of faith even if that means falling over a few times.

I'd go even further than this: teachers must actively encourage their students to make mistakes, they must foster a safe and secure environment in which falling over is not only accepted without criticism or humiliation, but it is actively encouraged as evidence of effective learning and of getting better at something.

In her book, 'Mindset', Dweck says that believing "your qualities are carved in stone – the fixed mindset – creates an urgency to prove yourself over and over. If you have only a certain amount of intelligence, a certain personality and a certain moral character – well then you'd better prove that you have a healthy dose of them…."

A person with a fixed mindset doesn't believe that 'If at first you don't succeed, try and try again', they believe, 'If at first you don't succeed, then give up because you probably don't have the ability'.

Dweck compares this fixed mindset with what she calls the 'growth mindset'. The growth mindset, by contrast, "is based on the belief that your basic qualities are things you can cultivate through your efforts. Although people may differ in every which way – in their initial talents and aptitudes, interests, or temperaments – everyone can change and grow through application and experience."

Dweck goes on: "Do people with [a growth mindset] believe that anyone can be anything, that anyone with proper motivation or education can become Einstein or Beethoven? No, but they believe that a person's true potential is unknown (and unknowable); that it's impossible to foresee what can be accomplished with years of passion, toil, and training."

This belief that one can develop important qualities actually fosters a deeper passion for learning. After all, why waste time proving over and over again just how great you are, when you could be getting better instead? Why hide your deficiencies when you could be overcoming them?

And if it is our jobs as teachers to foster a deeper passion for learning then we must embrace the notion of growth mindset teaching; we must instil in our students the belief that they can get better if they work hard and practice.

Everyone can get better at everything if they try.

- The IQ Myth, M J Bromley (2012)

So much for the theory… let's turn to some practical advice on how you can build a 'growth mindset' culture in your school or college in order to help facilitate equal access to the curriculum…

How to develop a growth mindset in school

As a kid I wanted to become a cliché when I grew up, so I bought a guitar and grew my hair. I successfully learnt all the chords but struggled to combine them in any meaningful way (perhaps I should've joined an experimental jazz band instead of churning out '80s power ballads). When my dreams of rock stardom eventually withered on the vine, I turned my attention to mastering magic, then to conquering chess, and to all manner of other hobbies.

What all these childhood endeavours had in common was this: I took it for granted that I'd have to work hard at each of them, I knew I'd have to practice endlessly and that I wouldn't become an expert overnight. I played that old six-string till my fingers bled, readily accepting that any improvement would be incremental.

Most of us feel this way about our interests. We know, for example, that to run a marathon we'd have to train hard for months beforehand (or, in my case, to walk to the pub without getting out of breath I'd have to stop eating chocolate).

And yet when it comes to education – to mastering English or maths or science – we often forget the importance of hard work and practice. We assume that academic ability, that one's IQ, is somehow fixed, innate. We might not do it consciously, but we say things like "maths isn't his forte" or "she's not a natural artist". That's why most pupils who start the year in the bottom set, end the year in the bottom set.

By creating a culture in which pupils and students believe that their abilities are preordained, and in which they are either good at a subject or not, we discourage them from taking risks, from making mistakes. After all, if ability is fixed, then if at first you don't succeed, you may as well give up.

In her book 'Mindset' (2012), Dr Carol Dweck calls a belief that "your qualities are carved in stone" the 'fixed mindset'. But does it really have to be this way?

What if we applied the same mindset to education as we do to our hobbies and interests? What if we taught our pupils and students that, although people may differ in every which way – in their initial talents and aptitudes, interests, or temperaments – everyone can change and grow through application and experience?

What if we used our curriculum to instil in our pupils and students what Dr Dweck calls the 'growth mindset', the belief that "your basic qualities are things you can cultivate through your efforts"?

As we've seen above, even Alfred Binet, the inventor of the IQ test, believed that education and practice could bring about fundamental changes in intelligence. He said, in his book Major Ideas About Children, that "a few modern philosophers assert that an individual's intelligence is a fixed quantity which cannot be increased. We must protest against this brutal pessimism …

with practice, training, and above all, method, we become more intelligent than we were before".

Practice, training, and method – these three words uttered a century ago – remain the perfect definition of what the best teachers do. They provide a safe and secure environment in which all pupils can learn without fear of failure and in which all pupils and students can increase their intelligence with deliberate practice.

So, let us look at five practical strategies that can be baked into our curriculum and which can help instil the growth mindset...

1. Use frequent formative feedback

Dr Dweck's research found that people with a fixed mindset "greatly mis-estimated their performance and their ability (while) people with the growth mindset were amazingly accurate".

Why should this be? Because, as Dr Dweck says: "If, like those with the growth mindset, you believe you can develop yourself, then you're open to accurate information about your current abilities, even if it's unflattering. What's more, if you're oriented towards learning, as they are, you need accurate information about your current abilities in order to learn effectively."

We should, therefore, ensure that our pupils are acutely aware of their strengths and areas for development. We should frequently assess our pupils and give them formative feedback so that they know what they do well and what they can do better. We should dedicate quality time in our lessons for our pupils to act on this feedback, to redraft work in order to improve upon it.

2. High levels of challenge for every pupil

Dr Dweck and Binet agree that everyone can improve with practice; they agree that effort is more important than "talent" or "innate ability". Therefore, we must challenge our pupils to be the best, we must have high expectations of all our pupils and must encourage them to take a leap of faith, even if that means falling over a few times.

Teachers' attitudes directly affect their pupils' learning and, ultimately, the grades they get. A teacher who has high expectations of every pupil in his or her class will reap the rewards: more pupils will rise to the challenge and succeed.

Many teachers think that lowering standards will give pupils a taste of success, boost their self-esteem, and raise their achievement. But all the evidence suggests it doesn't work. Instead, it leads to poorly educated children. Rather than lowering standards, we should believe in the growth of the intellect and talent. We should set high standards for all our pupils, not just the ones who are already achieving.

3. Explicitly welcome mistakes

Teachers must actively encourage their pupils to make mistakes, they must foster a safe and secure environment in which falling over is not only accepted without criticism or humiliation, but in which it is actively encouraged as evidence of effective learning and of getting better at something.

Every teacher knows that some pupils do not raise their hands in class to answer a question because they fear they will be criticised or made to feel embarrassed for being wrong. And yet the opposite should be true: pupils should be eager to raise their hands because to get an answer wrong is to learn from their mistakes; to get an answer wrong is to learn the correct answer. Equally, raising a hand to say, "I don't understand this ... can you help?" is not a sign of weakness or low intelligence, it is a means of increasing one's intelligence.

Of course, making a mistake – even if you have a positive mindset – can be a painful experience. But a mistake shouldn't define you; it's a problem to be faced and learnt from. We teach this by modelling it, by publicly making mistakes and by making explicit our own implicit learning.

4. Engaging in deliberate practice

In his book, 'Outliers' (2008), Malcolm Gladwell suggests that as a society we value natural, effortless accomplishments over achievement through effort. We endow our heroes with superhuman abilities that lead them inevitably towards greatness. People with the growth mindset, however, believe something very different. For them, even geniuses have to work hard for their achievements. After all, what's heroic about having a gift?

Thomas Edison is credited with inventing the lightbulb, but he wasn't an innate genius who single-handedly, effortlessly discovered his invention in –

forgive the pun – a lightbulb moment. This is what Professor Anders Ericsson calls the iceberg effect: beneath the visible tip of genius, Edison had 30 assistants, including highly trained scientists, often working around the clock in a corporate-funded state-of-the-art laboratory.

"His" invention was the culmination of a lot of time-consuming work involving mathematicians, chemists, physicists, engineers and glass-blowers. Yes, he was a genius; but he wasn't born one. He was, according to his biography, an ordinary boy. He just worked hard, tried and tried again. He never stopped being curious, never shied away from taking on a new challenge.

Similar stories could be told of many geniuses such as Charles Darwin – whose Origin of Species was the result of years of research, a lot of effort and toil involving hundreds of discussions with colleagues and mentors, and went through several drafts, taking Darwin half a lifetime to finalise. In other words, his book wasn't created in a big bang, it evolved over time.

Jack Nicklaus, the most successful golfer of all time, famously said: "Nobody – but nobody – has ever become really proficient at golf without practice, without doing a lot of thinking and then hitting a lot of shots. It isn't so much a lack of talent; it's a lack of being able to repeat good shots consistently that frustrates most players. And the only answer to that is practice."

Matthew Syed, author of 'Bounce' (2010), quantifies the amount of "purposeful practice" that is required to achieve excellence. He says that "from art to science and from board games to tennis, it has been found that a minimum of 10 years is required to reach world-class status in any complex task".

Malcolm Gladwell, meanwhile, asserts that most top performers practise for around 1,000 hours per year. We should, therefore, provide our pupils with plenty of opportunities to practise and perfect their knowledge and skills.

Professor Daniel Willingham says that deliberate practice "reinforces (the) basic skills required for more advanced skills, it protects against forgetting, and improves transfer". Professor Siegfried Engelmann says that pupils need "five times more practice than many teachers expect".

There are two kinds of practice proven to be the most effective: first, distributed practice which is "a schedule of practice that spreads out study activities over time", and second, interleaved practice which is "a schedule of practice that mixes different kinds of problems, or a schedule of study that mixes different kinds of material, within a single study session" (Dunlosky et al, 2013).

5. Reward effort not attainment

Dr Dweck conducted research with hundreds of pupils. She gave each pupil a set of 10 problems to solve from a non-verbal IQ test. Most of the pupils did well and when they'd finished, she praised some of the pupils for their ability ("you got a high score, you must be smart") and some for their effort ("you got a high score, you must have worked hard").

Both groups were exactly equal to begin with but, after receiving praise, they began to differ. The pupils whose ability was praised were pushed into the fixed mindset. When they were given a choice, they rejected a challenging new task that they could learn from, favouring more of the same instead because they didn't want to do anything which would expose flaws in their intelligence and bring their talent into question. In contrast, 90 per cent of the pupils whose effort was praised wanted to try the challenging new task precisely because they could learn from it.

Dr Dweck concluded that praising ability actually lowered pupils' IQs whereas praising effort raised them. She also said that praising children's intelligence harmed their motivation because, although children love to be praised, especially for their talents, as soon as they hit a snag their confidence goes out of the window and their motivation hits rock bottom. If success means they're smart, then failure means they're dumb.

This doesn't mean we shouldn't praise pupils, Dr Dweck argues. But it does mean we should only use a certain type of praise. We can praise our pupils as much as we want for the "growth-oriented process – what they accomplished through practice, study, persistence, and good strategies". But we should avoid the kind of praise that judges their intelligence or talent, and we should avoid the kind of praise that implies "we're proud of them for their intelligence or talent rather than for the work they put in".

To conclude, we should use the central tenets of the growth mindset in order to provide all pupils and students with equal access to our curriculum and instil in them a belief that they can reach the destination we set for them if they try hard, persevere when faced with setbacks, learn from their mistakes, and practice till their fingers bleed!

In the next chapter we will explore the importance of teaching to the top for every pupil and giving every pupil work to do that is hard but achievable...

CHAPTER NINETEEN
TEACHING TO THE TOP

In Chapter Eighteen we discussed the role that genetics might play in determining pupils' and students' starting points. Of course, nurture plays a big role and so we need to ensure that we do all we can to identify the barriers that some pupils face when trying to access our curriculum and then plan strategies to help them overcome those barriers.

In Part Six of this book I will dig deeper into this topic and share my advice for closing the attainment gap, including through the better use of the Pupil Premium Grant in schools and High Needs funding in colleges.

But first I'd like to advocate 'teaching to the top' for every pupil and student because if we don't do this – in other words, if we reduce the curriculum or dumb down for those pupils we consider to be in some way disadvantaged, then we only double that disadvantage and prevent those pupils from ever catching up and making good. In short, we condemn pupils by ensuring their birth is also their destiny.

So, what exactly is 'teaching to the top'?

Broadly speaking, we might say there are two approaches to teaching a class with a distribution of prior attainment and/or a class which includes disadvantaged pupils (which is to say, every class): teaching to the middle; and teaching to the top. (I limit the approaches to two because I don't think any teacher actively sets out to teach to the bottom, dumbing down for all but the lowest-performing pupils in their class).

Every class, whether set or streamed, will have a distribution of prior attainment; pupils will have a range of starting points and, although some gaps between pupils' performances will narrow through the course of the academic year, there will always be differences. Teaching to the middle means pitching the lesson to the centre of the bell curve - teaching what the 'average' pupil can do and what will fill the gaps in their current performance.

Scaffolding will be required for those pupils to the left of the bell curve in order to bridge the gap between their current performance and the performance of the average pupil in that class, whereas additional stretch and challenge will be needed for those pupils to the right of the bell curve in order to propel them further forwards from their more advanced starting points.

Teaching to the top, meanwhile, is about pitching learning at what the most able - or highest performing - pupils will be able to do with time, effort and support.

I'll return to the notion of 'teaching to the top' in a moment but before I go on, I have an admission to make: I don't like the terms 'less able' and 'more able'. Less able than what, exactly? Less able than the more able? That's a pretty banal and facile statement. Less able than they could be? Than we want them to be? Less able than the average pupil? If so, what's 'average'?

No one is 'average'; rather, we are all made up of myriad individual characteristics. If you take an average of each of us (height, weight, IQ, shoe size, etc), you won't find any individual who is average in all respects.

This is known as the 'jaggedness principle'…

The Jaggedness Principle

In the 1940s, the US Air Force had to refit fighter planes with adjustable seats because the cockpits had been designed around the average range of ten body measurements taken from a population of 4,063 pilots. But because no individual met all those criteria, they ended up with a seat which didn't fit a single pilot.

Not to be deterred by the jaggedness principle, as recently as 2011 the Australian Bureau of Statistics used the national census to find the average Australian. They announced that she was a 37-year-old woman with a son and a daughter aged six and nine. She was 5'4" and weighed 11 stone. She lived in a three-bedroom house, had about $200,000 still to pay on her mortgage and her family originally came from the UK. However, when they checked this description against the census data, they couldn't find a single person in the whole country who fit.

So 'average' doesn't exist and we'd be wise not to compare pupils to the average, deeming some to be 'less able' and others 'more'.

What's more, the term 'less able' implies a fixed state of affairs. The 'less able' are destined to remain less able ad infinitum. They will always reside to the left of our graph, there to languish in the shadow of the bell curve.

I prefer 'lower performing' or 'lower prior attainment' and even these terms niggle. But for all their faults, at least 'lower performing' and 'lower prior attainment' have the advantage of being less permanent, less immobile.

Someone who is lower performing can improve their performance and become a better performer or a higher performer.

But this still implies an arbitrary comparison. What are we using as our measuring stick? The most recent summative assessment data? But surely this only tested pupils on their mastery of the most recent topic? Key stage 2 SATs results? But surely this only tested pupils in English and maths, and even then, on a narrow field of study within these two subjects? Teachers' predictions for end of year or end of course outcomes? The latest university admissions data shows the weakness in that, with only 16% of A Level predictions bearing fruit.

Whatever stick we use to beat less able pupils with, it will be - like all sticks, I suppose - narrow. Someone who is deemed less able by one measure might well be more able by another. We are in danger of arbitrarily writing off some pupils because they didn't perform as well on a test than other pupils. We are defining them by way of a snapshot taken through a pinhole lens.

Whatever term we want to use - and I will stick with 'lower performing' for the purposes of this chapter - we must first accept that pupils and students cannot be pigeonholed in this way. All pupils and students - like all human beings - are different, unique, individual.

We should not pool the 'less able' into an homogenous group and assume that what works with one of them will work with all and that what has been proven to work with 'less able' pupils in another school or college, in another county, in another country, (according to research evidence and meta-analyses) will work in our classroom.

The danger of differentiation

As I say, I do not think teaching to the middle is very effective because differentiation in this guise (scaffolding for lower-performing pupils whilst stretching and challenging higher-performing ones - and therefore - by definition - expecting less of lower-performing pupils), carries with it an inherent danger…

It is, by any another name, 'dumbing down' and I have argued throughout this book against dumbing down and reducing our curriculum offer, and instead have suggested we offer every pupil and student, no matter their starting point and background, the same ambitious curriculum.

Differentiation of the 'dumbing down' kind is delivered by means of placing limits on learning, lowering a glass ceiling on top of pupils' ambitions. Differentiation of this kind might take the form of using Bloom's taxonomy to target questions at different pupils. For example, the teacher might start a classroom discussion by asking a question from the bottom of the taxonomy - a knowledge-based question which requires only a recall of facts - to a lower-performing pupil before moving up the taxonomy with higher performing pupils. But sticking to the bottom of Bloom's taxonomy does not allow lower-performing pupils to deepen their understanding; rather, it leads to surface learning. And, to complicate matters further, this approach is guilty of assuming that because the taxonomy grows in difficulty, the bottom end isn't as important and that higher-performing pupils don't need to waste their time down there. Instead, they should be floating around the pyramid's apex like Bisto kids following the gravy trail.

Yes, Bloom is a spectrum of task difficulty: it goes from easy - such as recalling knowledge - to harder - such as evaluating an argument. But it is a spectrum because it explores the full range of cognitive learning. Knowledge is just as important as evaluation. Without knowledge, pupils can't access the higher bits. In other words, without the bottom layers of the pyramid - the foundations - the whole structure crumbles and falls to the sandy desert plain.

In order to show their complete mastery of a topic, every pupil (no matter their current level of performance) should be able to answer a combination of recall-type questions (these are questions which can be answered in a short period regardless of prior learning) and developmental-type questions (these are questions which stretch pupils and develop the skills required for academic success).

Every pupil at every level of their academic development needs to answer questions on the full spectrum of Bloom's taxonomy; every pupil needs access to both mastery and developmental questions.

Let me cite a familiar example often used in teacher-training...

First read this extract from The Jabberwocky by Lewis Carroll:

'Twas brillig, and the slithy toves
Did gyre and gimble in the wabe;
All mimsy were the borogroves,
And the mome raths outgrabe.

Now answer me this:
1. What were the slithy toves doing in the wabe?

How about this:
2. How would you describe the state of the borogroves?

And:
3. What can you say about the mome raths?

I bet you had no difficulty answering these questions and you even, by default, used quotations from the text, didn't you? But did you need to understand the poem in order to answer these questions? Or were you simply regurgitating isolated facts?

Now try this question:
4. Were the borogroves justified in feeling mimsy?

And:
5. How effective was the mome raths' strategy?

You'll note that questions 1 to 3 were from the bottom of Bloom's taxonomy whereas 4 and 5 were from the top. This activity demonstrates the fact that questions and tasks which remain at the very base of Bloom's pyramid create the false impression of learning, or 'surface learning', without actually helping pupils to develop and deepen their understanding of a topic.

So, to summarise, we should ensure that every pupil moves up and down the taxonomy by asking questions and setting tasks which use the following stems:

- *Knowledge*: state; recall

- *Comprehension*: explain; interpret
- *Application*: apply; use
- *Analysis*: analyse; classify; compare; give reasons; explain the cause and effects
- *Synthesis*: solve; create; design; invent; suggest improvements for; provide constructive feedback on
- *Evaluation*: strengths / weaknesses; advantages / disadvantages; give the arguments for and against; compare and contrast.

In conclusion, we differentiate in the sense of 'dumbing down' at our peril. Placing artificial limits on what we expect our lower-performing pupils to do isn't the answer to the question of 'How do we teach less able pupils or students?'

…So, what is?

Teaching lower-performing pupils and students

I have argued that teaching to the middle of the bell curve - pitching learning to the average student whilst scaffolding for the lower-performing and stretching and challenging the higher-performing – is a form of dumbing down. I have said that a far more effective way to pitch learning and ensure every pupil and student achieves their potential is to teach to the top - pitch learning to the highest-performing pupil in the class, accepting that will take some pupils longer and that they will require more support but that every pupil will get there eventually.

Teaching to the top is a way of modelling high expectations for all our pupils, no matter their starting points and their most recent performance.

So, we should teach to the top, not the middle, and ensure our classrooms provide challenge for all and that this challenge is baked into our curriculum not left to individual teachers to determine on an ad hoc basis. Challenge of this kind must be embedded in the destination – or end points – we set for our pupils and in the waypoints through which pupils must pass and which will provide our measure of progress.

Of course, some pupils and students fear challenge. We need to eliminate - or at least mitigate - pupils' feelings of fear and hesitation by creating a classroom environment which encourages the making of mistakes as a sign of learning, and which explicitly says (through our choice of language, our modelling and thinking aloud, and the routines we engage in) there is nothing to fear by trying your best and pushing yourself to do hard work.

After all, challenge is innate...

In their lives outside the school gates, pupils and students are always seeking hard things to do such as Minecraft and Fortnite. They are the YouTube generation who spend hours watching video tutorials, looking at graphic organisers on Pinterest or reading articles on Buzzfeed so they can learn by increments and improve their performance in, say, gaming, baking, football, make-up and nail art, hair design, and so on.

They love challenge when it is private because, in the safety of their bedrooms, there isn't the fear of humiliation or peer pressure.

In order to promote challenge in the classroom, therefore, we need to reduce the threat level, we need to ensure no one feels humiliated if they fall short of a challenge. Rather, they need to know they will learn from the experience and perform better next time. They will learn by increments.

Of course, in order to set the right level of challenge for our pupils - hard but achievable with time, effort and support - we need to identify (perhaps through the use of low-stakes quizzing and hinge questions) pupils' zones of proximal development.

What else can we do to help lower-performing pupils learn and make progress?

First, we can put blocks in the way of pupils' initial learning (or encoding) - what Robert Bjork calls 'desirable difficulties' - in order to bolster their subsequent storage and retrieval strength.

Second, we can 'chunk' information, ensuring we teach knowledge before skill. And we can link new learning with prior learning so that pupils can cheat their limited working memories.

Third, we can provide opportunities for our pupils to engage in deliberate practice, repeating learning at least three times but doing so in a different way each time, allowing pupils to do something new with the learning every time they encounter it in order to forge myriad connections and improve 'transfer'.

And if all this works with lower-performing pupils then it will work with all pupils.

That's the beauty of this 'teaching to the top' approach to supporting lower-performing pupils: if you have high expectations of all your pupils and if you model grade 9 work rather than grade 5 work, then although some pupils will fall short, simply because they have aimed high they are more likely to achieve a better grade than if you'd placed artificial limits in the way of their learning.

What's more, why show pupils anything other than the very best? Why model the mediocre?

As Matthew Arnold said in 'Culture and Anarchy' – just as we discovered earlier in this book - "Culture…is a study of perfection, [it] seeks to…make the best that has been thought and known in the world current everywhere; to make all men live in an atmosphere of sweetness and light".

So, let's bring our all our pupils and students, no matter their starting points and current performance, out into the light and watch them grow and blossom. Let us ensure every learner, no matter their background, no matter their starting point, no matter the barriers they face, are given fair access to the same ambitious curriculum.

And helping them to access and achieve within this ambitious curriculum begins with high expectations…

CHAPTER TWENTY
HIGH EXPECTATIONS

If we are to ensure all our pupils and students have equal access to the same ambitious curriculum and if we are to teach that curriculum 'to the top', then we must have high expectations of all learners and anticipate that they will all succeed, albeit at differing speeds and with different levels of support.

So, what do high expectations look like in practice? How can we reinforce those expectations through our words and actions? Let's take a look...

The Pygmalion Effect

Research conducted by Robert Rosenthal and Lenore Jacobson in the 1960s showed that when teachers expected their students to perform better, they actually did so.

Their study supported the hypothesis – known as the Pygmalion Effect and named after a sculptor from Greek mythology who fell in love with one of his statues – that reality can be positively or negatively influenced by other people's expectations. In other words, the higher the expectations you have of somebody, the better they perform.

Rosenthal and Jacobson's research involved students in a Californian elementary school. They started by giving every student a covert IQ test. Without disclosing the scores, they gave the teachers the names of about 20 per cent of students chosen at random and told them that these chosen few were expected to do better than their classmates. At the end of the study all the students were tested again using the same IQ test. Every student had increased their IQ scores. However, the chosen 20 per cent (chosen at random, remember) showed statistically significant gains. This led Rosenthal and Jacobson to conclude that teachers' expectations actually influenced student achievement. Or, to put it another way, teachers' biased expectancies affected reality and created self-fulfilling prophecies. But why should this be?

Rosenthal believed that a teacher's attitude or mood positively affected his or her students because a teacher paid closer attention to so-called "gifted" students and treated them differently when they got stuck. For example, they were more willing to be patient and offer help when "gifted" students struggled because they believed that these students had the capacity to improve. This led Rosenthal to predict that teachers subconsciously behave in ways that facilitate and encourage their students' success. In other words, teachers perpetrate the Pygmalion Effect: when they have high expectations of their students, their students perform well.

It follows, therefore, that having high expectations of pupils and students is not only a nice thing to do, it also leads to demonstrably improved performances. But saying and doing are two very different things. After all, what do high expectations look like in practice? Well, as with most teaching strategies, having high expectations is simply about establishing a set of clear rules and routines. Doug Lemov shares a few such routines in his book, 'Teach Like a Champion'. For example, Lemov says that teachers who have high expectations often operate a "no opt out" policy. In other words, a teaching sequence that begins with a pupil unable to answer a question ends with the same pupil answering the question as often as possible.

Lemov also says that teachers who have high expectations always insist that "right is right" - they set and defend a high standard of correctness in their classroom. For example, they use simple positive language to express their appreciation of what a pupil has done and to express their expectation that he or she will now complete the task. They also insist that pupils answer the question they have asked not a different question entirely. These teachers are clear that the right answer to any question other than the one they have asked is, by definition, wrong.

As well as insisting on the right answer, teachers with high expectations insist that pupils answer the right question at the right time. They protect the integrity of their lesson by not jumping ahead to engage an exciting right answer at the wrong time. These teachers insist their pupils use precise, technical vocabulary. Lemov says that teachers who have high expectations "stretch it". In other words, a sequence of learning does not end with a right answer; these teachers reward right answers with follow-up questions that extend knowledge and test for reliability. For example, they ask how or why, ask for another way to answer, ask for a better word, ask for evidence, ask pupils to integrate a related skill, and/or ask pupils to apply the same skill in a new setting. Lemov says that, for the teachers who have high expectations of their pupils, "format matters". In other words, it is not just what their pupils say that matters but how they say it. To succeed, pupils must take their knowledge and express it in the language of opportunity.

As well as having high expectations of our pupils, we should insist that our pupils have high expectations of themselves, because only by believing in yourself and in your own ability to get better will you actually do so. So, what does this look like in practice...?

First, pupils should have a growth mindset and believe that they can get better at anything if they work hard. This means having a thirst for knowledge, this means accepting that work needs to be drafted and redrafted, and this means following the maxim that if it isn't excellent, it isn't finished (never settling for work that is less than their best). This also means setting aspirational goals for themselves and expecting to achieve them.

Second, pupils should embrace challenge and enjoy hard work because they know it will help them to learn. This means actively engaging in lessons and readily accepting any new challenges that are presented. It also means exerting a lot of effort and engaging in deliberate practice. It means pushing themselves in lessons, practising something over and over again, and regarding additional study opportunities such as homework as an important way of consolidating and deepening their learning rather than as an onerous chore.

Third, pupils should seek out and welcome feedback. They should value other people's opinions and advice and use it to help them improve their work. Feedback should be given and received with kindness in a manner that is helpful and not unduly critical, and yet it should be constructive and specific about what needs to be improved.

Fourth, pupils should be resilient. By being resilient – not giving up easily when things get hard – they will overcome obstacles. Moreover, they will be happy to make mistakes because they know they will learn from them. In practice, this means that pupils ask good questions in order to further their learning, this means pupils always try and solve problems for themselves before asking others for help.

Finally, pupils should be inspired by other people's success. They should seek out examples of great work, discovering what makes it great then using this knowledge to inform their own work. They should take collective responsibility for the work of the class and have a vested interest in everyone's success. This means that pupils support each other and encourage each other to succeed. This means that pupils work well in groups and are confident expressing their views and sharing their ideas. This means that pupils are good at giving each other feedback that is – as I say above – kind, specific and helpful.

The Pygmalion Effect gives teachers a reason to believe that having high expectations of their pupils actually helps them to perform better, but it does come with a health warning…

The opposite of the Pygmalion Effect is the Golem Effect – if we expect our pupils to perform badly, chances are they will. Both the Pygmalion Effect and the Golem Effect have their downsides: they are self-fulfilling prophecies in part because they encourage us to find evidence that supports our expectations regardless of whether or not such evidence exists. In other words, we are in danger of interpreting pupils' performances in line with what we think they will achieve rather than accurately and based on evidence. If we have high expectations of a pupil then we are more inclined to think they are performing well, irrespective of whether or not they actually are.

Equally, if we have low expectations of a pupil, we are eager to find evidence that they are performing badly and seize on the slightest sign of it. This is sometimes called the observer-expectancy effect and is the situation by which a researcher's cognitive bias causes them to unconsciously influence the participants of an experiment. Confirmation biases such as this can lead to the experimenter interpreting results incorrectly because of their tendency to look for information that conforms to their hypothesis, while overlooking information that argues against it.

So, we should have high expectations of all our pupils because this will encourage them to perform better. Moreover, it will help them to develop high expectations of themselves, and if they believe in themselves, they are more likely to succeed. But we should beware of false prophets: we should use empirical evidence to help us determine our pupils' actual performances; we should be attuned to our natural tendencies to find evidence that supports our beliefs, regardless of whether such evidence is accurate or fair.

Just as teachers' high expectations of pupils is a habit not an act, pupils' high expectations of themselves is also about tangible words and actions. So, what do high-performing pupils and students tend to do differently that leads to their academic success? Let's take a look…

The conspiracy of success

I don't believe in conspiracy theories, but Abraham Lincoln and John F Kennedy have always made my spine tingle. After all, they have an awful lot in common…

Abraham Lincoln was elected to Congress in 1846; John F. Kennedy was elected to Congress in 1946. Abraham Lincoln was elected president in 1860; John F Kennedy was elected president in 1960. The names Lincoln and Kennedy each contain seven letters. Both men were particularly concerned with civil rights. Both their wives lost children while living in the White House. Both presidents were shot on a Friday. Both were shot in the head. Lincoln's secretary, Kennedy, warned him not to go to the theatre; Kennedy's secretary, Lincoln, warned him not to go to Dallas. Both were assassinated by Southerners. Both were succeeded by Southerners. Both successors were named Johnson: Andrew Johnson, who succeeded Lincoln, was born in 1808; Lyndon Johnson, who succeeded Kennedy, was born in 1908. Both assassins were known by three names which comprised 15 letters: John Wilkes Booth was born in 1839; Lee Harvey Oswald was born in 1939. Having assassinated Lincoln, Booth ran from the theatre and was caught in a warehouse; having assassinated Kennedy, Oswald ran from a warehouse and was caught in a theatre. Both Booth and Oswald were assassinated before their trials.

Spooky, eh? I don't know about you, but the hairs on the back of my neck are standing up. But, as I say, I don't believe in conspiracy theories. I do, however, believe in coincidence. So, what's the difference? When you think about it, coincidences aren't spooky at all; they are, in fact, perfectly rational because they express a simple, logical pattern of cause and effect. Take, for example, academic achievement…

Several years ago, while working as a deputy headteacher, I interviewed fifty students in Years 11 and 13 who had achieved high grades in their GCSE and A level exams. I found something spooky – a series of apparent coincidences. For example, …

All the students I interviewed had an attendance of more than 93 per cent; 9 out of 10 students had a perfect attendance record. All the students I interviewed told me they used their planners regularly and considered themselves to be well-organised. As a result, all the students I interviewed completed their homework on time and without fail. All the students I interviewed told me they always asked for help from their teachers when they got stuck. They didn't regard doing so as a sign of weakness, rather a sign of strength. Admitting they didn't know something and asking questions meant they learnt something new and increased their intelligence.

Most of the students I interviewed were involved in clubs, sports, or hobbies at lunchtime, after school and/or at weekends. Though not all were sporting, they did all have get-up-and-go attitudes. They didn't spend every evening and weekend watching television. They were sociable and, in order to unwind, they read books. Lots of books. In fact, the school library confirmed that my cohort of high-achievers were among the biggest borrowers in school. All the students believed that doing well in school would increase their chances of getting higher paid and more interesting jobs later in life.

Many of them had a clear idea about the kind of job they wanted to do and knew what was needed in order to get it. They had researched the entry requirements and had then mapped out the necessary school, college, and/or university paths. They had connected what they were doing in school with achieving their future ambitions. School work and good exam results had a purpose, they were means to an important end.

Was it spooky that nearly all these high-achieving students had done the same things? Or was it a simple case of cause and effect: because these students shared these traits they went on to succeed? I believe it was the latter: it was because these students had attended school, were well organised, completed work on time, and had an end goal in mind that they had achieved excellent grades in their final exams. The cause was diligent study and determination; the effect was high achievement. As such, these young people can teach our pupils a valuable lesson - that the recipe for success is to:

- Have good attendance and punctuality.
- Be organised and complete all work on time.
- Be willing to ask for help when you're stuck.
- Have something to aim for and be ambitious.
- Map out your career path and be determined to succeed.

Let's explore the second of these ingredients in more detail: personal organisation. One means of becoming better organised is to acquire effective study skills. In Chapter Twelve I talked about identifying transferable and non-transferable skills and argued the importance of teaching these skills (or procedural knowledge) in context and in domain-specific ways. Of course, although context is key, there are some study skills which pupils need to acquire and use in most if not all subjects, albeit perhaps in different ways. According to Paul C Brown et al in their book, 'Make It Stick', the following study skills are proven to be particularly helpful to pupils and students right across the curriculum...

1. Self-quizzing

Self-quizzing is about retrieving knowledge and skills from memory and is far more effective than simply re-reading a text. When your pupils read a text or study notes, you should teach them to pause periodically to ask themselves questions – without looking in the text – such as:

- What are the key ideas?
- What terms or ideas are new to me? How would I define them?
- How do the ideas in this text relate to what I already know?

You should set aside a little time every week for your pupils to quiz themselves on the current week's work and the material you have covered in previous weeks. If this is to work, it needs to be built into the curriculum plan. Once they have self-quizzed, get your pupils to check their answers and make sure they have an accurate understanding of what they know and what they don't know. Your pupils need to know that making mistakes will not set them back, so long as they check their answers later and correct any errors.

You should space out your pupils' retrieval practice. This means studying information more than once and leaving increasingly large gaps between practice sessions. Again, this needs to be baked into the curriculum and not left to chance. Initially, new material should be revisited within a day or so then not again for several days or a week. When your pupils are feeling surer of certain material, they should quiz themselves on it once a month. They should also interleave the study of two or more topics so that alternating between them requires them to continually refresh their memories of each topic.

2. Elaboration

Elaboration is the process of finding additional layers of meaning in new material. It involves relating new material to what pupils already know, explaining it to somebody else, or explaining how it relates to the wider world. An effective form of elaboration is to use a metaphor or image for the new material.

3. Generation

Generation is when pupils attempt to answer a question or solve a problem before being shown the answer or the solution. The act of filling in a missing word (the cloze test) results in better learning and a stronger memory of the text than simply reading the text. Before reading new class material, ask pupils to explain the key ideas they expect to find and how they expect these ideas will relate to their prior knowledge.

4. Reflection

Reflection involves taking a moment to review what has been learned. Pupils ask questions such as:

- What went well? What could have gone better?
- What other knowledge or experience does it remind me of?
- What might I need to learn in order to achieve better mastery?
- What strategies could I use next time to get better results?

5. Calibration

Calibration is achieved when pupils adjust their judgment to reflect reality – in other words, they become certain that their sense of what they know and can do is accurate. Often when we revise information, we look at a question and convince ourselves that we know the answer, then move on to the next question without making an effort to actually answer the previous one. If we do not write down an answer, we may create the illusion of knowing when in fact we would have difficulty giving a response. We need to teach our pupils to remove the illusion of knowing and actually answer all the questions even if they think they know the answer and that it is too easy.

Here are some other useful study skills we could build into our curriculum plans:

1. Anticipate test questions during lessons.
2. Read study guides, find terms they can't recall or don't know and learn them.
3. Copy key terms and their definitions into a notebook.
4. Take practice tests.
5. Reorganise class material into a study guide.
6. Copy out key concepts and regularly test themselves on them.
7. Space out revision and practice activities.

And here are some handy teacher tips to help our pupils and students to study smarter:

Create desirable difficulties in the classroom by using tests frequently. Design study tools that make use of retrieval practice, generation and elaboration.

Return to concepts covered earlier in the term. Space, interleave and vary the topics covered in class so that pupils frequently have to "reload" what they already know about each topic in order to determine how new material relates to, or indeed differs from, prior knowledge.

Make learning transparent by helping your pupils to understand the ways in which you have incorporated desirable difficulties and other strategies into your lessons.

Plan for "free recall", whereby pupils spend 10 minutes at the end of each lesson filling a blank piece of paper with everything they can remember from that lesson.

Set a weekly homework whereby pupils create summary sheets (perhaps a side of A4) on which they summarise the previous week's learning in text, annotated illustrations, or graphical organisers. The purpose of this task is to stimulate retrieval and reflection, and to capture the previous week's learning before it is lost.

And finally, explain how learning works. Help your pupils to understand that creating some kinds of difficulties during the learning process helps to strengthen learning and memory because when learning is easy it is often superficial and soon forgotten. Help your pupils to understand that not all intellectual abilities are innate – in fact, when learning is "effortful", it changes the brain, making new connections and increasing intellectual ability. Pupils learn better when they struggle with new problems by themselves before being shown the solution, not vice-versa. Help your pupils to understand that, in order to achieve excellence, they must strive to surpass their current level of ability. This, by its very nature, often leads to setbacks and set-backs are often what provide the information that's needed in order to achieve mastery.

Finally, as I suggested in Chapter Twelve, it's important to identify the study skills we require our pupils to develop in order to access and succeed in our curriculum, and to build the explicit teaching, modelling and practice of these skills into our curriculum plan. By so doing, we not only ensure that every pupil is explicitly taught these skills, but that they're taught them before the skills are needed, and in context within a subject domain.

CHAPTER TWENTY-ONE
PITCH PERFECT

In Book Two in this 3-book series on school and college curriculum design, we will explore 'curriculum implementation' – the *'how?'* of education. We will talk about how to pitch learning in pupils' struggle zones so that work is always hard (requiring pupils to think and actively attend to curriculum content) but achievable (helping pupils to cheat the limitations of working memory and avoid cognitive overload).

For the purposes of this book on 'curriculum intent', however, I think it worth exploring some of the central tenets of 'pitch' as they relate to defining excellence and teaching to the top...

If I were to ask you to calculate 57 x 3489 in your heads, no cheating, and in the space of a minute, I'm pretty confident most of you would fail. And in the process of failing, you'd likely do one of two things...

Either: you'd decide the task was unachievable - especially with the time constraints attached - and therefore not even attempt it.

Or: you'd try and try to complete the task but fail to do so because to succeed would involve processing too much information all at once. Your working memory wouldn't be able to cope with the demands you'd placed upon it, and in just sixty seconds, and you'd reach the point of cognitive overload.

Whichever of these two paths you'd take, you wouldn't get the answer and would, therefore, have encoded nothing into long-term memory.

Put simply, you'd neither learn something new nor practice something that you already knew.

This complex thing called 'learning' would not occur.

The task would prove utterly pointless.

Now, if I were to ask you to calculate 2 x 10, once again in your heads and in the space of a minute, I'm confident all of you would succeed this time. And you wouldn't need a full minute to do so either! In fact, you'd proffer your answer instantaneously.

But, and here's the rub, you wouldn't have calculated anything; you'd have given your answer automatically. In other words, you wouldn't have engaged the attention of your working memory, at least not in any meaningful sense, because you've practised your times tables to the point of automaticity whereby you can reel them off through habit, without thinking about them, just as you tie your shoe laces or button your shirt without thinking about it. Most of the time, you drive your car without thinking about that, too; you've done it so many times that the task no longer needs to engage your active attention, which helps explain why you sometimes arrive at your destination with absolutely no memory of the journey.

And because you answered 2 x 10 without thinking about it, as was the case with the first sum, you didn't learn anything new or practice something that you already knew.

In other words, this task - though ostensibly a success - was also pointless. Learning did not occur.

In 'Thinking Fast and Slow' (2011), Daniel Kahneman summarises his own research - and that of other cognitive scientists - in mapping the roles of the two interacting systems of the human brain:

"System 1" thinks fast. That is to say it's instinctive and intuitive. It can react more quickly than conscious thought. But it is also prone to error. And we cannot turn it off. We cannot see a word in a language we speak and choose not to read it. "System 2" thinks slow. That is to say it works rationally and methodically. It can assess and analyse choices in a sophisticated and analytical way. But it is slower and because this thinking is hard work, our minds try to avoid it.

We are always trying to shut this system down to save energy. And if we overload this system, it's in danger of interfering with our basic functions (such as our perception).

For example, driving while talking on our mobile phone - even using hands free - increases the likelihood of having an accident because a conversation requires us to think and so we see and perceive less.

Kahneman argues that System 2 can shape System 1 by providing constant exposure to experiences that encode behaviours until they become more instinctual. We see a situation over and over and learn to recognise and react to it; ultimately it shapes our instinctual responses.

This is much of what we do when we engage in work that is pitch perfect - targeted at our 'sweet spot'.

Understanding the two systems and how they interact is incredibly useful for teachers because it helps us to understand how we can shape pupils' and students' thinking.

In particular, it shows that decision-making starts with perception, and so systematic exposure to situations where pupils and students learn to perceive and recognise viable solutions is critical. This is why it's necessary to build "knowledge" …

If we want to develop our pupils and students' problem-solving abilities, we must first teach them background knowledge. Indeed, problem-solving is not a skill our pupils and students can develop without background knowledge. In 'Practice Perfect' (2012), Doug Lemov says: "You essentially recognise a situation visually faster than you can consciously think. Then you associate this cue with knowledge of viable choices stored in long-term memory."

Herbert Simon, meanwhile, says, "Intuition is nothing more than and nothing less than recognition."

If we want our pupils to learn anything of our ambitious curriculum - by which I mean, encode information into their long-term memories - then we need to engage their active attention and get them thinking hard. We need to give them work to do that's challenging but achievable because: If the work's too easy, pupils will complete it through habit; if the work's too hard, pupils will be unable to complete it. In both cases, learning will fail.

So, we need to pitch work in pupils' 'struggle zone', what they can do with time, effort and support. This is sometimes referred to as the 'zone of proximal development', a term invented by the Russian psychologist Lev Vygotsky and defined by him in 1978 as "the distance between the actual developmental level as determined by independent problem-solving and the level of potential development as determined through problem-solving under adult guidance, or in collaboration with more capable peers".

In fact, that sentence is a perfect example of why we need to set hard work...

If you're like me, you probably had to read Vygotsky's definition a couple of times before you could make proper sense of it. His sentence is long and complex, it is just hard enough for me to be challenged by it but not too hard for me to be put off by it. If it contained lots of words with which I was unfamiliar, I'd likely give up or shy away from it, deeming it beyond my current reach. If it was short and simple, I'd probably skim over it without really taking it in because I didn't have to think about it. But it is difficult and achievable; it is just beyond my current ability but without my reach.

As such, I had to read it a couple of times to make the necessary connections between words I already knew and a context or meaning that was new to me. But I made sense of it eventually and, as a consequence, I learnt what Vygotsky meant by the term 'zone of proximal development'.

The fact I worked hard at understanding Vygotsky's definition, and had to stop and think about it, means I'm not just able to overcome a challenge and succeed, thus engaging the active attention of my working memory and helping me to learn, but I'm also much more likely to remember it later. In other words, because the work was pitched in my struggle zone, beyond my current abilities but within my reach, I improved the storage and retrieval strength of the information I encoded in long-term memory.

Working on problems that are too easy or too difficult is not enjoyable because there is no sense of progress, and thus we become frustrated. Working on problems that are pitched in our struggle zone, however, is rewarding.

This is why giving pupils work to do that is too easy for them and which they can therefore accomplish without thinking - in the misguided belief that it will give them a sense of success and thus motivate them - doesn't work. Instead, we are motivated by thinking hard and overcoming difficulty; we are motivated by overcoming challenges.

There's evidence from the field of neurochemistry to support this notion, too. When we solve a problem, we are rewarded with a small dose of dopamine which is a naturally-occurring chemical that's important to the brain's pleasure system. Indeed, alongside serotonin, dopamine is one of only two things that - chemically speaking - give us pleasure.

So, how can we ensure that our pupils are made to think hard?

Sometimes, we need to place artificial barriers in the way of their initial encoding of information so that the information is stored more effectively and can more easily be retrieved later. These artificial barriers, or road-blocks in our thinking, are what Robert Bjork called 'desirable difficulties'...

Desirable difficulties

Bjork, a cognitive psychologist at UCLA, coined the phrases 'storage strength' (SS) and 'retrieval strength' (RS) in order to help improve our understanding of how we learn (which is to say, how we commit things to long-term memory).

Storage strength is the measure of how effectively we have encoded something. Studying something in greater detail increases the chance of us storing it in our long-term memory. The better it is learned, the higher the SS. If it has a high SS, it is more likely to be stored in our long-term memory (rather than remain in our working memory to be quickly forgotten) and more likely to be ready to be 'retrieved' later.

Retrieval strength, meanwhile, is the measure of how easily we can access a memory of something we've learned. In other words, RS is our ability to recall information at a later date. RS decreases over time - which is why we forget things as we get older - and the lower the SS, the faster the RS will decrease.

Put simply, if we want to learn something well enough so that it will be accessible to us in the future (rather than quickly forgotten), then we need to learn it in greater depth, and we need to 'over-learn' it

Bjork identified a number of conditions which over time increase SS and RS and which therefore lead to information being retained for longer. These conditions, Bjork cautioned, "slow down the apparent learning, but under most circumstances help long term retention, and help transfer of knowledge, from what you learnt to new situations".

Bjork called these conditions 'desirable difficulties' because they are ways of teaching which are intentionally challenging to pupils because difficulty and hard work are what assists their long-term learning.

Put simply, then, Bjork argued that teachers should spend longer teaching fewer things but in greater detail. In other words, our pupils should learn less content but in more depth.

I'll give you an example in a moment but first answer me this question before we go on: How many animals of each kind did Moses take onto the Ark? The more quick-witted, eagle-eyed among you would have spotted the mistake and answered 'none'. But I bet some of you said 'two', didn't you? I've asked this question during several conference speeches and training events and some members of the audience always say 'two'.

If you said 'two' then you fell into the trap of skimming the question too quickly and offering the obvious answer. The fact is, the question asks you how animals Moses took onto the Ark when, in fact, Moses didn't build an ark; it was Noah.

That question was a perfect example of work that is too simple, too easy, too obvious. Because it has all the hallmarks of a straightforward question, some of you put two and two together and made five. You skimmed over the words and filled in the gaps then offered an answer out of habit. That answer happened to be wrong, but you were convinced of its accuracy.

There are several ways to help pupils avoid falling into this trap - each of which is an example of a desirable difficulty, a barrier that slows down the initial encoding of information so that it is stored better and more easily retrieved from long-term memory...

Firstly, we can use more complex language constructions. For example, instead of asking a question worded as a simple sentence ('How many animals of each kind did Moses take onto the Ark?'), we could ask it using a complex sentence ('In the biblical story, to save them from the flood, how many animals of each kind did Moses take onto the Ark?').

Secondly, we could put a deliberate block in the way - something incongruous that stops pupils in their tracks ('How many animals of each kind did Donald Trump take onto the Ark?').

Thirdly, and this is rather counter-intuitive, we could use a hard-to-decipher font for written information on the board or on handouts. If the font causes us to stop, slow down and concentrate more then we are forced to think harder and therefore more likely to encode information into long-term memory from where we can retrieve it later. If you want to try this, download a font called 'Sans Forgetica' from the internet, specifically designed with this purpose in mind.

In 'Visible Learning' (2012), John Hattie echoed Bjork's belief that teachers should slow down learning and set challenging work. He said that the best way for pupils to learn is not always pleasurable for them: "Learning is not always… easy; it requires over-learning at certain points, spiralling up and down the knowledge continuum, building a working relationship with others in grappling with challenging tasks".

Hattie went on to say that the most "accomplished teachers set tasks that [have] a greater degree of challenge".

Memory is the residue of thought

The cognitive scientist Daniel Willingham argues that a lack of space in working memory is a functional bottleneck of human cognition. In 'Why Don't Students Like School?' (2009), he says: "Working memory is more or less fixed – you get what you get, and practice does not change it… there are, however, ways to cheat this limitation".

One way to cheat the limited size of your working memory, so says Willingham, is through factual knowledge. The second way is to make the processes that manipulate information in working memory more efficient. Willingham uses the analogy of learning to tie our shoelaces. At first, tying our laces requires our full attention and thus absorbs all of our working memory, but with practice we can tie our shoes automatically whilst our working memory is otherwise engaged holding a conversation, for example.

I think another useful example which demonstrates the benefit of practice is that of learning to read…

Once we have 'mastered' reading in the sense that we know the sound each letter makes and how letters combine to make words, we still keep practising our reading not just to get faster at reading but in order to get so good at recognising the letters and words and the sounds they make that word recognition becomes automatic… we see words and understand them and how they sound without having to think about it and this automaticity frees up precious space in our working memories which used to be used to retrieve sounds and meanings from our long-term memories but which we can now devote to thinking about the meanings of sentences and texts.

Eventually, we get so good at reading that we have enough working memory to be able to recognise allusions and make other connections between the text we are reading and all the background knowledge we already possess.

What's true of reading is true of all the skills our pupils use in all the subjects we teach.

In conclusion, we should not be afraid to set our pupils work to do which is hard, which challenges them and makes them think. We should avoid setting work which is too easy and which pupils have already mastered. And we should avoid setting work which is too hard and which pupils cannot possibly master at the moment. Instead, we should ensure we set work that is pitched within the 'zone of proximal development': work that is hard but accessible; work that is challenging but achievable.

We should not set work which is too easy because if pupils do not have to think about it, they will not think about it. They will rely on their memory instead and complete tasks out of habit without engaging any cognitive processes, which is to say that their brains will not have to release dopamine in order to forge new connections, and they will not therefore feel any sense of reward and will become apathetic and bored.

Perhaps more importantly, if pupils complete tasks without having to think about them, new connections will not be made, information will not enter their long-term memories and they will not, therefore, be able to recall that information at a later time.

In short, if the work is too easy pupils will not learn.

Nor should we set work for our pupils to do which is too hard because if pupils cannot access it, they will be unable to forge new connections in their brains, their brains will not release dopamine and they will become frustrated and demotivated.

In short, if the work is too hard pupils will not learn.

And how do we make sure that the work we set falls squarely within the 'zone of proximal development'? Simply by knowing our pupils because regular assessment of our pupils will inform us where each of them is now - what they can and cannot do and, therefore, where the gaps in their learning are - and this, in turn, will inform us where their zone of proximal development sits currently.

Assessment is a form of planning. If you can confidently answer the following questions about each of your pupils, then you can plan for progress:

- Where are they now?
- Where do they need to be?
- How can they get there?

Planning for progress is at the heart of effective curriculum design and indeed integral to great teaching, and pupils only make progress when they are challenged and engaged. They are only challenged and engaged when the work they are asked to do is not too hard and not too easy but just right. Great teachers, therefore, are like Goldilocks: they know when the conditions are just right for learning to take place. Great teachers serve a rich diet of porridge that's heated to the optimum temperature - neither too hot nor too cold - each and every day.

Once we have defined excellence and set the bar high for every pupil, we need to actively attend to the differences between pupils' starting points and do all that we can to ensure our curriculum is accessible to all our pupils and that all have an equal chance of success – which, as I explained in Chapter Eighteen, means ensuring all pupils can understand curriculum content and the language in which – and through which – it is expressed, and that all pupils have the prior knowledge and schema (or mental maps) to achieve, incrementally, the destinations we set for them.

As I said earlier, not all pupils are equal. We know that pupils will come to our curriculum knowing different things, being able to do different things, and with differing capacities to know and do more. I have argued against dumbing down or reducing our curriculum for those pupils who have lower starting points or disadvantages. I have said we should teach to the top and have high expectations of all. But by so doing we must not leave some pupils and students to flounder and fall behind their peers. We must help to close the gap between disadvantaged pupils and their peers.

So, how can we close the gap? How can we help disadvantaged pupils and pupils with SEND or High Needs fill the gaps in their knowledge and language capabilities and provide more equal access to education?

In the final part of this book we will consider how to do just that: diminish disadvantage…

PART SIX

DIMINISH DISADVANTAGE

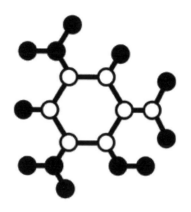

CHAPTER TWENTY-TWO
CLOSING THE GAP

In Chapter Fourteen, I argued the case for developing a consistent language *of* and *for* learning. I said that we need to provide planned opportunities for our pupils and students to develop their language capabilities so that they can access and make progress through our ambitious curriculum.

Language is crucial to curriculum success because pupils and students gain access to, comprehend, and demonstrate their understanding of curriculum content through their use of language.

In March 2018 I attended the National Ofsted and Pupil Premium Conference in Birmingham to give a speech about cultural capital. The speaker on stage before me was Peter Humphries, Ofsted's senior HMI for schools in the West Midlands region.

Humphries used his speech to emphasise the key role that literacy plays in the curriculum. Under the new EIF, a school's curriculum, he said, will be evaluated for the extent to which it helps close the gap.

Humphries pointed to American research that shows children in richer families experience 45 million words, while those in working class families and those in families on welfare experience just 20 and 13 million respectively.

He told delegates, "We know that literacy is an issue for disadvantaged pupils and it's sometimes a bit of a surprise that it's not being addressed more rigorously in schools. Ninety per cent of words will only be experienced in books. It's important to read because that's where we develop vocabulary."

As such, in the next chapter on cultural capital I will argue that a primary – though not only – means of closing the attainment gap and providing equal access to our curriculum is to develop pupils' language and literacy skills.

In Chapter Twenty-Five I will discuss literacy across the curriculum in more detail.

But first I'd like to explore the Pupil Premium Grant – the additional monies given to schools in England to help them diminish the attainment gap between disadvantaged pupils and their peers. I do so for illustrative purposes but my 3-point plan for Pupil Premium success applies equally to the use of other funding streams including monies given to High Needs Learners in FE colleges.

Diminishing disadvantage through the Pupil Premium

What is the Pupil Premium?

The Pupil Premium was introduced by the Coalition Government in 2011 and is money given to schools to help support disadvantaged pupils. 'Disadvantage' is defined by three categories:

Firstly, the Pupil Premium is awarded to pupils who are categorised as 'Ever 6 FSM'. In other words, it is given to pupils who are recorded in the January school census who are known to have been eligible for free school meals (FSM) in any of the previous six years, as well as those first known to be eligible that month.

Secondly, Pupil Premium funding is also awarded to pupils who are adopted from care or who have left care. In other words, the funding is given to pupils who are recorded in the January school census and alternative provision census who were looked after by an English or Welsh local authority immediately before being adopted, or who left local authority care on a special guardianship order or child arrangements order (previously known as a residence order).

Finally, Pupil Premium funding is awarded to pupils who are categorised as 'Ever 5 service child' which means a pupil recorded in the January school census who was eligible for the service child premium in any of the previous four years as well as those recorded as a service child for the first time in the January school census.

Does the Pupil Premium work?

Since the Pupil Premium was introduced in 2011, its success has been variable…

The gap has closed fastest in schools with the highest concentration of disadvantaged pupils.

In contrast, schools with the lowest proportions of disadvantaged pupils have seen the gap widen, particularly at key stages 2 and 4, suggesting that disadvantaged children are not prioritised when they are in the extreme minority.

What's more, the overall gap has widened. One in three children in the UK now grows up in poverty and the attainment gap between rich and poor is detectable at an early age. White working-class pupils (particularly boys) are among the lowest performers and the link between poverty and attainment is multi-racial.

The limited impact of the Pupil Premium can, I believe, be attributed to several factors…

Firstly, as I explained above, the Pupil Premium (which I will now refer to as PP for the sake of brevity) is awarded to pupils who are eligible for free school meals (as well as those in care and care-leavers, and children from service families) but FSM eligibility is a poor proxy for educational and social disadvantage. Indeed, as many as 50-75% of FSM children are not in the lowest income households. What's more, it's often the time-poor and the less educated who are not as engaged and motivated at school, rather than those facing economic deprivation.

That's not to suggest that a majority of pupils from poorer households do not have difficulties at school and are not deserving of additional funds to help close the gap between them and their better-off peers, but it is important to note that other pupils not currently in scope for the PP are also academically disadvantaged and are equally deserving of our attention.

Secondly, PP children are not a homogenous group. Indeed, the group mean often masks significant differences amongst all those eligible for the PP.

Thirdly, closing the gap is more difficult for some schools because the size of the 'gap' is necessarily dependent on the non-PP demographic in a school. Put simply, the more advantaged the non-PP cohort, the harder it is to close the gap. And yet we too often focus on measuring the disadvantage and do not consider the make-up of those pupils in a school who are not eligible for PP funding.

Finally, PP data is often meaningless because assessments change and the PP cohort itself changes over time - not least as a result of benefits reforms which have taken a large number of pupils out of eligibility despite no discernible differences in their circumstances. In other words, pupils who were previously eligible for the PP are no longer so but are just as disadvantaged socio-economically. Further, in-school sample sizes are usually too small to make inferences, and this also means that a school's closing the gap data is largely meaningless.

All of which is not to suggest that we should abandon the PP altogether or indeed all hope of closing the gap. But we need to recognise the limitations of the funding and use common sense and pragmatism when analysing our data. Most importantly of all, we need to ensure that we focus on every child in a school not just those eligible for discrete funding, and work on a case-by-case basis to understand the barriers that some pupils face at school. Talking of which...

The 3-point plan

I will now explore my 3-point plan for PP success. The plan is as follows:

1.   Identify the barriers
2.   Choose the intervention strategies
3.   Set the success criteria

Let's start, sensibly enough, with step one...

Identifying the barriers

Before you can put in place any Pupil Premium intervention strategies aimed at supporting your disadvantaged pupils, you must first understand why a gap exists between the attainment of disadvantaged pupils and non-disadvantaged pupils.

In short, you need to ask yourself: What are the barriers to learning faced by your disadvantaged students?

This may sound obvious but it's a step often missed by schools who assume all pupils eligible for PP funding must be disadvantaged and similarly disadvantaged.

However, when identifying the barriers to learning in your school, it is important to remember that not all the children who are eligible for the PP will face all, or even some, of the barriers I set out below, and there is no such thing as a typical pupil premium child.

Rather, each child must be treated on an individual basis and the support given must be tailored to meet their needs, not the needs of a homogenous group of 'Pupil Premium kids'.

As such, schools should identify, on a case by case basis, what, if any, barriers to learning those pupils eligible for PP face.

Let me emphasise this: not all pupils from come from socio-economically deprived homes will struggle at school and do less well than their affluent peers. A majority will, but it's not set in stone.

Likewise, not all pupils who come from affluent families will do well in school. It may be that some of these pupils have time-poor parents and spend their evenings plugged into a device rather than talking at the dinner table or reading books.

In short, avoid stereotypes and work hard to understand the truth for each of your pupils.

When seeking to identify barriers to learning, here are some possible answers to look out for...

- Pupils for whom English is an additional language having limited vocabulary;
- Poor attendance and punctuality;
- Mobility issues caused by a pupil moving between schools;
- Issues within a pupil's family unit;
- Medical issues, sometimes undiagnosed;
- A lack of sleep or poor nutrition;
- A lack of family engagement with learning;
- Education not being valued within local community;
- A lack of role models, especially male role models;

- A lack of self-confidence and self-esteem;

Planning solutions

Once you have identified the barriers your disadvantaged pupils face towards learning, you need to plan the solutions.

1 in 3 young people grows up in poverty in the UK. What's worse, a report by the Resolution Foundation in February 2019 predicted that by 2023 37% of children would live in poverty. The highest proportion since the early 1990s.

The academic achievement gap between rich and poor is detectable from an early age - as early as 22 months in fact - and the gap continues to widen as children travel through the education system.

Children from the lowest income homes are half as likely to get five good GCSEs and go on to higher education as the national average. And white working-class pupils (particularly boys) are amongst our lowest performers.

What's more, the link between poverty and attainment is multi-racial - whatever their ethnic background, pupils eligible for free school meals underperform compared to those who are not.

In short, if you're a high ability pupil from a low-income home (and, therefore, a low social class), you're not going to do as well in school and in later life as a low ability pupil from a higher income home and higher social class.

In other words, it is social class and wealth - not ability - that defines a pupil's educational outcomes and their future life chances.

The gap does not grow at a consistent rate. The gap at age sixteen can be broken into fifths: two were already present by age five, one developed during primary school and two developed during secondary school.

The component of the gap that emerges during primary school is half the size of the early years and secondary components, despite primary education lasting two years longer than pre-16 secondary education, or than the maximum length of time between birth and starting school.

Two-thirds of the primary school component develops during reception and key stage 1; only one-third of the primary progress gap emerges during key stage 2, despite this stage being four years in length compared with less than three years between the early years foundation stage (EYFS) assessment and the end of key stage 1.

In other words, educational disadvantage starts early - certainly before a child enters formal education. In fact, two fifths of the attainment gap at age 16 was present before the child started school. These gaps are particularly pronounced in early language and literacy.

By the age of 3, more disadvantaged children are – on average – already almost 18 months behind their more affluent peers in their early language development. Around two fifths of disadvantaged five-year-olds are not meeting the expected literacy standard for their age.

The Pupil Premium should, therefore, be spent on improving children's literacy and language skills. We will explore this issue further in Chapter Twenty-Three when we consider the vital role of cultural capital in our curriculum.

Agreeing the strategies and evaluating their impact

The second action in my 3-point plan is to choose the strategies. Once we have identified the barriers each pupil faces, we must decide what action we can take to overcome those barriers and afford each pupil equal access to our ambitious curriculum and an equal chance of success at school and college.

There are, I believe, some common principles we need to consider when deciding which strategies to use...

Firstly, we should ensure our strategies promote an ethos of attainment for all pupils, rather than stereotyping disadvantaged pupils as a group with less potential to succeed.

Secondly, we should take an individualised approach to addressing barriers to learning and emotional support and do so at an early stage, rather than providing access to generic support as pupils near their end-of-key-stage assessments.

Thirdly, we should focus on outcomes for individual pupils rather than on providing generic strategies for whole cohorts.

Fourthly, we should deploy our best staff to support disadvantaged pupils; perhaps develop existing teachers' and teaching assistants' skills rather than using additional staff who do not know the pupils well.

Fifthly, we should make decisions based on frequent assessment data, responding to changing evidence, rather than use a one-off decision point.

And finally, we should focus on high quality teaching first rather than on bolt-on strategies and activities outside school hours and outside the classroom.

Earlier, I articulated one such strategy: the building of cultural capital by closing the vocabulary gap. In addition to building cultural capital, I believe that PP funding should be focused on:

1. Improving pupils' transition from primary school
2. Developing pupils' cross curricular literacy skills
3. Developing pupils' cross curricular numeracy skills

Why use PP to improve transition?

In Chapter Thirteen, I cited Galton (1999) who found that almost forty per cent of children fail to make expected progress during the year immediately following a change of schools. I also quoted data from the DfE (2011) which shows that average progress drops between key stage 2 and key stage 3 for reading, writing and maths.

I also said that the effects of transition are amplified by risk factors such as poverty and ethnicity.

Those pupils eligible for PP are, therefore, amongst the most likely to suffer when they change schools. Although schools cannot mitigate all the social and emotional effects of transition, they can do more to help pupils make the academic leap.

Why use PP to improve literacy?

I've already talked about vocabulary, but literacy development is much more than this…

PP funding can be used to provide opportunities for the word poor to mingle with the word rich, to hear language being used by pupils of their own age and in ways that they might not otherwise encounter. It might also be used to run interventions in which teachers or mentors model higher-order reading skills because, as the literate adults in the room, we teachers use these skills unconsciously all the time, so we need to make the implicit explicit. For example, interventions could be used to model:

- Moving quickly through and across texts
- Locating key pieces of information.
- Following the gist of articles
- Questioning a writer's facts or interpretation
- Linking one text with another
- Making judgments about whether one text is better than, more reliable than, or more interesting than another text

PP funding could also be used to promote the love of reading for the sake of reading, too; encouraging our pupils to see reading as something other than a functional activity. It is the responsibility of every adult working in a school and college (not just teachers, and certainly not just English teachers) to show that reading because we like reading is one of the hallmarks of civilised adult life.

We'll explore literacy in more detail in Chapter Twenty-Five.

Why use PP to improve numeracy?

PP funding can be used to fund teacher professional development to raise awareness of how to teach numeracy across the curriculum.

For example, in English, numeracy can be developed by using non-fiction texts which include mathematical vocabulary, graphs, charts and tables. In science, pupils will order numbers including decimals, calculate means, and percentages, use negative numbers when taking temperatures, substitute into formulae, rearrange equations, decide which graph to use to represent data, and plot, interpret and predict from graphs. In ICT, pupils will collect and classify data, enter it into data handling software to produce graphs and tables, and interpret and explain the results. When they use computer models and simulations, they will draw on their abilities to manipulate numbers and identify patterns and relationships. In art and design and technology, pupils will use measurements and patterns, spatial ideas, the properties of shapes, and symmetry, and use multiplication and ratio to enlarge and reduce the size of objects. In history, geography and RE, pupils will collect data and use measurements of different kinds. They will study maps and use coordinates and ideas of angles, direction, position, scale, and ratio. And they will use timelines similar to number lines.

PP funding can also be used for numeracy intervention strategies. At the whole-school level, PP funding may also be used to help create a positive environment that celebrates numeracy and provides pupils with role models by celebrating the numeracy successes of older pupils. At subject level, PP funding may be used to help provide high quality exemplar materials and display examples of numeracy work within a subject context. Departments could highlight opportunities for the use of numeracy within their subject and ensure that the learning materials that are presented to pupils match both their capability in the subject and their numerical demands.

Again, we will explore numeracy still further in Chapter Twenty-Five.

When interventions work best

For each of the above areas, it's important to consider the best individual approach. For example, evidence suggests that interventions work best when they are short term, intensive, focused, and tailored.

Short term
The best interventions help pupils to become increasingly independent over time. In other words, the scaffolds slowly fall away as the pupil develops confidence and ability. Interventions should, therefore, be planned to run for a finite amount of time, ideally less than a term. Of course, if the evidence shows the intervention is working but that further improvement is needed, then the intervention can be extended, but to slate an intervention for a year, say, is often misguided.

Intensive
Similarly, interventions should be intensive, perhaps with three or more sessions a week rather than just one. And those sessions should also be intensive in the sense of being short, say 20 to 50 minutes in length rather than an hour or more.

Focused
Interventions should be keenly focused on a pupil's areas of development rather than be generic. For example, rather than setting a goal of, say, 'improving a pupil's literacy skills', an intervention strategy should be focused on a specific aspect of literacy such as their knowledge of the plot of Stone Cold or their ability to use embedded quotations in an essay.

Tailored

Interventions need to be tailored to meet the needs of those pupils accessing them. They must be as personalised as any classroom learning and not be 'off the peg' programmes. Assessment data should be used to inform the intervention and to ensure it is being pitched appropriately to fill gaps in the pupil's knowledge.

Putting it into practice

By way of an example, consider this scenario: immediately after a maths lesson, pupils might access additional tutoring in those areas of study with which they struggled in class. If the intervention is to be effective, there must be close liaison and effective communication between the classroom maths teacher and the tutor/TA who leads the intervention and this communication must occur both before and after the intervention to ensure classroom learning and intervention support are connected. This communication must not be left to a chance encounter in the staffroom but must be a planned part of the weekly timetable.

As I say above, it should be the aim of any intervention strategy to develop pupils' independence so that the scaffolds can gradually be taken down. If the same pupils are repeatedly in these maths intervention sessions, questions must be asked about the effectiveness of the sessions in meeting their needs.

Monitoring and evaluating

Any intervention strategy must be monitored as it's happening and not just evaluated once it's finished. The monitoring may involve more anecdotal data such as pupil and teacher feedback, but evidence must be gathered throughout the timespan of the intervention in order to ensure it is working – or working as well as it could – and so that timely decisions can be taken to stop or tweak an intervention if it is not having the desired effect on pupil progress. Waiting until the intervention has finished to evaluate its success is too late: if it did not work or did not work as well as it could have done, then time and money have been wasted.

Setting the success criteria

The third and final action on our 3-point plan for Pupil Premium success is to set the success criteria.

Once you've identified the barriers to learning faced by those eligible for the Pupil Premium and have chosen the best strategies to help them overcome these barriers, you need to be clear about what success will look like. Ask yourself: what do I expect to see as an outcome? What is my aim here? For example, is it to:

- Raise attainment;
- Expedite progress;
- Improve attendance;
- Improve behaviour;
- Reduce exclusions;
- Improve parental engagement;
- Expand upon the number of opportunities - including extra-curricular activities - afforded to disadvantaged pupils...?

Whatever your immediate goal is, ultimately you should be seeking to diminish the difference between the attainment of disadvantaged pupils in your school and non-disadvantaged pupils nationally, as well as narrowing your within-school gap.

Here's an important caveat though: if your initial aim is pastoral in nature, for example to improve behaviour and attendance, or reduce exclusions, then you must take it a step further and peg it to an academic outcome. Although pastoral outcomes are important, all our PP activity must ultimately lead to an academic success criteria - in other words, improving attainment. The PP exists to close the attainment gap, after all.

Common pitfalls to avoid

In those schools where the Pupil Premium isn't used effectively and is not tracked well enough, there tends to be a lack of clarity about the intended impact of interventions.

These schools run the same intervention strategies year after year because that's just what they're used to doing or have the staff and resources for, irrespective of whether or not they work. There is no real monitoring of the quality and impact of the interventions and no real awareness of what works and what offers the best value for money.

These schools also tend to spend the money indiscriminately on teaching assistants, but they are not well utilised.

The schools whose PP practice is ineffective also tend to have an unclear audit trail. They tend to spend the funding in isolation, it does not feature as part of the whole school development plan and decisions about it are not therefore taken in the round. These schools also compare their performance to local, not national, data.

Pupil Premium funding is used for pastoral interventions, but they are vague and not focused on desired outcomes for pupils. And, finally, in these schools, governors are not involved in taking decisions about PP spending and are not informed about its use and impact.

Good practice

Schools that use PP funding effectively and close the gap tend to conduct a detailed analysis of where pupils are underachieving and why. They make good use of research evidence when choosing support and intervention activities. However, they focus on high quality teaching, rather than relying on interventions to compensate because they know that pedagogy trumps all - getting it right first time is the best approach and teaching matters more than curriculum.

They ensure that their best teachers lead English and maths intervention groups. They make frequent use of achievement data in order to check the effectiveness of interventions and they do this early and continue to do it throughout the year rather than waiting until the intervention has finished and it's too late to change it. These schools also tend to have a systematic focus on clear pupil feedback and pupils receive regular advice to help them improve their work.

These schools have a designated senior leader with a clear overview of the funding allocation and a solid understanding of how the funding works and how it needs reporting. All the teachers in these schools are aware of the pupils who are eligible for PP funding and they take responsibility for those pupils' progress. These schools have strategies in place for improving attendance, behaviour and links with families and communities if these are an issue, as well as for improving academic performance. And, finally, these schools ensure that the performance management of staff includes discussions about the PP and about individual pupils in receipt of the funding and how they are progressing.

What works?

In Book Two of this series I will explore in more detail the research evidence about which teaching approaches work best and I will focus on the Educational Endowment Foundation's Teaching and Learning Toolkit. For the purposes of this chapter, however, here is a summary of my thoughts on evidence-informed approaches to teaching disadvantaged pupils in order to diminish the difference...

Evidence-informed approaches

When I started teaching, we were not what you would call an evidence-informed profession. We did what teachers had been doing for decades, what our teacher-training lecturers told us to do and what our own teachers had done to us when we were at school. And we did these things irrespective of whether they were the best things, or the right things, to do.

Truth was, we simply didn't know what the best or right things to do were because no one really analysed teachers' methods or sought to compare one approach with another.

These days, however, there's a surfeit of research evidence about what works and what doesn't. From the darkness there is light.

Of course, evidence can only take us so far...

We need to be discerning in our diet of evidence; we need to regard external data as a starting point not a destination; evidence is not a tablet of stone handed down from a higher authority, it is to be questioned and disputed and weighed against our own professional judgment.

Evidence, then, is the start of the conversation. But which evidence to use? I will focus on the Education Endowment Foundation's teaching and learning toolkit. Before we delve into the detail, however, let's explore who the EEF are and where their toolkit comes from...

What is the EEF toolkit and how does it work?

The teaching and learning toolkit, much like John Hattie's Visible Learning, is based on meta-analyses of other studies. A meta-analysis is a way of collating the outcomes of similar studies and converting the data into a common metric, then combining those in order to report an estimate which represents the impact or influence of interventions in that given area.

There are a number of advantages of meta-analyses when conducted as part of a systematic review. For example, they allow large amounts of information to be assimilated quickly. They also help reduce the delay between research 'discoveries' and the implementation of effective strategies. Meta-analyses enable the results of different studies to be compared, and in so doing highlight the reasons for any inconsistencies between similar studies.

However, meta-analyses are not without their problems…

Firstly, it is a misconception that larger effect sizes are associated with greater educational significance. Secondly, it is a misconception that two or more different studies on the same interventions can have their effect sizes combined to give a meaningful estimate of the intervention's educational importance because studies that used different types of 'control group' cannot be accurately combined to create an effect size (not least because what constitutes 'business as usual' in each control group will be different to the others). Likewise, unless the studies used the same range of pupils, the combined effect size is unlikely to be an accurate estimate of the 'true' effect size of a particular strategy. Also, the way in which researchers measure the effect can influence the effect size. For example, if you undertake an intervention to improve pupils' ability to decode words, you could choose to use a measure specifically designed to 'measure' decoding, or you could use a measure of general reading competence that includes an element of decoding. The effect size of the former will be greater than the latter, due to the precision of the measure used.

What's more, increasing the number of test items can influence the effect size. If the number of questions used to measure the effectiveness of an intervention is increased, this may significantly increase the effect size.

Is the toolkit any good?

So, should we ignore meta-analyses, effect sizes and the EEF toolkit altogether and go back to doing what we've always done? Of course not. As I say above, we are finally becoming an evidence-informed profession that uses data to ensure we get better at what we do and, ultimately, improve pupils' life chances. But, as I also said above, we should always exercise caution. We should not regard the data as an oracle; rather, we should contest it and balance what the evidence suggests with what we know from our own experiences.

We should also dig beneath the meta-analyses and analyse the original studies on which the effect sizes are based because the averages may hide huge variations depending on the nature of the intervention and the context in which it was used.

Caution is most needed when looking at the bottom of the 'league table' of what works.

For example, according to the first iteration of the EEF toolkit, teaching assistants are 'not worth it' because they are costly and have little effect on pupil progress. As a result, many schools began cutting TA posts in a bid to tackle budget cuts. However, delve beneath the headlines and you'll find the picture is a little more nuanced...

Firstly, although the positive effects of teaching assistants on pupils' academic learning are small, there is strong evidence that when teachers delegate routine administrative tasks to TAs it allows them to focus more time on teaching, planning, and assessment tasks. TAs have also proven beneficial in terms of reducing teacher workload and improving teachers' job satisfaction.

Those teachers featured in the EEF evidence base were also positive about the contribution TAs make in their classrooms. They said the presence of additional adults in the room helped increase pupils' attention and supported the learning of pupils who struggled most. Results from observations made as part of the DISS project also suggested that TAs had a positive effect in terms of reducing disruptions and therefore afforded teachers more time to teach.

Secondly, the poor effects related to the use of teaching assistants tend to derive from situations where the TA has been used poorly or not at all. Naturally, if not well utilised TAs will have little positive impact on pupil progress.

In short, we must not take at face value claims that certain interventions are 'not worth it' and immediately stop doing them. We should consider what we know of our contexts and take a long-term, pragmatic, nuanced view.

So, in terms of teaching assistants, for example, if you are to continue to employ them, what works best? Here are five tips...

1. Teachers need to spend at least as much time working with lower-performing pupils as they spend with other pupils which means that TAs should also work with a range of pupils within the class rather than work exclusively with lower-performing pupils. What's more, TAs should sometimes provide whole-class instruction from the front of the room whilst the teacher supports targeted pupils or engages in one-to-one feedback.

2. Teachers and TAs need to work together and communicate with each other effectively and frequently. Teachers may need training on how to manage, organise and work with TAs. Teachers and TAs may need to set aside time to plan and review lessons together and to feedback on pupils' learning. TAs need to approach lessons with a clear understanding of the concepts and information that will be taught, and they need to know the intended learning outcomes of the lesson and be aware of any specific learning needs of pupils they work with.

3. TAs should ensure pupils retain ownership of their learning and responsibility for their work. This means offering the least amount of support possible and allowing pupils to become increasingly independent. TAs should provide a healthy mix of support and challenge but allow the weighing scales to tilt away from support and towards challenge as time progresses.

4. When asking questions, TAs should afford sufficient wait time for pupils to think about and articulate their responses rather than proffer an answer themselves after just a few seconds, tempting though that may be.

5. When delivering intervention sessions outside the lesson, TAs should ensure these are well-structured, and that they explicitly consolidate and extend pupils' classroom-based learning. Intervention sessions should be kept brief (certainly no longer than 30 minutes), and they should be regular and sustained. Each session should have a clear objective, and they should be well-paced, well-resourced and carefully timetabled to minimise the time spent away from other lessons or activities. There needs to be planned opportunities for teachers and TAs to discuss the intervention sessions in order to ensure that they are focused and impactful, and that they remain closely aligned to classroom teaching.

To facilitate these five practices, it may be necessary to adjust TAs' working hours, for example to enable them to start early and finish early or start late and finish late in order to run before- and after-school interventions. It may be necessary to timetable free time for TAs that coincides with teachers' PPA time. It may be necessary to pay TAs to attend CPD days or events in order to train them in delivering interventions and in order to ensure they have the requisite knowledge and skills to support the teaching of the lessons in which they provide support.

Pupils can become over-reliant on TAs, particularly if they regularly work one-to-one with an adult, and this can lead to learned helplessness. It's important, therefore, that TAs slowly remove the scaffolds, provide less support and more challenge, and enable pupils to become increasing independent. Here are some strategies – adapted from The teaching assistant's guide to effective interaction: How to maximise your practice (2016) by Bosanquet, P., Radford, J. and Webster, R. - that TAs can use to help pupils take greater ownership of their learning and progress:

Correcting – here, the TA provides pupils with the answers when they get stuck. Pupils do not work independently and rely on the TA.

Modelling – here, TAs show pupils how to complete a task by producing an exemplar and thinking aloud. Pupils observe the TA then produce a model of their own. Pupils become more independent through practice but still rely on the TA to model the process first.

Clueing – here, TAs ask questions that provide cues to information stored in pupils' long-term memories. This is based on the notion that pupils know the answer but cannot actively recall the information from memory. The TA provides a cue that helps the pupil retrieve the correct information and relieve a bottle-jam in their thinking. Pupils are more independent and have to think for themselves.

Prompting – here, TAs provide prompts (less detailed then clues and thereby encouraging pupils to think for themselves) to pupils that encourage them to use their own knowledge to solve a problem. This is similar to coaching whereby the TA encourages pupils to find the answers from within themselves by challenging their thinking, posing questions, and providing hints, but does not provide the answers or do the work for them.

Self-scaffolding – here, TAs observe pupils and afford them sufficient time to process, think and articulate their understanding. Pupils are at their most independent at this stage.

In conclusion, if teaching assistants are to be used effectively to aid differentiation, then they must not be used as an informal teaching resource for lower-performing pupils, thus replacing the teacher and encouraging learned helplessness. Rather, TAs should be used to add value to the teacher and not to replace them. Indeed, under-performing pupils need as much access to the teacher as any other, perhaps more.

Feedback

Feedback tops the EEF charts as the most impactful strategy at a teacher's disposal and so it would follow that PP funding should be used to improve the effectiveness of feedback...

What is it? The EEF say that feedback is "information given to the learner or teacher about the learner's performance relative to learning goals or outcomes. It should aim towards (and be capable of producing) improvement in students' learning. Feedback redirects or refocuses either the teacher's or the learner's actions to achieve a goal, by aligning effort and activity with an outcome. It can be about the output of the activity, the process of the activity, the student's management of their learning or self-regulation, or them as individuals (which tends to be the least effective). This feedback can be verbal or written or can be given through tests or via digital technology. It can come from a teacher or someone taking a teaching role, or from peers (see Peer tutoring)."

Is it effective? According to the EEF, studies tend to show very high effects of feedback on learning. However, some studies show that feedback can have negative effects and make things worse. It is therefore important, the EEF say, to understand the potential benefits and the possible limitations of feedback as a teaching and learning approach. In general, research-based approaches that explicitly aim to provide feedback to learners, such as Bloom's 'mastery learning', tend to have a positive impact.

Metacognition

Metacognition and self-regulation take equal top-billing on the EEF toolkit and, like feedback, can add an extra eight months' of learning per year.

What is it? Metacognitive approaches aim to help pupils think about their own learning more explicitly, often by teaching them specific strategies for planning, monitoring and evaluating their learning.

The PP might be used to fund interventions designed to give eligible pupils a repertoire of strategies to choose from and the skills to select the most suitable strategy for a given learning task.

Is it effective? The EEF say that metacognition and self-regulation approaches have consistently high levels of impact, with pupils making an average of seven months' additional progress. These strategies are usually more effective when taught in collaborative groups so that learners can support each other and make their thinking explicit through discussion. The potential impact of these approaches is high but can be difficult to achieve in practice as they require pupils to take greater responsibility for their learning and develop their understanding of what is required to succeed. The evidence indicates that teaching these strategies can be particularly effective for low achieving and older pupils.

If using PP funding to help develop pupils' metacognitive abilities, you should consider which explicit strategies you can teach your pupils to help them plan, monitor, and evaluate specific aspects of their learning? You should also consider how to give them opportunities to use these strategies with support, and then independently, and ensure you set an appropriate level of challenge to develop pupils' self-regulation and metacognition in relation to specific learning tasks. In the classroom, you should consider how you can promote and develop metacognitive talk related to lesson objectives, and what professional development is needed to develop teachers' knowledge and understanding of these approaches.

I will explore metacognition in more detail in Chapter Twenty-Six.

At the start of this chapter I said I would focus on the primary – though not only – means of closing the attainment gap: the development of cultural capital. So, let's do just that...

CHAPTER TWENTY-THREE
CULTURAL CAPITAL

As I explained in the introductory chapter entitled 'The Ofsted context', one of the driving forces behind the new education inspection framework is a desire to tackle social injustices.

In particular, Ofsted wish to ensure that disadvantaged pupils – including those with SEND, those from deprived backgrounds and vulnerable groups such as pupils eligible for the Pupil Premium or High Needs funding, pupils from minority ethnic groups and so on – are afforded the same ambitious curriculum as their more advantaged peers.

In practice, inspectors will judge the extent to which all pupils have access to a challenging curriculum, rather than a dumbed down or reduced offer. Inclusion, therefore, is at the very heart of the new framework.

I'm sure no one would disagree with this aim. No one would actively argue that we should lower a glass ceiling over the heads of our disadvantaged pupils and limit what they can achieve. Likewise, no one would argue that we should lower our expectations of SEND pupils. And yet, as I explained in Chapter Twenty-Two, achieving an inclusive curriculum in practice is tough because not all pupils are equal: they each face different challenges and they each have differing levels of knowledge and skills.

As such, understanding why some pupils are at a disadvantage in school and why they do not yet have equal access to our curriculum is crucial if we are to tackle that disadvantage and help those pupils to do better in school and college, and then in life.

So, what is the cause of academic disadvantage?

Well, as you may have guessed, there is no simple answer. There is certainly not one answer. The causes of disadvantage are complex and myriad; the causes will be different for each child and each child is very complex. I do not seek to simplify or reduce this complex issue; I want us to recognise its complexity and accept that we all need to do more to understand each pupil's disadvantages and to plan individual solutions, as I outlined in my 3-point plan in Chapter Twenty-Two.

However, as a starting point, I think it will be helpful to consider *when* the effects of academic disadvantage first emerge because this can help inform the *why*…

As I explained in the previous chapter, educational disadvantage starts early - certainly before a child enters formal education – and the attainment gap at this early age is most pronounced in language and literacy skills. In fact, by the age of 3, more disadvantaged children are – on average – already almost 18 months behind their more affluent peers in their early language development. Around two fifths of disadvantaged five-year-olds are not meeting the expected literacy standard for their age.

So, let us now delve a little deeper into the issue of language and literacy as a means of building cultural capital…

Language and literacy

Black and William (2018) explain: "Children from working class families, who are only familiar with the restricted code of their everyday language, may find it difficult to engage with the elaborated code that is required by the learning discourse of the classroom and which those from middle class families experience in their home lives."

Children born into families who read books, newspapers and magazines, visit museums, art galleries, zoos, and stately homes and gardens, take regular holidays, watch the nightly news and documentaries, and talk - around the dinner table, on weekend walks, in the car - about current affairs and about what they're reading or doing or watching - develop cultural capital.

These children acquire, unknowingly perhaps, an awareness of the world around them, an understanding of how life works, and - crucially - a language with which to explain it all. And this cultural capital provides a solid foundation on which they can build further knowledge, skills and understanding.

The unlucky ones - those children not born and brought up in such knowledge-rich environments, and who therefore do not develop this foundation of cultural capital - don't do as well in school because new knowledge and skills have nothing to 'stick' to or build upon.

These children may come from broken or transitory homes, be in care, have impoverished parents who work two or more jobs and so spend little time at home or are too exhausted when they get home from work to read to or converse with their children.

These parents may not themselves be well educated and so possess very little cultural capital of their own to pass on to their children. Maybe these parents came from disadvantaged backgrounds and so books and current affairs never featured in their lives and remain alien to them. Maybe they did not do well at school or did not enjoy their schooling and so do not know how to - or do not wish to - help prepare their child for the world of education.

Let's be clear - educational disadvantage is an accident of birth. It is not about ability, innate or otherwise. But, unfortunately, a child's birth is often their destiny...

The Matthew Effect is a term coined by Daniel Rigney in his book of the same name, using a title taken from a passage in the Bible (Matthew 13:12) that proclaims, 'The rich shall get richer and the poor shall get poorer".

In the context of academic disadvantage, the Matthew Effect posits that disadvantaged pupils shall get more disadvantaged because they do not possess the foundational knowledge, they need in order to access and understand the school and college curriculum.

It is not, as I said earlier, that these young people are less able, but that they don't have the same amount of knowledge about the world as their more fortunate peers with which to make sense of new information and experiences.

Put simply, the more you know, the easier it is to know more and so the culturally rich will always stay ahead of the impoverished, and the gap between rich and poor will continue to grow as children travel through our education system.

The best course of action, therefore, is to help disadvantaged pupils to build their cultural capital.

Once you're clear about this solitary aim, all the hard work of action planning, implementing, monitoring and evaluating intervention strategies, and reporting the impact of your activities becomes easier…

The next big question, then, is 'how?'

One tangible form that this 'cultural capital' takes is a pupil's vocabulary…

The size of a pupil's vocabulary in their early years of schooling (the number and variety of words that the young person knows) is a significant predictor of academic attainment in later schooling and of success in life.

Most children are experienced speakers of the language when they begin school but reading the language requires more complex, abstract vocabulary than that used in everyday conversation.

Young people who develop reading skills early in their lives by reading frequently add to their vocabularies exponentially over time.

In 'The Matthew Effect' (2010), Daniel Rigney explains: "While good readers gain new skills very rapidly, and quickly move from learning to read to reading to learn, poor readers become increasingly frustrated with the act of reading and try to avoid reading where possible.

"Pupils who begin with high verbal aptitudes find themselves in verbally enriched social environments and have a double advantage."

Furthermore, E D Hirsch, in his book 'The Schools We Need' (1996), says that "The children who possess intellectual capital when they first arrive at school have the mental scaffolding and Velcro to catch hold of what is going on, and they can turn the new knowledge into still more Velcro to gain still more knowledge".

Data (see, for example, Biemiller 2004) suggests that, by the age of seven, the gap in the vocabulary known by children in the top and bottom quartiles is something like 4,000 words (children in the top quartile know around 7,000 words; those in the bottom quartile just 3000).

For this reason, when planning ways to build cultural capital we need to understand the importance of vocabulary and support its development so that children who do not develop this foundational knowledge before they start school are helped to catch up.

So, what can we do to help the word poor become richer and, with it, to diminish the difference between the attainment of disadvantaged pupils and their non-disadvantaged peers?

One answer, which I mentioned earlier, is to plan group work activities which provide an opportunity for the word poor to mingle with the word rich, to hear language being used by pupils of their own age and in ways that they might not otherwise encounter. This runs counter to the approach taken by many schools - setting. Most schools place disadvantaged children together in a 'bottom set' and 'dumb down' the curriculum to make it more easily accessible. They assume that the best way to close the gap is to expect less of these pupils and to provide more scaffolding. Sometimes this also means a narrowing of the curriculum because disadvantaged pupils are withdrawn from classes to attend more English and maths lessons.

Unfortunately, this doesn't work very well and often widens the gap because the word poor get poorer and the word rich get richer, and - what's more - the word poor become increasingly reliant on the scaffolds and less able to cope with the demands of the curriculum.

A better approach is to ensure disadvantaged pupils have equal access to a knowledge-rich diet and provide cultural experiences in addition to, not in place of, the school curriculum. This might involve spending part of the Pupil Premium Grant, SEND monies, or High Needs funding on museum and gallery visits, or on mentors who talk with pupils about what's happening in the world, perhaps reading a daily newspaper with them before school or at lunchtime.

Another answer is to provide additional intervention classes for the disadvantaged (taking place outside the taught timetable to avoid withdrawing pupils from classes) in which we teach and model higher-order reading skills because, as the literate adults in the room, we teachers use these skills subconsciously all the time so we need to make the implicit explicit.

As I said earlier, it is the responsibility of every adult working in a school (not just teachers, and certainly not just English teachers) to show that reading because we like reading is one of the hallmarks of civilised adult life.

Finally, it's worth remembering that, although Pupil Premium funding is for the purposes of the school it is awarded to, it can also be used for the benefit of pupils registered at other maintained schools or academies and on community facilities such as services whose provision furthers any charitable purpose for the benefit of pupils at the school or their families, or people who live or work in the locality in which the school is situated.

We know that the attainment gap emerges early in a child's life and that, therefore, the child's family is crucial in helping to close that gap. We know, too, that reading books from an early age is a vital weapon in the battle for social mobility. As such, Pupil Premium funding can legitimately - and wisely - be used to support community projects such as reading mentor schemes, helping improve parents' literacy levels and encouraging parents and members of the community to engage with education.

The Pupil Premium grant can be used, for example, to fund a community outreach officer who helps educate disadvantaged or hard-to-reach parents in the locality about the work of the school, how best to support young people with their education, and as an advocate for the use of community facilities such as libraries, museums and galleries. They could lead cultural visits after school, at weekends and in the holidays for those children who would not otherwise enjoy such experiences. If the impact of such activity can be linked to an increase in literacy levels and cultural capital, then it is money well spent and will help to close the gap in a sustainable way.

Admittedly, this will involve some bravery - secondary schools will not know with absolute certainty which pre-school or primary-age pupils are likely to attend their school aged 11 but they can make an educated guess and, even if some Pupil Premium money is spent on young people who do not go on to attend that school, it is still money well spent within the school community and schools have a duty to look beyond their gates and be a force for good in society.

CHAPTER TWENTY-FOUR
THREE WAVES OF INTERVENTION

Inclusion often takes the form of differentiation – doing different things for different pupils in order to include them all in our curriculum. We will explore some aspects of differentiation in more detail in Book Two of this series when we consider how to teach our curriculum in a way that leads to long-term learning. But, for the purposes of our present discussion on diminishing disadvantage to give all pupils equal access to an ambitious curriculum, I'd like to focus on three waves of intervention:

1. Quality first teaching;
2. In-class differentiation; and
3. Additional interventions and support.

I wish to do so because these approaches to differentiation need to be baked into our curriculum not left to chance or to individual teachers. Consistency is key, after all...

Collective autonomy

Although teacher autonomy is important - teaching is a profession after all - pupils undoubtedly benefit from a degree of consistency in approaches to pedagogy. Pupils like routine, after all.

In her book 'Student-Centred Leadership' (2011), Vivianne Robinson argues, although "feet of varying shapes should not be shoved into the same ill-fitting shoe", in the sense of professional practice – teaching and teacher-learning – one size *does* fit all. In other words, although it is assumed that any loss of teacher autonomy is undesirable because it somehow reduces the professionalism of teachers, this isn't necessarily the case...

Although there can be no question that increased coherence (requiring teachers to teach in a consistent manner) means reducing autonomy, this does not necessarily imply a decrease in professionalism. After all, doctors are regarded as professionals precisely *because* they have mastered complex sets of shared diagnostic and treatment practices. They exercise their judgment about how those procedures are to be applied in any individual case and are held accountable for those judgments.

Teachers, too, need sufficient autonomy within which to exercise professional judgment about how to use the framework they're given and to contribute to evaluative discussions about its adequacy. But that autonomy should also be constrained by the need to ensure effective teaching practice – that is, practice under which all pupils achieve to a high level.

We may encourage collective autonomy (teachers working together to improve their practice) but curtail individual autonomy (teachers working in a purely idiosyncratic way) because standard professional practice provides the scaffolding that's required for the exercise of truly professional rather than idiosyncratic judgment. In other words, although we should not eradicate *individuality*, we should eliminate *individualism* (habitual or enforced patterns of working alone). Eliminating individualism should not be about making everyone the same and plunging them into groupthink; it should be about achieving collective responsibility.

In his book, 'Good to Great' (2001), Jim Collins expounds the importance of having a set of consistent systems and structures which dictate what staff can and cannot do and which governs how they should and should not operate. He uses the analogy of an airline pilot. A pilot, he says, operates within a very strict system and does not have the freedom to go outside of that system. Yet at the same time, the crucial decisions – whether to take off, whether to land, whether to abort, whether to land elsewhere – rest with the pilot. Collins says that great organisations have a culture of discipline which involves a duality. On the one hand, it requires people to adhere to a consistent system; yet, on the other hand, it gives people freedom and responsibility within the framework of that system.

In other words, schools and colleges can excel at delivering a great curriculum if they do so in a consistent manner. They must have strong values and high expectations. Their achievements will not happen by chance but through highly reflective, carefully planned strategies. There needs to be a high degree of internal consistency.

So, what 'routines' enable teachers to deliver the curriculum in the most effective manner and, furthermore, what teaching strategies best ensure a differentiated approach to curriculum delivery that meets the needs of every pupil? I'm glad you asked because I recommend a 4-step teaching sequence...

The 4-step teaching sequence

As I've already explained, all mental activity – and *all* activity is mental activity, of course - is a delicate balance between intrinsic load (the space in working memory dedicated to performing a task), germane load (the space in working memory dedicated to trying to understand the task), and extraneous load (the space in working memory dedicated to understanding and responding to the instructional context).

Making the instructional context familiar helps to automate these processes which, in turn, frees up space in working memory to focus more on performing the task. This explains why, when we first learn to drive a car, we must focus on the various actions required to, say, change gear and we cannot do this well whilst also holding a conversation. As we grow used to changing gear, however, we free up the space used to understand the instructional context, and this enables us to multi-task.

As such, when teaching the curriculum in a differentiated way, we can free up much needed space in pupils' working memories by following a familiar pedagogical routine – by using a consistent teaching sequence - in every lesson and in every subject across the curriculum.

What's more, pupils with learning difficulties and disabilities, and other vulnerable learners, benefit even more from a consistent routine so following a familiar teaching sequence is the first step towards effective differentiation.

My 4-step teaching sequence is as follows:

1. Telling
2. Showing
3. Doing
4. Practising

Telling is the most effective, expedient way for pupils to acquire new information. And the best teacher explanations – or direct instruction - are often formed of three features:

Firstly, good teacher explanations involve metaphors and analogies because this enables the teacher to contextualise new information so that abstract ideas or hitherto alien concepts are made concrete, tangible, and real, and so that they are related to pupils' own lives and experiences.

Secondly, good explanations make effective use of dual coding. In other words, teachers' verbal instructions, as well as any text-based explanations displayed on the board or in handouts, are paired with and complemented by visuals such as diagrams, charts, graphics and moving images.

Finally, good explanations are reciprocated, with pupils explaining concepts back to the teacher as well as to each other. This works on the basis that only once you teach something do you truly learn it. Learning by teaching works because, by teaching, pupils gain feedback and make better sense of a topic. Learning by teaching also works because it is a form of learning by doing, of practising, and thus provides a source of both intrinsic and extrinsic motivation.

Showing is the effective and plentiful use of models – exemplars of both good and bad work, as well as exemplars from a range of different contexts – which show pupils what a final product should look like and what makes such products work. It is important to show pupils what excellence looks like by sharing models of the very best work, giving them something to aspire to and an understanding of how to produce high quality work of their own. But it is equally important to show pupils models of ineffective work, work that isn't quite the best (or perhaps is so very far from being the best) so that pupils can learn what not to do and how to avoid making the same mistakes themselves. Whilst modelling, the teacher should think aloud in order to make visible the invisible decision-making process and to make explicit what experts do implicitly.

Doing works well because by engaging in co-construction the teacher engages pupils' thought processes and helps them by questioning their decisions and by prompting further decision-making. The teacher's role is not to construct another model herself but to ask targeted questions of pupils to encourage them to complete the model together, as well as to provide corrections and feedback along the way, and drip-feed key vocabulary into the mix. During co-construction, the teacher will mostly be engaged in asking open questions such as, 'Why did you choose that word?' 'Is there another word which might fit better or have more impact?' 'Why is this word better than this one?' 'Should we use a short sentence here?' 'Why? /Why not?' and 'What is the effect of this, do you think?'

Practising is the opportunity for pupils to complete work independently. Independent practice enables pupils to demonstrate their own understanding and for the teacher to assess the extent to which they have 'got it'. Until a pupil completes a task by themselves, we - and perhaps they - cannot be certain they can do so or that information has been encoded in long-term memory. If pupils succeed, the teacher can move on. If not, the teacher can use the feedback information to guide further teaching of the subject, perhaps re-teaching key elements of it or engaging those pupils who have succeeded in teaching those who have not.

Of course, the teaching sequence does not end here. Rather, pupils need to garner feedback on their independent practice and then act on that feedback in order to improve by increments. As such, once pupils have practised new learning, we need to provide planned opportunities for them to be assessed (by themselves, by each other, and/or by the teacher) and receive feedback on what they have mastered and what they still need to practice. Then, crucially, we need to provide planned opportunities in class for them to act upon that feedback.

Pupils learn through practice, by making mistakes, and by experimenting. They also learn best when engaged in a process of trial and error and when they repeat actions several times, making incremental improvements each time. And so, if we do not provide lesson time for pupils to respond to feedback and improve their work, we send a negative message about the importance of redrafting work and learning from our mistakes. What's more, if pupils do not respond to feedback in class, the teacher cannot see progress being made and cannot, therefore, recognise and celebrate it.

No such thing as average

When we talk about differentiation, we often have in mind ways of scaffolding learning for our 'less able' learners. But learners – like learning – are complex and no pupil is uniformly 'less able' than another. Rather, some pupils have acquired more knowledge and skills in one area than another pupil or have practised a task more often. Of course, some pupils have additional and different needs – such as those young people with learning difficulties or disabilities – and they require a different approach. But to say they are 'less able' is, I think, an unhelpful misnomer.

As I explained in Chapter Nineteen, to suggest a pupil is 'less able' implies there is an average pupil against which we are comparing all others. But there is no such thing as 'average'; rather, we are all made up of myriad individual characteristics. If you take an average of each of us (height, weight, IQ, shoe size, etc), you won't find any individual who is average in all respects. This, I said, is known as the jaggedness principle.

When approaching differentiation, therefore, we would be wise to remember that all pupils – like all human beings – are different, unique, individual. Differentiation, therefore, should not be about treating 'less able' pupils – or indeed those with SEND or eligible for Pupil Premium or High Needs funding – as a homogenous group. Rather, we should treat each pupil on an individual basis. Nor should we assume that what works with one pupil will work with all and that what was proven to work with 'less able' pupils in another school, in another district, in another country, (according to research evidence and meta-analyses) will work in our classroom.

Mastery learning

As I explained in Chapter Twenty, rather than expecting different outcomes of different pupils, we should have high expectations that all our pupils will reach the same destinations, albeit some will take a different route and need more time to do so. This notion that all pupils achieve the same outcome forms the basis of 'mastery learning'…

Mastery learning is founded on the belief that all pupils are capable of learning anything if that learning is presented in the right way. Mastery learning works on the basis that understanding is the result of intention and effort, and that difficulty is enjoyable.

In practical terms, mastery learning, which was first introduced into the UK system in maths and modelled on practices popular in China and Singapore but which is now gaining traction in other subjects, is about pupils demonstrating they have mastered something before being able to move on to the next thing. The teacher decides the level of mastery required – 80 or 90 per cent, say – and pupils are given opportunities to learn through a variety of instructional methods before taking a test. If pupils do not attain the right level of mastery in the test, they are given additional instructional activities to complete before retaking the test (which is usually in a different form or uses different questions).

One benefit of the mastery approach is that it avoids the negative effects of differentiation which can translate as lower expectations of what the so-called 'less able' pupils are able to achieve. With traditional differentiation, activities can also be oversimplified. Mastery, however, allows teachers to genuinely challenge pupils. Here's how it works...

In a traditional classroom, as I have already explained, the teacher tends to teach to the middle and when the middle is ready, the teacher moves on to the next topic. This sends a signal to the class that everyone learns in the same way and requires the same activities. This approach also tells pupils that once the majority of the class has learnt something, all pupils move on. Many pupils learn nothing but are compelled to move on whether they are ready to do so or not. Those pupils who are ready to move on faster than the middle, meanwhile, have to wait for the majority to catch up.

But with mastery learning, the teacher sends a very different signal to their pupils: that everyone will learn and succeed, that the teacher is not going to move on until everyone is ready to do so. With mastery, the teacher also makes it explicit that every pupil will get a minimum of, say, 80 per cent in tests and that the teacher and/or teaching assistant will keep working with them until they do so.

The teacher can tell the faster pupils that they can move on whenever they are ready, that they will not be held back. The teacher makes it clear that people learn different things in different ways and at different paces.

Although, at its heart, mastery learning is about handing over responsibility for learning to pupils, it is not the same as independent learning or self-teaching. In fact, teachers who employ a mastery approach tend to interact more not less with individual pupils compared to more traditional instructional methods. By using a variety of resource materials (such as texts at different reading levels) and addressing various learning styles (by presenting information visually, verbally, and in writing), teachers can address differences in preferred learning styles and achievement levels.

By allowing pupils some options about how they work (for example, independently or in groups) or how they communicate their learning (visually, verbally, or in writing), teachers can personalise the learning still further.

A mastery approach like this works particularly well when combined with a progression model such as the one I described in Chapter Seventeen. After all, pupils are headed for the same destination but may pass through the waypoints or threshold concepts at different rates.

Same destination, different route

In short, then, differentiation should be about ensuring every pupil is headed toward the same destination. We should not 'dumb down' or expect less of lower-performing pupils; rather, we should articulate the same high expectations of all – expectations regularly reinforced through our language and our actions – but accept that some pupils, some of the time, will need different levels of support, different kinds of support, and to be afforded different timescales to reach that destination.

Of course, as I've already explained, some pupils fear challenge. If we are to have high expectations of all and teach to the top for all, we must therefore eliminate – or at least mitigate – their feelings of fear and hesitation by creating a classroom environment which encourages the making of mistakes as an integral part of the learning process, and a pedagogical culture which explicitly says (through our choice of language, our modelling and thinking aloud, and the routines in which we engage) that there is nothing to fear by trying your best and pushing yourself to do hard work.

To promote challenge in the classroom, therefore, we need to reduce the threat level, we need to ensure no-one feels humiliated if they fall short of a challenge. Rather, they need to know that they will learn from the experience and perform better next time. They will learn by increments.

Comfortable with discomfort

When I talk about reducing the threat level, I mean we need to create a positive learning environment in which pupils' senses are stimulated so that they pay attention to the right things and are made to think hard but efficiently about curriculum content. I refer, too, to an environment in which pupils are challenged by hard work but know that they are safe to take risks and make mistakes. What I do not mean to imply is that our classroom should be regarded as an easy, fun place to be. There's nothing wrong with pupils enjoying themselves whilst they learn, and we certainly wouldn't want school to be a dull and boring place. However, fun is never the goal. Rather, we need pupils to think and work hard.

What then, if not fun, are the hallmarks of a positive learning environment? To my mind, as I explained in Chapter Six, a positive learning environment is one in which all pupils:

- Feel welcomed,
- Feel valued,

- Are enthusiastic about learning,
- Are engaged in their learning,
- Are eager to experiment, and
- Feel rewarded for their hard work.

As I also explained in Chapter Six, behind all these characteristics - and any more we care to mention - is a simple, albeit oxymoronic, aim: to ensure pupils are comfortable with discomfort. In other words, we want our pupils to know that the work they'll be asked to do in our classrooms will be tough, that they will be challenged with hard work and made to think. We want our pupils to know that there will be no hiding place in our classrooms; they must ask and answer questions and attempt everything we ask of them.

Talking of which…let's now explore some ways – in addition to – some ways to enable differentiated instruction.

Finding the right level of challenge for our pupils – work that is hard but achievable with time, effort and support – is not easy. For practical advice on how to locate pupils' 'struggle zones', I would refer you back to Chapter Fifteen and the section on KWL charts, exit tickets and hinge questions.

Types of in-class differentiation

Differentiation, as we have seen, wears many guises. To conclude this chapter, therefore, I'd like to review eight of the most common forms of differentiation in use in our classrooms today and analyse their advantages and disadvantages, then examine the role teaching assistants can play in ensuring that learning is differentiated.

Differentiation by task

What is it? The teacher gives different pupils different tasks, the level of difficulty of which is determined by the pupil's 'ability'.

What are the advantages? It allows the task to be set to test the mastery of skills of different groups of pupils dependent on their needs.

What are the disadvantages? It can be time-consuming, and it can lead to difficulties comparing pupils' achievements because we can't assess the same things. It also places a limit on what some pupils can achieve.

Differentiation by resource

What is it? The teacher gives different pupils different resources to support their learning, such as scaffolded worksheets or texts at differing word levels.

What are the advantages? It allows pupils of different abilities to access the curriculum but in a manner appropriate to them.

What are the disadvantages? It can be time-consuming.

Differentiation by assessment

What is it? The teacher gives different pupils different assessment tasks based on what they need them to demonstrate.

What are the advantages? It allows an assessment task to be set to test the mastery of skills of different groups of pupils dependent on their needs. It can be quick to prepare because it can simply consist of different questions

What are the disadvantages? It can be time-consuming and can lead to difficulties in comparing pupil achievements because different assessments may not be testing the same thing. What's more, it runs counter to current examination practice in most subjects whereby papers are no longer tiered, and every pupil is assessed in the same manner.

Differentiation by pace

What is it? The teacher allows pupils differing timescales to read the end goal, accepting that every pupil learns at a different pace.

What are the advantages? It allows pupils to work at their own pace whilst striving towards the same destination.

What are the disadvantages? It may mean that some pupils do not reach their destination and therefore do not cover all the curriculum content.

Differentiation by support

What is it? The teacher offers different levels of support to different pupils.

What are the advantages? Pupils receive personalized support from the teacher, teaching assistant or other pupils.

What are the disadvantages? It is difficult for the teacher to manage whole class progress and know exactly what has been taught and learnt so they can assess pupil progress and move through the curriculum.

Differentiation by extension

What is it? The teacher provides additional tasks to pupils who finish soonest, enabling them to move on to more difficult content whilst the rest of the class catches up.

What are the advantages? It allows the teacher to set a task that tests pupils' mastery of skills. It can be quick to prepare if it takes the form of questions of differing difficulty.

What are the disadvantages? It can be time-consuming if it takes the form of different detailed activities. It can lead to difficulties in comparing achievement because different tasks may not be testing the same thing.

Differentiation by dialogue

What is it? The teacher uses one-to-one or small group discussions – such as verbal feedback – to provide assessment information and support which enables pupils to make progress.

What are the advantages? It is an integral part of the lesson, builds rapport, enables the teacher to gain crucial assessment information and personalise the learning, and can be applied to all.

What are the disadvantages? It is sometimes difficult to carve out sufficient time in a lesson to talk to pupils on an individual basis without slowing the flow of the curriculum. Some pupils may receive a lot of feedback information whilst others – whom the teacher deems to be making sufficient progress – are largely ignored.

Differentiation by grouping

What is it? The teacher places pupils into different groups depending on their current progress and their strengths and weaknesses, in order to carry out different tasks, use different resources, undertake different assessments, work at a different pace, access a different level of support, work on extension tasks, and so on.

What are the advantages? Differentiated grouping allows different groups to be tracked differently, it encourages collaborative learning and allows pupils to support each other. Sometimes, pupils are placed in groups of similar 'ability'; other times, 'less able' pupils are placed with their 'more able' peers who offer support, perhaps in the form of peer-teaching.

What are the disadvantages? It can lead to stigmatisation if some groups are deemed 'less able'. Like all group work, it can lead to off-task learning or to some pupils doing all the work whilst others 'coast' if it is not tightly controlled and if the teacher doesn't explicitly teach group work skills or behaviours first.

Additional interventions

Even when pupils have access to quality first teaching and effective in-class differentiation, some will require additional interventions and support in order to access our ambitious curriculum. As I explained in Chapter Twenty-Two, where additional interventions are used to support lower-performing pupils outside of lessons, these should be highly structured and have close links to what's happening in the lesson. They should consolidate and extend classroom-based learning, and this requires close communication between the teacher and the teaching assistant.

Intervention sessions should be brief (up to 30 minutes), often (several times a week) and sustained over the long-term (at least a half-term, ideally a term or two). TAs should be trained to deliver interventions and be afforded time to plan them and to review them with the teacher. Interventions should be subject to regular monitoring, not just reviewed at the end but evaluated as often as possible to ensure they are having the desired effect – which, in turn, means that they should have a clear objective.

Here are some suggested intervention strategies at Waves 1, 2 and 3...

Suggested Wave 1 interventions

Cognition and Learning
* Quality first teaching
* Differentiated curriculum planning
* In-class teaching assistant and targeted teacher support
* Use of visual timetables and other visual aids
* Use of support materials such as task boards and first/then boards
* Use of writing frames
* Guided group teaching within lessons

- Access to ICT support
- Regular staff training as appropriate

Social, Emotional and Mental Health
- Whole-school behaviour policy incorporating a range of strategies
- Regular feedback to parents as well as the use of rewards, praise and celebration
- Individualised class reward systems
- Focused work to support children with their personal, social, health and emotional development
- Ongoing development of the social emotional aspects of learning
- Weekly achievers assembly and half term merits
- Class circle time
- Regular staff training as appropriate

Communication & Interaction
- Use of modified language
- Use of visual prompts/ timetables
- Use of structured school and class routines
- Regular staff training as appropriate

Sensory and Physical
- Flexible teaching and support arrangements
- Access to writing slopes, pencil grips and posture supports
- Moving and handling training
- Dedicated pupil welfare assistant trained to deliver medication for conditions such as ADHD, epilepsy or anaphylactic shock
- Regular staff training as appropriate

Suggested Wave 2 interventions

Cognition and Learning
- Access to specific time-limited interventions
- Use of literacy and numeracy catch-up programmes
- Targeted booster lessons
- Targeted in-class support from the Teacher/Teaching Assistant
- Referral to and support from the Learning Language Service (LLS)

Social, Emotional and Mental Health
- Access to specific time-limited interventions
- Group circle time sessions

- In-class support for supporting behaviour targets/access/safety
- Use of individual support plans and reward systems as appropriate (as discussed with parents /carers)
- Referral to nurture group or CAMHs Service
- Inclusion in the talking and drawing programme
- Referral to and support from the Behaviour Support Outreach Services

Communication and Interaction
- Access to specific time-limited interventions
- Pre-teaching of subject specific vocabulary, as appropriate
- Access to a social skills group
- Referral to and advice from the speech and language therapy service and the Learning Language Service (LLS)

Sensory and Physical
- Access to specific time-limited interventions
- Additional fine motor skills practice
- Completion of individual risk assessments
- In-class support for supporting pupil access/safety
- Access to sensory areas and equipment
- Referral to (and advice) from the OT and physio services

Suggested Wave 3 interventions

Cognition and Learning
- Additional in-class teaching support as recommended in EHCP
- Targeted small group or one-to-one literacy and/or numeracy support
- Reduced or tailored timetable
- Exam concessions, e.g. extra time or use of a scribe/reader
- Ongoing advice from specialist teachers (as appropriate) and subsequent delivery of recommended programmes
- Use of specialised equipment and resources to support identified learning needs
- Advice from the educational psychologist

Social, Emotional and Mental Health
- Individualised behaviour support plan
- Small group or one-to-one support to support the development of social skills
- Use of individualised behaviour support plan

- Use of Pastoral support plan
- Implementation of targeted strategies such as 'time out'
- Social skills training or anger management support
- Advice from the educational psychologist/specialist teacher/ outreach teacher/ ADHD nurse / etc

Communication and Interaction
- Small group or one-to-one support for language in order to address specifically identified pupil targets
- Access to social skills group and social skills teaching
- Speech and language service support/advice
- Access to additional ICT teaching such as touch typing, Dictaphone, tablet
- Ongoing advice from specialist teachers (LLS/BS/PSSS)
- Advice from educational psychologist

Sensory and Physical
- Individual support for appropriate subjects, (e.g. science, PE) in class and/or during lunchtimes
- Delivery of Physiotherapy and Occupational Therapy programme Sensory Diet Programmes
- Ongoing advice from Specialist teachers (LLS/BS/PSSS) Ongoing support with personal care needs
- Advice from Educational Psychologist

CHAPTER TWENTY-FIVE
CROSS-CURRICULAR LITERACY AND NUMERACY

So far in this section of the book on diminishing disadvantage, we have discussed ways of using the Pupil Premium Grant and High Needs funding to better effect and homed in on the development of pupils' cultural capital – particularly in the guise of language and literacy skills – as a means of providing more equal access for all our pupils and students to the same ambitious curriculum. We have also examined three layers of intervention and support: quality first teaching; in-class differentiation; and additional interventions and support.

Running through this section of the book like the letters in a stick of seaside rock is literacy: the centrality of spoken and written language to the curriculum. As I have already argued, if pupils do not acquire the requisite level of language skills, they will not be able to access, understand and make progress within our curriculum. What's more, they will not be able to articulate – either verbally or in writing – their understanding of that curriculum.

And so let us now take a closer look at the role of literacy within our curriculum, before examining the part numeracy can also play in enabling pupils to access and understand our curriculum, and therefore be better prepared for the next stages of their education, employment and lives.

Why does literacy matter?

Y Kassam's 1994 paper 'Who Benefits from Illiteracy?' argues that "To be literate is to gain a voice and to participate meaningfully and assertively in decisions that affect one's life.

"To be literate," Kassam goes on, "is to gain self-confidence. To be literate is to become self-assertive. Literacy enables people to read their own world and to write their own history. Literacy provides access to written knowledge and knowledge is power.

"In a nutshell, literacy empowers."

Accordingly, I will share some proven strategies for embedding oracy, reading, and writing within our exciting new curriculum. But first I'd like to make the case for literacy as a whole-school and cross-curricular concern because, as George Sampson said (as long ago as 1922 in his book 'English for the English'), "Every teacher is a teacher of English because every teacher is a teacher in English."

In other words, literacy is not the sole responsibility of English teachers; rather, literacy is the language of learning in every curriculum subject. In schools, literacy skills must be actively taught by teachers of every curriculum subject. In FE colleges, meanwhile, vocational teachers are responsible for embedding English and maths into their lessons in a way that is both relevant and contextualised.

What is grammar?

According to the Newbolt Report of 1921, it is "impossible to teach English grammar for the simple reason that no one knows exactly what it is".

So, before we go any further - and bearing in mind how integral an understanding of English grammar is to the development of literacy skills - it might be wise (if not foolhardy) to attempt a definition…

It's possible to define 'grammar' in myriad ways but, in my humble opinion, it is a combination of:

Syntax - which is the study of sentence structure, an analysis of main and subordinate clauses, of simple, compound and complex sentences, of subjects, verbs and objects, and so on;

Morphology - which is the study of word structure, an analysis of stem (or root) words, of prefixes and suffixes, inflections for tense, number and person, and so on;

Semantics - which is the study of meaning, an analysis of the things, people, and events we refer to when we're talking, as well as how meanings - both literal (denotation) and implied (connotation) - are conveyed, and how words can mask their true meaning (e.g. through the use of euphemism).

Grammar teaching, therefore, should include the linguistic structure of words, sentences and whole texts, and should cover:

- the word classes (or parts of speech) and their grammatical functions;
- the structure of phrases and clauses and how they can be combined (by coordination and subordination) to make complex sentences;
- paragraph structure and how to form different types of paragraph;
- the structure of whole texts, including cohesion, and the conventions of openings and conclusions in different types of writing; and
- the use of appropriate grammatical terminology in order to reflect on the meaning and clarity of both spoken and written language.

Why is grammar important?

So, if that's what grammar is, why is it important that we teach it and - crucially - do so in every curriculum subject?

Well, according to the now-defunct resource that is the National Literacy Strategy, the only explicit justification for teaching grammar is its contribution to writing skills.

Whilst this is undoubtedly important, I'd go further and argue that grammar teaching also promotes pupils' understanding and helps them to know, notice, discuss and explore language features.

Grammar teaching may also provide a tool for learning other languages.

Why is literacy a cross-curricular concern?

Of course, many teachers persist in thinking that grammar teaching - and, more widely, teaching literacy - is an English teacher's job not theirs. And yet both the National Curriculum and Ofsted make clear that all teachers, not just teachers of English, should regard themselves as teachers of grammar, irrespective of their subject specialism.

What's more, teaching grammar is not the same as teaching English. Grammar - and literacy more generally - is about helping pupils to access the whole curriculum.

Literacy is about helping pupils to read subject information and it's about helping pupils to write in order that they can assimilate this subject information and then demonstrate their learning.

Still unconvinced? Then consider the Ofsted report 'Removing Barriers to Literacy' (2011) which concludes that "teachers in a secondary school need to understand that literacy is a key issue regardless of the subject taught".

The report goes on to say that literacy is an important element of teachers' effectiveness as a subject specialist.

'Removing Barriers to Literacy' also explains how literacy supports learning because "pupils need vocabulary, expression and organisational control to cope with the cognitive demands of all subjects".

The report argues that writing helps pupils to "sustain and order thought", that "better literacy leads to improved self-esteem, motivation and behaviour", and that literacy "allows pupils to learn independently" and is therefore "empowering". Moreover, it argues that "better literacy raises pupils' attainment in all subjects".

Another Ofsted report, 'Moving English Forward' (2013), has this to say about literacy across the curriculum:

"Schools need a coherent policy on developing literacy in all subjects if standards of reading and writing are to be improved. Even with effective teaching in English lessons, progress will be limited if this good practice is not consolidated in the 26 out of 30 lessons each week in a secondary school that are typically lessons other than English."

The debate is, of course, long established and formed a central point of the Bullock report on English published in 1975.

The All-Party Parliamentary Group for Education recently reported that "schools should be developing cross-departmental strategies to develop literacy".

As we have already seen, the new Education Inspection Framework takes a different view of literacy than did the old framework. The EIF now focuses, as we saw in Chapter Twenty-Three, on the notion of "knowledge and cultural capital" rather than on the development of literacy skills.

To be precise, Ofsted say that they will judge the extent to which "schools are equipping pupils with the knowledge and cultural capital they need to succeed in life".

Ofsted say that their definition of this knowledge and cultural capital matches that found in the aims of the national curriculum: namely, that it is "the essential knowledge that pupils need to be educated citizens, introducing them to the best that has been thought and said and helping to engender an appreciation of human creativity and achievement".

Of course, as we saw earlier, one of the most important and tangible forms this 'essential knowledge' takes is vocabulary in particular and language in general and so literacy is still central to inspection and central to the curriculum.

An approach to cross-curricular literacy

Literacy is, then, a cross-curricular concern and should feature in the curriculum plans of every subject discipline we teach in school and college but that is not to say that literacy will take the same form in every subject. Rather, literacy must be taught within the context of every school subject and in a domain-specific way.

For example, a teacher of, say, science, has a responsibility to help pupils learn about science, but they also have a responsibility to help them speak, listen, read and write like a scientist.

In practice, this means that science teachers must possess some specialist knowledge of – for example - the conventions of scientific report-writing and of the ways scientists themselves write about science.

But, perhaps more importantly, it means they must develop an analytical self-awareness which enables them to identify how they speak, listen, read and write about science so that those skills can be made explicit for their pupils. And this is best done by explaining, demonstrating, modelling, teaching, and giving feedback.

Of course, every school and college are different and, as such, each is likely to face the challenge of improving literacy in a different way, a way borne out of its unique context. Accordingly, your approach to literacy should be influenced by the evidence of what works elsewhere but it should also be informed by your unique context.

What is true of all schools and colleges, however, is that the best way to improve literacy is neither extravagant nor exotic; it is always simple, and it is always concerned with the fundamentals.

For example, each school and college should:

- Involve all teachers and demonstrate how they are all engaged in using language to promote learning in their subject or vocational area
- Identify the particular needs of all pupils in reading, writing, speaking and listening
- Make strong links between school and home
- Plan for the longer term, emphasising the integral relationship between language for learning and effective teaching in all subjects.

What's also true of all schools and colleges, is that literacy learning should:

- Be enjoyable, motivating and challenging;
- Be actively engaging;
- Activate prior learning, secure understanding and provide opportunities to apply skills; and
- Develop pupils' functional and thinking skills.

Literacy across the curriculum in all schools and colleges should also operate across three domains: speaking and listening (or oracy); reading; and writing. Teaching literacy in each subject domain is about teaching pupils how to speak, read and write like an expert in that subject. For example, literacy in history is about pupils being able to speak, read and write like a historian.

Let's consider some of the general skills and techniques required of literacy and language learning…

In order for our pupils to be literate, we need to:

- Activate prior knowledge in order to build on what pupils already know;
- Model in order to make language conventions and processes explicit;
- Scaffold in order to support pupils' first attempts and build confidence;
- Explain in order to clarify and exemplify the best ways of working;
- Question in order to probe, draw out and extend pupils' thinking;
- Explore in order to encourage critical thinking;
- Investigate in order to encourage enquiry and self-help; and

- Discuss and engage in dialogue in order to shape and challenge developing ideas).

Further, here are five tips for making a success of cross-curricular literacy...

1. Put literacy centre-stage

Literacy across the curriculum needs to be seen as an integral part of teaching, learning and assessment.

In order to highlight this, you could stop calling it literacy, referring to it as 'language for learning' instead which might help divorce literacy from the domain of English teachers and place it firmly in the mainstream of teaching, learning and assessment.

Literacy (or 'language for learning') also needs to be on the agenda whenever teaching, learning and assessment are discussed. All teachers need to routinely ask 'How can I use language for learning effectively in order to improve achievement in my subject?'

2. Rome wasn't built in a day

Literacy needs to become a permanent feature of the school's development plan or college's quality improvement plan.

Literacy cannot be addressed with a one-off training day or by displaying key words around classrooms; it has to become an integral part of the longer-term improvement agenda and it has to inform the content of development plans in each subject.

This improvement planning process should also involve governors and developing literacy should became a performance management target for all teachers.

In short, there is no 'quick fix' where literacy is concerned. Instead, there needs to be a set of clear aims and a genuine commitment from all staff - including the support of the headteacher and senior team - as well as a sense of urgency.

3. What's in it for me?

Teaching is a tough job that requires a lot of mental and physical strength and, often, proffers little semblance of a work life balance. Accordingly, when planning any literacy activity, you should remember that, like you, your colleagues are busy, hard-working people with challenges of their own.

You should not assume that all teachers will welcome your cross-curricular initiatives. Instead, you need to make clear and explicit the link between literacy and more effective learning in every subject.

Your starting point should be to ask every teacher what literacy skills the pupils in their subject need and what approaches to literacy learning will help them to become a more effective teacher of their subject.

You will need to consider the different forms and purposes of reading and writing in each subject and tailor your approach accordingly. For example, writing will look very different in history than it does in, say, science and maths.

4. Share and share alike

Sharing good practice across all subjects is the key to success in raising standards of literacy in your school or college. It's also a great way of highlighting and celebrating the various forms of literacy that already exist in your school which, in turn, will help you to win over hearts and minds.

For example, teachers of PE are likely to plan and facilitate effective class discussions and group work. By highlighting this you are showing your colleagues in PE that literacy does indeed apply to them and that they are already doing aspects of it well.

By sharing this good practice with other subject areas, you are also helping others to develop effective strategies for discussion and group work - but, crucially, these strategies are not handed down to them in the form of a decree.

If good practice comes from other teachers who are using these strategies in their daily teaching practice rather than in the form of a policy document, it is more likely to be welcomed and adopted by others.

5. The best laid schemes...

Cross-curricular literacy needs to run deeper than simply sharing some teaching strategies, however. And it must be more than an occasional token activity such as sharing key words or marking SPaG. In fact, though it may be an unpopular opinion, I don't believe teachers should routinely mark

SPaG because this rarely helps pupils to improve their literacy skills within subjects other than English and many teachers of subjects other than English do not have the skills to do this well. What's more, teachers do not like marking SPaG and feel it detracts from more impactful marking and feedback that will lead to more significant academic gains for pupils.

Instead of marking SPaG, I would advise you encourage all teachers to design and deliver subject-specific activities that develop pupils' reading, writing, and speaking and listening which does not have 'improving literacy' as their learning objective.

More is not enough

'Doing more literacy', however, is not enough. For example, the fact that there is more extended writing taking place in school or college does not in itself ensure that the quality of that writing is improving.

Imaginative initiatives might look good on an action plan, but they mean nothing if they don't lead to genuine and sustained improvements.

Accordingly, you need to be clear about the impact of your initiatives on pupil outcomes, as well as whether or not the initiatives represent good value for money and effective deployment of resources (including staffing).

For example, Ofsted say that a school policy of setting aside twenty minutes every day for reading begs the following questions:

1. Are all groups of pupils engaged?
2. What about the poor reader who sits and pretends to read?
3. What about the keen reader who reads for hours outside school?
4. What about the teacher who is not a keen reader and remains uncommitted to the idea?

The three domains of literacy

As I've already said, literacy can helpfully be divided into three domains:

1. Speaking and listening (or oracy);
2. Reading; and
3. Writing.

Let's now focus on each of these in turn. But first, a word of warning...

It is common for any one of these strands – speaking and listening, reading, or writing – to be used as if it were synonymous with the wider concept of 'literacy'. However, your approach to literacy across the curriculum should encompass all three - and more besides - and it should also make connections between each of the three and across different subjects...

The Department for Education, for example, say that in order to make a success of literacy across the curriculum schools should offer opportunities for pupils to: "engage in specific activities that develop speaking and listening skills as well as activities that integrate speaking and listening with reading and writing".

The DfE also say that schools should also offer opportunities for pupils to develop speaking and listening skills, reading skills, and writing skills "through work that makes cross-curricular links with other subjects".

And, finally, schools should provide opportunities for pupils to "work in sustained and practical ways, with writers where possible, to learn about the art, craft and discipline of writing"; to "redraft their own work in the light of feedback [which could include] self-evaluation using success criteria, recording and reviewing performances, target-setting and formal and informal use of peer assessment"; and to redraft in a purposeful way helping pupils to move "beyond proofreading for errors to the reshaping of whole texts or parts of texts".

Making connections between the three domains of speaking and listening, reading and writing calls for pupils to develop their thought processes and understanding, as well as their abilities to recall, select and analyse ideas and information; and it calls for pupils to communicate in a coherent, considered and convincing way both in speech and in writing.

In practice, this means that - in order to develop their literacy skills - all pupils should be encouraged to:

- Make extended, independent contributions that develop ideas in depth;
- Make purposeful presentations that allow them to speak with authority on significant subjects;
- Engage with texts that challenge preconceptions and develop understanding beyond the personal and immediate;
- Experiment with language and explore different ways of discovering and shaping their own meanings; and

- Use writing as a means of reflecting on and exploring a range of views and perspectives on the world.

Cross-curricular speaking and listening

Speaking and listening is about developing the ability to:

- Listen and respond to others (adding to or arguing against);
- Speak and present (with increasing formality);
- Participate in group discussion and interaction;
- Engage in drama, role-play and performance.

The Russian psychologist Lev Vygotsky said that speaking and thinking were intricately linked because the process of speaking helps us to learn by articulating our thoughts and developing the concepts, we use to understand the world. He argued that, "Up to a certain point in time, [thought and speech] follow different lines, independently of each other [but] at a certain point these lines meet, whereupon thought becomes verbal and speech rational".

Furthermore, Stricht's Law tells us that "Reading ability in children cannot exceed their listening ability" and Myhill and Fisher assert that "Spoken language forms a constraint, a ceiling not only on the ability to comprehend but also on the ability to write, beyond which literacy cannot progress".

Classroom talk, therefore, is an important part of literacy development because comprehension derives, not solely from writing and creating, but also from talking. Moreover, communication and understanding improve with practice. Therefore, providing pupils with an opportunity to talk in the classroom is vital if they are to develop their understanding.

Talking also helps build pupils' vocabulary knowledge - a process that continues across all years and levels of schooling and which is not, therefore, solely in the domain of the early years teacher and not solely in the domain of English teachers. Indeed, every teacher in the secondary and FE phases has a duty to help pupils develop their spoken language and they should continue to help pupils to become more articulate and sophisticated users of the English language.

Here are seven practical ways of achieving this:

Firstly, we should allow more 'wait time' following a question. Typically, waiting at least 3 to 5 seconds for pupils to respond to a question is effective because it allows for the thinking time that some pupils need in order to process information before composing an answer. When wait time is increased, answers tend to be more complex.

Secondly, we should model the clear and correct use of spoken language. In other words, we should give unambiguous instructions, use accurate descriptive and positional language, utilise precise terminology where appropriate, and give clear feedback.

Thirdly, we should regularly check for understanding until we have a clear idea of the level of our pupils' language skills. Sometimes, pupils who have trouble concentrating in class - particularly when the teacher is talking - may not actually understand what the teacher is saying. When we become aware of this, we can monitor our pupils' understanding and adjust our language when necessary.

Fourthly, we should use simple, direct language and place verbs at the beginning of instructions. 'Teacher talk' is not necessarily better than the language pupils access in other environments but it is different. As a result, pupils' language proficiency might be different from that required to access the curriculum, or even to understand simple classroom instructions.

Confusion and disobedience can result from the fact that pupils are unfamiliar with the language structures and 'lexical density' of the more formal teacherly language of the classroom. This does not mean that we should use the same language as our pupils, but that we may sometimes need to use simpler language and emphasise important words.

Fifthly, we should teach active listening skills. Most pupils can hear but are not naturally active listeners. Active listening requires selective and sustained attention, working memory, cognitive processing, and information storage and recall mechanisms. We can help pupils develop these skills by giving them tasks such as listening for specific or key information, listening to answer specific questions, and listening to follow instructions.

Next, we should teach note-taking skills whereby pupils have to write down the key points ascertained from a piece of spoken language.

Finally, we should build on pupils' language by elaborating on their answers to questions, adding new information, extending the conversation through further questioning, or reinforcing the language through repetition. We should also develop communication skills such as turn-taking and the use of eye contact.

Build oracy into daily routines

In addition to the above, we should make sure that the development of spoken language permeates the school day. After all, spoken language is used all day, every day so we should take advantage and build spoken language activities into daily routines such as during tutor time (e.g. ask a question of each pupil that must be answered in a sentence), when handing out materials, when pupils enter and leave the classroom, and when giving instructions.

We should also make sure that pupils have a regular opportunity to speak. The teacher tends to dominate classroom discussion - and it is right that teachers talk a lot because they are the experts in the room in possession of the knowledge and experience that pupils need. But it is also important that pupils get a chance to interact with the teacher and with each other and to do so beyond responding to closed questions.

What's more, we should plan opportunities for one-to-one discussion. Spoken language develops best through paired conversation and when one of the people in the pair has a better developed vocabulary. Therefore, it is worth investigating ways of pairing up pupils with people with more sophisticated language skills, perhaps an older pupil or a parent or volunteer. This could be a case of volunteers reading a book with a pupil or simply engaging in conversation. One to one conversation also enables young people to develop conversational skills such as turn-taking, intonation and eye contact.

Books are the bridge from misery to hope

Jackie Onassis once said, "There are many little ways to enlarge your child's world. Love of books is the best of all."

Accordingly, we should read lots of books with our pupils. Reading is the best way of developing a young person's vocabulary, particularly if we use the book as a stimulus, a means of initiating conversation by asking questions about the writer's intentions, about the characters' motivations, and about the structure and plot, theme and genre, style and so on.

Open questions such as 'What do you think is going to happen next and why?' are the most effective because they encourage pupils to develop their language and their cognition. For example, pupils have to make inferences and engage in critical thinking.

Asking pupils to re-tell a story is also effective because it encourages them to master tense, sequencing, and logical reasoning, as well as expanding the imagination.

We should never assume that pupils and students are too old to be read to: older learners, including those in the sixth form and college, enjoy being told a story and they can still learn from the experience because the teacher can highlight sophisticated vocabulary and syntactic structures which pupils may not pick up on if reading alone.

Thinking allowed

As well as reading aloud, we should 'think aloud' with our pupils. This involves modelling our cognitive processes, and our logic and reasoning, by making visible the invisible act of thinking - in other words, by making the implicit explicit.

Self-talk is also useful in mediating situations - hearing how we process difficult situations helps pupils to use words to resolve an issue and encourages them to engage in their own self-talk, calming themselves down with language rather than with a physical act.

To conclude this section on speaking and listening, here are six 'quick wins' for developing pupils' and students' speaking and listening skills...

1. Use fewer 'what?' questions and use more 'why?' and 'how?' questions
2. Give pupils time to rehearse answers to questions, perhaps by discussing their answers in pairs before sharing them more widely
3. Give pupils thinking time after each question has been asked before they are expected to share their answers
4. Enforce a 'no-hands-up' policy as often as possible
5. Model the kind of language you expect pupils to use in group discussions and answers
6. Build pupils' vocabularies by explicitly teaching the key words in your subject and by repeating key words as often as possible; give key words as homework, and test pupils on their spelling and meaning so that they become the expected discourse of all pupils

Cross-curricular reading

Reading is about developing the ability to:

- Decode increasingly complex and challenging words across the curriculum;
- Read for meaning (through the use of reading strategies such as prediction, skimming, scanning, inference, summarising, etc.);
- Understand a writer's craft (analysing the effect of the use of features of form, structure and language);
- Read and engage with a wide variety of texts; and
- Research for a wide range of purposes.

One of the key aspects of teaching reading skills is the use of subject-specific vocabulary. In order for pupils to understand and be able to use with accuracy words with which they are unfamiliar, we need to introduce those words in a careful sequence.

For example, we could begin by reading aloud a sentence in which the new word appears. Then we could show pupils the word written down and ask them to say it aloud before asking pupils to repeat the word several times. Next, we could debate possible meanings with the class and point out any parts of the word which might help with meaning, for example a prefix or Greek or Latin root.

After this, we could reread the sentence to see if there are any contextual clues and explicitly explain the meaning of the word through simple definition and the use of synonyms. We could provide several examples of the word being used in context, emphasising the word, and ask questions to determine whether or not pupils have understood the word.

We could also provide some sentences for pupils to judge whether or not the word is used correctly and get pupils to write their own sentences using the word. And, once the word has been introduced and reinforced in the lesson, we could explicitly use the word during the course of the next few days in order to reinforce its meaning.

One of the advantages of this sequence is that it ensures pupils are exposed to new vocabulary several times and get to see, hear and use new words in context.

Developing pupils' fluency

Once new subject-specific words have been introduced, we need to help pupils to read these words quickly and accurately, adopting the appropriate intonation. This is called fluency.

Fluency requires a background knowledge of words and a text, as well as a rapid retrieval of the requisite vocabulary. Fluency also requires a knowledge of syntax and grammar in order to predict the words that are likely to appear next.

The ability to adapt one's vocabulary and intonation according to a text's syntax and grammar, and the ability to read ahead assists with both speed and accuracy. Experienced readers integrate these processes so that reading becomes automatic - done without thinking - which allows their cognitive energy to be focused on the task of discerning meaning.

A useful analogy to return to here is that of learning to tie your shoelaces. When you first learn to tie your laces, because it is unfamiliar, you have to dedicate all your attention to it. However, once you have mastered the art of lace-tying - through repeated exposure to it - you begin to do it automatically, without having to think about it and so can do so whilst holding a conversation.

There is a strong correlation between fluency and reading comprehension; indeed, it is such a strong link that fluency and comprehension can be regarded as interdependent. After all, fluency only occurs when a reader understands the text; if reading is hesitant and disjointed, meaning is lost.

It is impossible to be a fluent reader if you have to keep stopping to work out what a word is. To be fluent you have to move beyond the decoding stage to accurately read whole words. Therefore, one of the first skills to teach in order to achieve fluency is accuracy.

A fluent reader has ready access to a vast bank of words which can be used in different contexts. The words to which a reader has immediate access are called their 'sight vocabulary'. Even complex words that originally had to be decoded – like 'originally' and 'decoded' rather than monosyllabic function words like 'that' and 'had' – but which can now be recognised on sight, become a part of the fluent reader's lexicon.

But recognition is not enough for fluency: as well as being in the reader's sight vocabulary, words must also be stored in their 'receptive vocabulary' - that is to say, words which the reader knows the meaning of. The larger the bank of words that are both recognised and understood on sight, then the broader the range of texts which are accessible.

For this reason, developing pupils' sight vocabularies and receptive vocabularies are the most effective ways of developing both fluency and reading comprehension.

Once you've developed accuracy, you need to develop speed, increasing the rate at which your pupils can access texts. Reading speed is not the same as reading fast. People who read too quickly and therefore show no regard for punctuation, intonation or comprehension are not fluent readers.

Reading speed is about being able to process texts quickly whilst understanding the text and taking account of punctuation and adopting an appropriate intonation. In short, improving pupils' reading speed is important but it must not be at the expense of comprehension.

After accuracy and speed, prosody - that is to say, reading with expression - is the third component of reading fluently. Prosody is more difficult to achieve than accuracy and speed because it involves developing stress, pitch, and rhythm. However, prosody is essential in rendering reading aloud meaningful.

Poor prosody can cause confusion and has an impact on readers' interest and motivation to read. Good prosody, meanwhile, makes reading aloud come alive and reflects the author's message more accurately and more meaningfully.

So how can we help pupils and students to develop prosody? Here are three suggestions...

1. Read aloud to pupils in an engaging and motivating way in order to model fluency for them.

2. Display high frequency irregular words from your subject around the classroom. Word walls - when they are referred to and used in competitions or quizzes - help build pupils' automatic recognition of words.

3. Read a text repeatedly in order to provide the practice needed to develop accuracy, speed and confidence.

Developing pupils' comprehension

Understanding what a text means is about much more than decoding or word recognition. The depth of understanding differentiates the weak reader from the strong.

Comprehension is an active process which is heavily dependent on the reader's spoken language skills, as well as their understanding of word meanings and the syntactic and semantic relationships between words. Comprehension is the ability to engage with a text at a deep level.

Active engagement with a text depends not only on the skill of the reader, but also on the nature of the text…

Broadly speaking, texts can be divided into three levels of comprehension: independent; instructional; and frustration. It's important to know which kind of text to give to pupils in different situations.

Texts at the 'independent level'

At this level, the reader is able to read most or all of the text with fluency, finding no more than about one word out of every twenty challenging. Pupils should be given texts which are at their independent level for independent reading activities.

By reading fluently, pupils will be able to engage with the material and take meaning from it. They may need strategies in order to decode the odd unfamiliar word, but they should be able to do so independently and without losing their thread.

Texts at the 'instructional level'

At this level, the reader finds the text challenging - with one word in ten proving difficult - but manageable and can read it with support. Support enables pupils who are reading at this more difficult level to access more sophisticated vocabulary and sentence structures.

Texts at the 'frustration level'

At this level, the reader has difficulty with more than one word in ten, and thus finds the text frustrating to read. Ideally, pupils should not be asked to read texts at this level - even with support - because interrupting the text every time they struggle with a word means they grow frustrated and so lose their motivation and enthusiasm.

When working independently, pupils should be given texts to read that fall within their independent level. When involved in guided reading aimed at developing pupils' vocabulary, pupils should be given texts to read that fall within their instructional level. Texts which appear at a pupil's frustration level can still be used in class but only if they are read to them by the teacher. This helps expose pupil to more sophisticated vocabulary and syntax.

To conclude, here are five 'quick wins' for developing pupils' and students' reading skills…

1.   Teach the reading skills needed in your subject – e.g. skimming, scanning, analysis, and research.
2.   Present hand-outs in an attractive and accessible way, taking account of pupils' reading ages
3.   Include a list of key words at the start of hand-outs
4.   Include a 'big picture' question or statement at the start of hand-outs which helps pupils to understand why they are reading it and what help it will provide
5.   Ensure that the questions you ask about a text move beyond straightforward comprehension towards exploratory talk involving 'why' and 'how' questions

Cross-curricular writing

Writing is about developing the ability to:

- Generate, plan and draft ideas for composition;
- Select, shape and construct language for expression and effect in composition;
- Proof-read and redraft written work, drawing on conventions and structures; and
- Use accurate grammar, punctuation and spelling.

Writing has traditionally been one of the weakest areas of literacy teaching because, all too often, teachers assume that imparting knowledge – making sure pupils know stuff – is enough.

In reality, of course, the most common and effective means by which most knowledge is demonstrated and assessed - whether that be in exams or through assignments, and class and homework - is through pupils' and students' writing.

Writing, therefore, needs to be taught by every teacher who uses writing as a means of demonstrating and assessing learning.

This is not a case of asking teachers to do anything technical or beyond their comfort zones; it's simply about helping pupils to write like a designer or artist or musician or historian or mathematician or scientist and so on...

Teaching writing by reading

The quality of pupils' writing is usually better when it emerges from reading other people's writing. That doesn't mean simply displaying a good model of a text on the board, however. Rather, it involves:

1. Modelling: sharing information about a text.
2. Joint construction: working with pupils to create a text collaboratively.
3. Independent construction: pupils constructing a text in a new genre independently of others, albeit with support.
4. Active teaching of vocabulary and sentence structures.

However, here's a word of warning: we can't teach writing simply by showing model texts, even if we annotate them to show what makes them work. Instead, we teach writing by writing...

Teaching writing by writing

If we simply show writing exemplars on the board, we are in danger of giving pupils the mistaken impression that writing is a product rather than a process.

Pupils need to see that writing is something that involves making decisions and, for that matter, making mistakes. Pupils need to see their teacher – and that means their teachers in all subjects – writing. This might involve:

Contemplating the 'what' and the 'how' of a text – what is its purpose and who is its audience? The answers to those questions will affect how the text is written both in terms of its language and its presentation.

Examining the conventions of a text – again, this is both in terms of language (formality, style, sentence structure, etc.) and presentation (paragraphs, sequence, bullet points, images, etc.).

Demonstrating how the text might be written - this involves pupils observing the teacher as they 'think aloud', explaining the decisions they take. For example, thinking aloud might sound like this: "I need to write this like a historian would write it. It will need to be in the third person, so 'he/she' and 'they' not 'I'. It will need to be formal not colloquial but not too stuffy either, it has to be accessible to a wide audience. Now talk to your partner about what your first sentence might say. Then we'll listen to some of your examples and compare them with what I write down." This articulation moves from modelling to composition to assessment.

Writing a text whilst providing a running commentary - this involves explaining the decisions that are made, and how words are selected and rejected.

Let's explore these strategies in more detail...

First, let's consider how we might help pupils to write texts appropriate to their audience and purpose...

We could use a sequence for teaching writing such as 1 establish clear aims – APT (Audience, Purpose, Technique), 2 provide examples of the text type being produced, 3 explore the main features of presentation and language in the example text.

Then we could read and discuss word, sentence and text-level features and define the conventions of the text type being produced – agree on the main 'ingredients' for this kind of writing. We could demonstrate how a text is written by modelling the thought processes (thinking aloud) and compose a text (or the introduction to a text) together as a class.

We could also scaffold pupils' first attempts – e.g. use writing frames, lists of key words, the beginnings of sentences - and provide time for pupils to write independently.

Second, let's consider how we might help pupils to sequence and structure information, ideas, and events effectively...

We could, for example, model the planning process for pupils, introducing them to a variety of writing frames including templates for note-making. We could teach the main features of different text types (e.g. instructions are chronological). And we could make explicit a sequence for planning which might include: 1 Write initial thoughts and ideas on Post-it notes or cards, 2 Identify key words or phrases which need to be included, 3 Draft the topic sentences and/or sub-headings, and 4 Organise these sentences/sub-headings into a logical sequence.

We could also use visual organisers such as flowcharts, mind maps, graphs and tables, in order to support the planning and writing process.

Third, in order to help pupils construct paragraphs and to make links within and between paragraphs, we could share a paragraphed text with pupils and ask them to identify why each paragraph starts where it does. We could share a paragraphed text with pupils and ask them to give each paragraph a sub-heading which summarises the subject of the paragraph.

Fourth, to help pupils vary their sentences for clarity, purpose and effect, we could encourage them to change the openings of their sentences. For example, we could ask them to write a text in which at least one sentence:

- Starts with a verb ending in ing...
- Starts with a verb ending in ed...
- Starts with an adverb ending ly...
- Starts with a preposition e.g. over, at, on,
- Starts with an adjective e.g. Cold and weary they sank ...

We could encourage pupils to vary the lengths of their sentences, too. For example, we could ask them to write a text in which there is at least one:

- Simple sentence
- Compound sentence
- Complex sentence

We could also encourage pupils to vary the purpose of their sentences. For example, we could ask them to write a text in which there is at least one:

- Declarative sentence
- Exclamative sentence
- Inquisitive sentence
- Imperative sentence

And we could encourage pupils to use a range of connectives which go beyond 'and' and to use connectives in order to:

- Combine sentences
- Start sentences (with a comma)
- Link sentences and paragraphs
- Express thinking more clearly

Fifth, we could help pupils to write with accurate syntax and punctuation in phrases, clauses and sentences by giving them a series of sentences written in 'hangman' style with underscores and punctuation but no letters and ask them to identify the sentence types.

We could also get pupils to use sequencing when reviewing and previewing learning to get used to using time prepositions such as:

- Before last lesson, I knew…
- During last lesson, I learnt…
- Since last lesson, I found out…
- By the end of this lesson, I want to know…

What's more, we could give pupils a text and ask them to highlight the main and subordinate clauses in different colours and then explain the effect. And we could give pupils three complex sentences which make different uses of main clauses and subordinate clauses (main + subordinate, subordinate + main, and main + embedded subordinate) and ask them to identify the different clauses and explain their answers.

Sixth, in order to help pupils to select appropriate and effective vocabulary, we could teach the use of synonyms – e.g. identify a word in a sentence and ask pupils to think of a list of alternative words which have the same meaning. This will improve their vocabulary and the quality of their writing. We could focus on providing alternatives for high frequency words such as 'said' and 'walked'.

We could also get pupils to play word detectives using thesauruses and dictionaries to find the meaning of words.

Finally, in order to help pupils to use the correct spelling, we could teach them how to:

- Break words into sounds/phonemes (p-a-r-t-y)
- Break words into syllables (dem-oc-ra-cy)
- Break words into an affix and root word (un + happy)
- Use a mnemonic (Big Elephants Can Always Upset Small Elephants for BECAUSE or one Collar two Sleeves for neCeSSary)
- Refer to different words in the same family (chemical, chemist, chemistry)
- Over-articulate silent or hidden letters (Wed-nes-day)
- Identify words within words (GUM in argument)
- Refer to a word's etymology / history (tri = three, pod = foot)
- Use analogy (through, rough, enough)

- Use a key word (I'm – to remember an apostrophe can replace a missing letter)
- Apply spelling rules (hopping = short vowel sound, hoping = long vowel)
- Learn by sight (look-say-cover-write-check)
- Use a 'mind palace' of visual memories (recall images, colour, font)

To conclude, here are three 'quick wins' for developing pupils' and students' writing skills…

1. Model how to write the first paragraph of an essay/evaluation/description, etc.
2. Teach the essential connectives of writing such as however, because, as, so, although, while, despite, on the other hand.
3. Encourage pupils to use short sentences at the start and end of paragraphs

Numeracy across the curriculum

In the 2015 report 'Key Stage 3: The Wasted Years', Ofsted expressed concerns about the development of pupils' numeracy skills.

A majority of the headteachers Ofsted spoke to as part of the research for the report were able to explain how they were improving literacy but only a quarter could do the same for numeracy. This was reflected in inspection evidence, for example from monitoring inspections, where inspectors reported improvements in literacy nearly three times more than they did in numeracy.

Ofsted recommended that school leaders put in place numeracy strategies that ensure pupils build on their prior attainment.

In my own experience of working with schools and colleges, I'd say it's true that numeracy is often regarded as literacy's poor relation, not given the same amount of time, resources and priority as its close cousin.

Many teachers struggle to understand their role in developing pupils' and students' numeracy skills and fail to see how their subject or vocational area presents the same opportunities for embedding numeracy as it does for embedding literacy.

Let us first, then, look at what numeracy means and provide some examples of numeracy at play in various subjects.

I would suggest that numeracy can be meaningfully divided into four categories:

1. Handling information;
2. Space, shape and measurements;
3. Operations and calculations; and
4. Numbers.

Handling information is about graphs and charts, comparing sets of data and types of data, processing data, and probability. Within graphs and charts, you might look at pie and bar charts. You might look at interpreting information, you might look at data in lists and tables, and you might look at reading scales. Within comparing sets of data and types of data, you might look at measures of averages, measures of spread, discrete data and continuous data. Within processing data, you might look at decision trees and VENN diagrams. Within probability, you might look at using a probability scale, estimating probability from statistical information, and experimental probability.

Space, shape and measurements is about both space, shape and measure, and solving problems with space, shape and measure. Within measurements, you might look at standard units of measurements for length, mass, capacity, time, temperature, and area and perimeter, and consider both metric and imperial measurements. You might select and use measuring instruments and look at how to interpret numbers and read scales. You might also look at volume. Within shape and space, you might look at coordinates to describe a position. You might look at simple positional language. You might look at symmetry. You might look at 2D and 3D shapes. And you might look at angles. Solving problems with space, shape and measurements might involve selecting and using appropriate skills to solve geographical problems. It might involve using geographical notation and symbols correctly.

Operations and calculations are about addition and subtraction, multiplication and division, number operations, and the effective use of calculators. Within addition and subtraction, you might look at knowing plus and minus facts to twenty, at mental methods to one hundred, and at whole numbers to one thousand and beyond. Within multiplication and division, you might look at knowing multiply and divide facts to twenty, and remainders and rounding. Within number operations you might look at inverse operations, interrelationships and order of operations. And within the effective use of calculators you might look a calculations with fractions, decimals and percentages, and calculations with negatives.

Numbers (and the use of the number system) is about using numbers, whole numbers, size and order, place value, patterns and sequences, and numbers 'in between' whole numbers. Within using numbers, you might look at reading and writing using symbols and labels, at ratio and proportion, at using numbers for measuring and for counting, and for ratio and proportion. Within whole numbers and size and order you might look at comparing and ordering and using number lines. Within place value you might look at zero as a place holder, at money context, at measures and at estimation. Within sequences and patterns, you might look at odd and even, at square numbers, at factors and multiples and at prime numbers. And within numbers 'in between' whole numbers you might look at fractions, decimals and percentages.

I would also proffer that numeracy encompasses three sets of skills:

1. Reasoning;
2. Problem-solving; and
3. Decision-making.

Reasoning might involve identifying structures, being systematic, searching for patterns, developing logical thinking, and predicting and checking. Problem-solving might involve identifying the information needed to carry out a task, breaking down a problem or task into smaller parts, interpreting solutions in context, and making mental estimates to check the reasonableness of an answer. And decision-making might involve choosing appropriate strategies, identifying relevant information and choosing the right tools and equipment.

In English, numeracy can be developed by using non-fiction texts which include mathematical vocabulary, graphs, charts and tables.

In science, pupils will order numbers including decimals, calculate means, and percentages, use negative numbers when taking temperatures, substitute into formulae, rearrange equations, decide which graph to use to represent data, and plot, interpret and predict from graphs.

In ICT, pupils will collect and classify data, enter it into data handling software to produce graphs and tables, and interpret and explain the results. When they use computer models and simulations, they will draw on their abilities to manipulate numbers and identify patterns and relationships.

In art and design and technology, pupils will use measurements and patterns, spatial ideas, the properties of shapes, and symmetry, and use multiplication and ratio to enlarge and reduce the size of objects.

In history, geography and RE, pupils will collect data and use measurements of different kinds. They will study maps and use coordinates and ideas of angles, direction, position, scale, and ratio. And they will use timelines similar to number lines.

Hopefully, if you were in any doubt, you can already see how numeracy is a whole-school or college concern and encompasses skills that apply across the curriculum.

So how can we ensure that numeracy is taught effectively throughout the school?

At the whole-school or college level, you need to create a positive environment that celebrates numeracy and provides pupils with role models by celebrating the numeracy successes of older pupils. You also need to ensure that planned activities allow pupils to learn and practice their numeracy skills. You should publicly display examples of high-quality numeracy work from across the curriculum around the school. And you should ensure that every department adheres to the school's numeracy policy or college's English and maths policy.

Individual departments should provide high quality exemplar materials and display examples of numeracy work within their subject context. Departments should also highlight opportunities for the use of numeracy within their subject and ensure that the learning materials that are presented to pupils match both their capability in the subject and their numerical demands.

Individual teachers, meanwhile, should have high expectations of all their pupils and ensure that the numerical content of their lessons is of a high standard. They should encourage pupils to show their numerical working out where relevant and encourage the use of estimation, particularly for checking work. Teachers should also encourage pupils to write mathematically-correct statements and to vocalise their maths. They should also encourage pupils to use non-calculator methods wherever possible. Teachers and departments should inform the maths department as soon as possible if any numeracy problems are identified.

CHAPTER TWENTY-SIX
METACOGNITION AND SELF-REGULATION

Having argued in favour of subject-specific curriculums and the importance of subject specialists designing curricular that look different to each other, I think – in addition to literacy and numeracy – there is one other 'skill' which pupils might benefit from developing across the whole-school curriculum, albeit taught within context and in domain-specific ways. That skill is metacognition… or, more accurately, metacognition *and* self-regulation.

In Chapter Twenty-Two I outlined the main findings of the Educational Endowment Foundation's Teaching and Learning Toolkit. I said that the teaching strategies considered 'top of the league' in terms of their impact on pupil learning, are feedback and metacognition. In that chapter I briefly summarised those strategies but now I'd like to delve deeper into the latter…

As educators today, we have access to a wealth of research evidence about what works and what does not work in the classroom. Teaching is much more of an evidence-informed profession than it used to be. But knowing what evidence to look at and what it means in practice is the real challenge. The Educational Endowment Foundation's toolkit says that metacognition has 'consistently high levels of impact, with pupils making an average of eight months' additional progress'. The toolkit also states that 'teaching these strategies can be particularly effective for low achieving and older pupils'.

But what, exactly, does metacognition look like within our curriculum and in the school and college classroom?

Before we can answer the question 'What is metacognition?' I think it will be helpful to state what it is not…

Firstly, metacognition is not simply 'thinking about thinking', despite the morphology of the word. Although metacognition does indeed involve thinking about one's thinking, it is much more complex than this; rather, metacognition is actively monitoring one's own learning and, based on this monitoring, making changes to one's own learning behaviours and strategies.

Secondly, not every strategy used whilst performing a cognitive task can be described as metacognitive. Indeed, Flavell (1981) made a useful distinction. He said that strategies used to make cognitive progress are 'cognitive strategies'; strategies used to monitor cognitive progress, meanwhile, are 'metacognitive strategies'.

Thirdly, metacognition is not solely in the domain of the learner and not solely for the benefit of older learners. Although it's true that a metacognitive approach typically focuses on allowing the learner rather than the teacher to take control of their own learning, this is not to say that the teacher has no role to play. Indeed, the teacher is still required to help in the development of learners' metacognitive skills. For example, in order for pupils to become metacognitive, self-regulated learners, the teacher needs to set clear learning objectives, demonstrate and monitor metacognitive strategies, and prompt and encourage their learners. And metacognition can be developed from an early age, certainly whilst pupils are at primary school.

So, if that is what it is not, what is it?

Metacognition describes the processes involved when learners plan, monitor, evaluate and make changes to their own learning behaviours. Metacognition is often considered to have two dimensions:

1.   Metacognitive knowledge, and
2.   Self-regulation.

Metacognitive knowledge refers to what learners know about learning. This includes:

- The learner's knowledge of their own cognitive abilities (e.g. 'I have trouble remembering key dates in this period of history')
- The learner's knowledge of particular tasks (e.g. 'The politics in this period of history are complex')

- The learner's knowledge of the different strategies that are available to them and when they are appropriate to the task (e.g. 'If I create a timeline first it will help me to understand the overall period of history').

Self-regulation, meanwhile, refers to what learners do about learning. It describes how learners monitor and control their cognitive processes. For example, a learner might realise that a particular strategy is not yielding the results they expected so they decide to try a different strategy.

Put another way, self-regulated learners are aware of their strengths and weaknesses, and can motivate themselves to engage in, and improve, their learning.

According to the EEF, we approach any learning task or opportunity with some metacognitive knowledge about:

- our own abilities and attitudes (knowledge of ourselves as a learner);
- what strategies are effective and available (knowledge of strategies); and
- this particular type of activity (knowledge of the task).

When undertaking a learning task, we start with this knowledge, then apply and adapt it. This, the EEF say, is metacognitive regulation. It is about "planning how to undertake a task, working on it while monitoring the strategy to check progress, then evaluating the overall success".

A metacognitive cycle

Metacognition and self-regulation might take the following form:

1. *The planning stage:*

During the planning stage, learners think about the learning goal the teacher has set and consider how they will approach the task and which strategies they will use. At this stage, it is helpful for learners to ask themselves:

- 'What am I being asked to do?'
- 'Which strategies will I use?'
- 'Are there any strategies that I have used before that might be useful?'

2. *The monitoring stage:*

During the monitoring stage, learners implement their plan and monitor the progress they are making towards their learning goal. Pupils might decide to make changes to the strategies they are using if these are not working. As pupils work through the task, it is helpful to ask themselves:

- 'Is the strategy that I am using working?'
- 'Do I need to try something different?'

3. The evaluation stage:

During the evaluation stage, pupils determine how successful the strategy they've used has been in terms of helping them to achieve their learning goal. To promote evaluation, it is helpful for pupils to ask themselves:

- 'How well did I do?'
- 'What didn't go well?' 'What could I do differently next time?'
- 'What went well?' 'What other types of problem can I use this strategy for?'

4. The reflection stage:

Reflection is an integral part of the whole process. Encouraging learners to self-question throughout the process is therefore crucial.

The EEF offer a slightly different version of this process which they call the metacognitive regulation cycle. Helpfully, they posit some concrete examples. For instance, they introduce us to John who is set a maths question to answer. John starts with some knowledge of the task (word problems in maths are often solved by expressing them as equations) and of strategies (how to turn sentences into an equation). His knowledge of the task then develops as it emerges from being a word problem into a simultaneous equation. He would then continue through this cycle if he has the strategies for solving simultaneous equations. He could then evaluate his overall success by substituting his answers into the word problem and checking they are correct. If this was wrong, he could attempt other strategies and once more update his metacognitive knowledge.

In another example, Amy's geography teacher asks the class to prepare a short presentation about rainforest ecosystems. To plan this, Amy reflects on how she learned best on the last topic (using the school textbooks) and decides to read the relevant chapter before drafting her presentation. However, when reading it she decides that the chapter does not really improve her understanding. She starts to panic as she was relying on this.

Then Amy remembers a geography website her teacher mentioned. She adapts her strategy and searches the website. This provides a more useful overview and she uses the information to summarise some interesting facts. She reflects on the experience and decides that next time she will gather a range of resources before starting to research a topic rather than relying on one source.

Most learners, say the EEF, go through many of these thinking processes to some extent when trying to solve a problem or tackle a task in the classroom. The most effective learners, however, will have developed a repertoire of different cognitive and metacognitive strategies and be able to effectively use and apply these in a timely fashion. They will, in other words, self-regulate and find ways to motivate themselves when they get stuck. Over time, this can further increase their motivation as they become more confident in undertaking new tasks and challenges.

Teaching metacognition

The EEF argue that metacognition and self-regulation must be explicitly taught. This might look as follows:

1. *The planning stage:*

The teacher encourages pupils to think about the goal of their learning (set by the teacher, or themselves) and to consider how they will approach the task. This might include:

- ensuring they understand the goal,
- activating relevant prior knowledge about the task,
- selecting appropriate strategies, and
- considering how to allocate their effort.

2. *The monitoring stage:*

Here, the teacher emphasises the need for pupils to assess their own progress. This might include self-testing and self-questioning, as well as making changes to their chosen strategies. Teachers can explicitly teach these skills by prompting pupils with examples of the things they should be considering at each stage of a learning task.

The EEF use the example of pupils drawing or painting a self-portrait in art. Effective teacher questioning while modelling a self-portrait, they say, can aid the development of metacognitive reflection as follows:

Planning:

- 'What resources do I need to carry out a self-portrait?'
- 'Have I done a self-portrait before and was it successful?'
- 'What have I learned from the examples we looked at earlier?'
- 'Where do I start and what viewpoint will I use?'
- 'Do I need a line guide to keep my features in proportion?'

Monitoring:

- 'Am I doing well?'
- 'Do I need any different techniques to improve my self-portrait?
- 'Are all of my facial features in proportion?'
- 'Am I finding this challenging?'
- 'Is there anything I need to stop and change to improve my self-portrait?'

Evaluation:

- 'How did I do?'
- 'Did my line guide strategy work?'
- 'Was it the right viewpoint to choose?'
- 'How would I do a better self-portrait next time?'
- 'Are there other perspectives, viewpoints or techniques I would like to try?'

Some of the above 'planning' questions activate prior knowledge (resources, previous exemplars) whereas others model the use of the best cognitive strategies (viewpoint, line guides). The 'monitoring' questions, meanwhile, emphasise both general progress (proportion, editing) alongside checking general motivation (meeting goals and dealing with challenge). The 'evaluation' questions concentrate on assessing the relative success of the cognitive strategies used (line guide, viewpoint, comparison with other techniques) and on what can be learnt from the experience.

The EEF suggest that these prompts are accompanied by explicit instruction in the relevant cognitive strategies. In the self-portrait example, for instance, pupils will only be able to consider these questions and approaches if they understand the importance of perspective and the different techniques.

The EEF proffers a handy 7-step guide to teaching metacognitive strategies, as follows:

1.   Activating prior knowledge;
2.   Explicit strategy instruction;
3.   Modelling of learned strategy;
4.   Memorisation of strategy;
5.   Guided practice;
6.   Independent practice; and
7.   Structured reflection.

Here's an example from a history lesson that the EEF use to put some meat on the bones…

Activating prior knowledge – here, the teacher discusses with pupils the different causes that led to World War One while making notes on the whiteboard.

Explicit strategy instruction – here, the teacher explains how a 'fishbone' diagram will help organise their ideas, with the emphasis on the cognitive strategy of using a 'cause and effect model' in history that will help them to organise and plan a better written response.

Modelling of learned strategy – next, the teacher uses the initial notes on the causes of the war to model one part of the fishbone diagram.

Memorisation of learned strategy – here, the teacher tests if pupils have understood and memorised the key aspects of the fishbone strategy, and its main purpose, through questions and discussion.

Guided practice – next, the teacher models one further fishbone cause with the whole group, with pupils verbally contributing their ideas.

Independent practice follows whereby pupils complete their own fishbone diagram analysis.

Finally, in structured reflection the teacher encourages pupils to reflect on how appropriate the model was, how successfully they applied it, and how they might use it in the future.

So, what other teaching approaches help pupils to develop metacognition and self-regulation…?

Thinking aloud

One of the most effective teaching strategies to promote metacognition is 'thinking aloud' whereby the teacher makes explicit what they do implicitly and makes visible the expertise that is often invisible to the novice learner.

The best thinking aloud occurs when the teacher is modelling excellence. For example, a teacher may write a short paragraph of persuasive text to model how to use rhetorical devices. As she is writing, the teacher explains every decision she is taking, and articulates the drafting and re-drafting process that is essential to all good writing.

There is some evidence, at least in terms of metacognition, that modelling and thinking aloud should not be too specific as this may inhibit pupils' reflection. Indeed, as the EEF says, "some 'deliberate difficulty' is required so that pupils have gaps where they have to think for themselves and monitor their learning with increasing independence".

Thinking hard

Teachers need to set an appropriate level of challenge if they are to help develop pupils' metacognition and self-regulation because if pupils are not given hard work to do – if they do not face difficulty, struggle with it and overcome it - they will not develop new and useful strategies, they will not be afforded the opportunity to learn from their mistakes and they will not be able to reflect sufficiently on the content with which they are engaging. Moreover, if pupils are not made to think hard, they will not encode new information into long-term memory and so learning will not occur.

The EEF offers some useful questions for pupils to ask that gauge the difficulty level of the work they're doing:

Knowledge of task:

* Is this task too challenging for me?
* What are the most difficult aspects of this task?
* How much time should I devote to this task?
* Are there easy bits I can get 'done'?

Knowledge of self:

* Is this task asking for subject knowledge I can remember?
* Do I understand the concept(s) that underpins this task?
* Am I motivated to stick at this tricky task?
* What can I do to keep myself focused?

Knowledge of strategies:

- Are my notes effective for understanding this task?
- Do I need to ask the teacher for help?
- What strategies can I deploy if I am stuck?
- What can I do to ensure I remember what I've learned?

Thinking efficiently

As well as thinking hard, pupils need to think efficiently if they are to cheat the limitations of working memory. Yes, pupils must be challenged and must struggle with new concepts if they are attend to them actively and therefore encode them into long-term memory, but if the work's too hard, they're likely to hit cognitive overload whereby they try to hold too much information in working memory at one time and therefore thinking fails.

The trick, then, is to ensure the work is hard but achievable. The work must be beyond pupils' current capability but within their reach. They must struggle but must be able to overcome the challenge with time, effort and support.

The concept of cognitive load theory (which was first espoused by John Sweller) is crucial to metacognition and self-regulation because:

- When we draw on existing knowledge from long-term memory to support working memory, creating what's called 'schema', we increase working memory capacity and overcome its limited size. This explains why knowledge is important and why pupils must be encouraged to try and activate prior knowledge before asking for help.
- We understand new concepts within the context of what we already know. The more pupils know and can draw from their long-term memory, the more meaningful new knowledge will become and the more they will be able to process and apply it.
- To ensure that learning activities don't demand too much of working memory and cause cognitive overload, we need to teach pupils coping strategies such as using mind-maps, taking effective notes (perhaps using the Cornell method), thinking aloud to work through problems, and breaking tasks down into smaller steps. Teachers can support this process through the use of structured planning templates, teacher modelling, worked examples, and breaking down activities into their constituent parts, revealing one part at a time and in sequence. Teachers can also help by being mindful of the fact that metacognitive tasks – such as asking pupils to reflect on their learning – can, if not well-timed,

distract pupils from the task at hand. In other words, teachers shouldn't expect pupils to develop new cognitive and metacognitive skills simultaneously, rather one must follow the other.

Thinking positively

Research suggests that an important factor in the effective use of metacognitive strategies is the ability to delay gratification. In other words, pupils who are better able to delay rewards in favour of studying are better at planning and regulating their learning, and vice versa. This is nothing new, of course. Walter Mischel began his now-famous 'marshmallow tests' back in 1960. He gave young children a challenge of delaying their gratification by offering them a choice of one small reward – a single marshmallow - or waiting 15 minutes and receiving two marshmallows instead. During the experiment, children used a number of metacognitive strategies such as not looking at the marshmallow and closing their eyes and thinking of something completely different. Pupils need to be taught strategies for delaying gratification and for motivating themselves if they are to master metacognition. There are two types of motivation: extrinsic and intrinsic.

Extrinsic motivation refers to the performance of an activity in order to attain a desired outcome. Extrinsic motivation comes from influences outside an individual's control; a rationale, a necessity, a need. Common forms of extrinsic motivation are rewards (for example, money or prizes), or - conversely - the threat of punishment. To build extrinsic motivation, and therefore improve metacognition, we can provide pupils with a rationale for learning by sharing the 'big picture' with them. In other words, we can continually explain how their learning fits in to the module, the course, the qualification, their careers and to success in work and life. For example, we can explain how today's lesson connects with yesterday's lesson and how the learning will be extended or consolidated next lesson, as well as how it will be assessed at a later stage. We can explain how this learning will become useful in later life, too. And we can connect the learning in one subject with the learning in other subjects, making explicit the transferability of knowledge and skills and the interconnectedness of skills in everyday life.

Intrinsic motivation, meanwhile, is the self-desire to seek out new things and new challenges, in order to gain new knowledge. Often, intrinsic motivation is driven by an inherent interest or enjoyment in the task itself and exists within an individual rather than relying on external pressures or necessity. Put simply, it's the desire to do something even though there is no reward except a sense of accomplishment at achieving that thing. Intrinsic motivation is a natural motivational tendency and is a critical element in cognitive, social, and physical development.

Pupils who are intrinsically motivated are more likely to engage in a task willingly as well as work to improve their skills through metacognition and self-regulation which - in turn - increase their capabilities. Pupils are likely to be intrinsically motivated if:

1. They attribute their educational results to factors under their own control, also known as autonomy.
2. They believe in their own ability to succeed in specific situations or to accomplish a task - also known as a sense of self-efficacy.
3. They are genuinely interested in accomplishing something to a high level of proficiency, knowledge and skill, not just in achieving good grades - also known as mastery.

Thinking together

Our job as teachers is to help pupils move from novice to expert. Part of this process is to ensure our pupils become increasingly independent over time. In short, we need to begin with lots of scaffolds in place but slowly remove those scaffolds as pupils develop their knowledge and skills. Asking challenging questions and guiding pupils with verbal feedback, prompting dialogue, and productive 'exploratory' talk is a great way to do this.

In practice, the teacher might achieve this by encouraging pupils to think in advance of a task about what could go wrong then, afterwards, to discuss what they found hard about the task.

Of course, it's not just about the teacher interacting with pupils; pupils must also interact with each other in order to test their metacognitive strategies and knowledge.

'Dialogic teaching' is a particularly effective method of managing these interactions because it emphasises classroom dialogue through which pupils learn to reason, discuss, argue, and explain. As the EEF explains, "A key element of [dialogic teaching] is to encourage a higher quality of teacher talk by going beyond the closed 'teacher question–pupil response–teacher feedback' sequence... [instead], dialogue needs to be purposeful and not just conversation, with teachers using questions to elicit further thought."

Dialogic teaching is the brainchild of Professor Robin Alexander whose most recent research identified six basic talk 'repertoires': talk settings, everyday talk, learning talk, teaching talk, questioning, and extending. The most relevant repertoires for developing metacognitive skills, so say the EEF, are learning talk and teaching talk. Learning talk includes narrating, questioning, and discussing; teaching talk, meanwhile, includes instruction, exposition, and dialogue.

Thinking alone

As pupils move from novice towards expertise, they become independent learners and, with a greater degree of autonomy, make active choices to manage and organise their own learning. But even as pupils become independent, they need their teachers to provide them with timely feedback and to help them to plan, monitor, and evaluate their progress.

According to Zimmerman, independent learners use a number of strategies to help them, including:

- setting specific short-term goals;
- adopting powerful strategies for attaining the goals;
- monitoring performance for signs of progress;
- restructuring one's physical and social context to make it compatible with one's goals;
- managing time-use efficiently;
- self-evaluating one's methods; and
- attributing causation to results and adapting future methods.

Russian psychologist Lev Vygotsky developed the idea of the Zone of Proximal Development which lies between what a learner can achieve alone and what a learner can achieve with expert guidance. The expert, in this case the teacher, initially takes responsibility for monitoring progress, setting goals, planning activities and allocating attention for example. Gradually, the responsibility for these cognitive processes is given over to the learner. The learner becomes increasingly capable of regulating his or her own cognitive activities.

- What do the students know already?
- What will they know with support from you?
- What remains to be known?

The four levels of metacognitive learners

David Perkins (1992) defined four levels of metacognitive learner which provide a useful framework for teachers when identifying where on the novice-expert continuum their pupils are and how much support is required:

1. Tacit learners are unaware of their metacognitive knowledge. They do not think about any particular strategies for learning and merely accept if they know something or not.

2. Aware learners recognise some of the thinking processes they use such as generating ideas, finding evidence, etc. However, thinking is not necessarily deliberate or planned.

3. Strategic learners organise their thinking by using problem-solving, grouping and classifying, evidence-seeking and decision-making, etc. They know and apply the strategies that help them learn.

4. Reflective learners are not only strategic about their own thinking, but they also reflect upon their learning whilst it is happening, considering the success or failure of their strategies and revising them as appropriate.

A useful checklist

The following checklist may be of use to classroom teachers when implementing the curriculum plan – there is more advice like this in Book Two of this series which focuses on how to teach the curriculum in a way that leads to long-term learning.

1. Have I included clear learning objectives? Pupils need to understand what their learning objectives are so that they can plan how to achieve them. The process of planning should involve pupils identifying which strategies they already know that could be applied in a new situation.

2. How am I going to encourage my pupils to monitor their learning? Effective learners commonly use metacognitive strategies whenever they learn. However, they may fail to recognise which strategy is the most effective for a particular learning task. Teachers can ask questions to prompt pupils to monitor the strategies that they are using. For example, before pupils begin a task, the teacher can prompt them to identify where the task might go wrong and how they could prevent this from happening. During the task, the teacher could encourage pupils to focus on the learning objectives and encourage them to think about how they can maintain that focus. This will encourage pupils to think more actively about where they are now, where they are going and how to get there.

3. How can I create opportunities for pupils to practise new strategies? When teachers introduce pupils to a new strategy, it helps to give them the opportunity to use it first with support and then independently. It is important to monitor pupils' progress and provide them with feedback on the specific strategies they are using to help shape their learning process.

4. How can I allow time for pupil self-reflection? Personal reflection enables pupils to critically analyse their performance in relation to a particular task and consider what they might do differently to improve their performance in future tasks. It is important that teachers dedicate time for pupils to reflect and provide them with the tools to do so. One way of doing this is to use thinking journals.

5. Does the classroom environment support metacognitive practices? Teachers are instrumental in shaping the culture of learning in their classrooms. By establishing a supportive learning environment that fosters and anticipates metacognitive practices, these practices will become an integral part of the learning process. Teachers should ensure they model metacognitive practices effectively, affording pupils plenty of opportunities to work collaboratively with their peers, encouraging reflection and evaluating their progress.

CONCLUSION

We have now reached the 'end point' of this book and so allow me to summarise what we have learnt along the way…

Agree the vision

The first step towards designing an effective curriculum is to agree the vision. This requires each school and college to consult on and then communicate a shared definition of what is meant by the word 'curriculum', as well as a working definition of what that curriculum encompasses in practice within the context of that school or college. This working definition might include, where relevant, aspects of the national, basic, local and hidden curriculums.

Agreeing the vision is also about defining what a school or college interprets as being a 'broad and balanced' curriculum. It means deciding upon and articulating the purpose of education within that school or college (why do we exist, what is our hope for all pupils and students?) and using this to write a vision against which all future curriculum decisions can be measured.

Talking of measurements, agreeing the vision is also about designing a meaningful assessment system which uses the curriculum as the progression model rather than relying on arbitrary grades, levels or numbers. This progression model should clearly show where each pupil and student is at any point in time by cataloguing what they know and can do, and what they do not yet know and cannot yet do – in other words, which aspects of the curriculum they have mastered and which they have not.

Senior leaders have several roles to play at this stage of the curriculum design process including working hard to create a whole-school or -college culture in which the curriculum can thrive. This culture, I argued, has three layers: the staff culture; the pupil and student culture; and the learning culture.

Senior leaders must also ensure their middle leaders and teachers are afforded sufficient time to engage in the curriculum planning process and are equipped with the knowledge and skills required for this complex task, including through the provision of quality professional development that performs the dual functions of developing subject knowledge *and* pedagogical content knowledge.

Set the destination

The second step towards designing an effective curriculum is to set the destination which is about identifying what we want all pupils and students to know and be able to do at the end of their curriculum journeys – be that at the end of a module or topic, at the end of a year, key stage or phase, at the end of their school or college studies, or indeed in ten years' time.

This stage begins by developing a shared understanding of the importance of knowledge – including cultural capital – and then agreeing, within subject disciplines or curriculum areas, *what* knowledge matters most to our pupils' and students' future successes.

Knowledge is needed, not simply to pass qualifications, but also to enable pupils and students to be genuinely prepared for the next stages of their education, employment and lives. As such, the knowledge base must be broad, encompassing employability and enrichment skills, cross-curricular skills such as literacy and numeracy, and research and study skills such as note-taking, and approaches to learning such as metacognition and self-regulation. What's more, the knowledge base must be suitably challenging for all.

A part of the process of setting the destination is identifying the key concepts that must be taught – and learnt – in each subject discipline. These 'foundational' concepts – a combination of knowledge *and* skills – provide the 'end points' or 'body of knowledge' towards which all pupils are headed.

Assess the starting points

The third step towards designing an effective curriculum is to assess the starting points and this, broadly speaking, takes two forms: the starting points of the *taught* curriculum and the starting points of the *learnt* curriculum.

The taught curriculum is that which is written down in curriculum plans (national curriculum documents, awarding body specifications, schemes of work, and so forth) and taught by teachers. The learnt curriculum, meanwhile, is that which each pupil or student has actually acquired, what they really know and can do – including their misconceptions and misunderstandings.

In terms of the *taught* curriculum, it's important to know the end points of the previous curriculum – what pupils are expected to know and be able to do by the time they begin studying your curriculum because you need to ensure, as far as is possible, that there is curriculum continuity – that each stage of education flows smoothly and naturally into the next and that each new year, key stage and phase of education consolidates and builds upon what has gone before rather than needlessly repeating prior content. This can be achieved, in part, by ensuring that transition arrangements are improved and that teachers and middle leaders in each phase work more closely with their counterparts in the preceding and succeeding phases in order to share data and engage in joint professional development and curriculum planning.

In terms of the *learnt* curriculum, it's important to understand what each pupil knows and can do and what they do not yet know and cannot yet do. This can be achieved, in part, through better data-sharing but also by using ongoing assessments such as class discussions, hinge questions, multiple-choice quizzes, and exit tickets in order to ascertain where each pupils' 'struggle zone' is positioned as well as to activate their prior learning.

Identify the waypoints

The fourth step towards designing an effective curriculum is to identify the waypoints. Once the destination and the starting points are known, the curriculum must carve a path between the two and this path must grow ever steeper as pupils near the end. In other words, the curriculum needs to be increasingly complex and challenging as pupils travel through it, and it must help pupils to develop as independent learners, too. One way to do this is to identify the threshold concepts that pupils must acquire at each stage – the checkpoints through which they must pass on the way to their destination. These thresholds concepts can also act as a source of meaningful assessment – a progression model – which measure pupils' progress.

Define excellence

The fifth step towards designing an effective curriculum is to define excellence so that our curriculum is ambitious for all but that each pupil and student is afforded equal access to the curriculum and is supported to travel through it and achieve.

This is, in part, about developing a growth mindset, believing that every pupil and student is capable of achieving excellence, no matter their starting points and backgrounds. But it is also about 'teaching to the top' for all pupils and not dumbing down or reducing the curriculum offer for disadvantaged pupils for that is only to double their disadvantage.

Defining excellence and providing equal access to an ambitious curriculum is also about having high expectations of every pupil and about explicitly teaching them the study and research skills – including how to take notes and revise – that they need to succeed.

Delivering excellence requires the curriculum – and teachers – to pitch learning at the appropriate level, which is to say hard but achievable because if the work is too easy or too difficult then pupils simply will not learn.

Diminish disadvantage

The sixth and final step towards designing an effective curriculum is to diminish disadvantage because if we are to provide an ambitious curriculum for all we must also accept that not all pupils and students start from the same point and that some will require more support and more time to reach their destination.

We diminish disadvantage by closing the gap between disadvantaged pupils – including those with SEND or High Needs – and their peers. This can, in part, be achieved by identifying the academic barriers that each pupil and student faces, then choosing the appropriate strategies to support them to overcome those barriers, and finally setting the success criteria for them. Intervention strategies work best when they are short term, intensive, focused and tailored. What's more, there is no substitute for quality first teaching and so improving teacher and teaching quality must always take precedence.

One way to support disadvantaged pupils is to use research evidence such as the EEF toolkit which posits that feedback and metacognition are the most impactful strategies at a teacher's disposal. But the application of such evidence must be carried out carefully because each pupil is different, just as each teacher, each class and each school or college is different, and so what works for one might not necessarily work for others.

We can also help to diminish the disadvantage by better understanding the root cause of that disadvantage. One such cause – though by no means the only cause – is a lack of cultural capital. One of the most tangible forms that cultural capital takes is vocabulary and so our curriculum should be a means of explicitly teaching vocabulary – the language *of* and *for* learning – in order to equip pupils and students with the tools they need to access the curriculum and achieve.

The journey's end

And those are the six steps I would recommend you follow when embarking upon your own 'curriculum intent' journey and indeed when reviewing the effectiveness of your existing curriculum.

Of course, curriculum intent is only really the start… pupils and students experience the curriculum, not through specifications, schemes of work and lesson plans, but through the teaching, learning and assessment that takes place in the classroom and, as such, it is crucial that our broad, balanced and ambitious curriculum is taught in a way that's effective and leads to long-term learning…

Teaching for long-term learning

Once we've designed a broad, balanced, and ambitious curriculum to which all our pupils and students have access and are supported to achieve its destinations, we must translate it into practice for this is how pupils encounter a curriculum: in the interactions that take place between teachers and learners, and between different learners, in the classroom, on the sports field, and in workshops and labs.

The secret to teaching our curriculum in a way that leads to long-term learning, I think, is to follow three steps, namely:

1. Create a positive learning environment in order to stimulate sensory memory

2. Make pupils think hard but efficiently in order to gain the attention of - but cheat - working memory

3. Plan for deliberate practice in order to improve storage in, and retrieval from, long-term memory

Allow me to explain…

We learn by means of an interaction between our sensory memory (sometimes referred to as our 'environment') and our long-term memory. Our sensory memory is made up of: what we see - this is called our iconic memory; what we hear - this is called our echoic memory; and what we touch - our haptic memory. Our long-term memory is where new information is stored and from which it can be recalled when needed, but we cannot directly access the information stored in our long-term memory. As such, the interaction that takes place between our sensory memory and our long-term memory occurs in our working memory, or short-term memory, which is the only place where we can think and do.

It might be helpful to think of our sensory memory as a haulage truck, our long-term memory as a warehouse, and our working memory as the holding bay where new deliveries are received, processed and labelled ready for stowing. The payload cannot be passed directly into the warehouse, it must first pass through the holding bay to be sorted.

In order to stimulate our pupils' sensory memories and thus engage the active attention of their working memories and make them think, we need to create classroom conditions conducive to learning, conditions that stimulate pupils' iconic, echoic and haptic memories. In other words, we need to engage pupils' senses in order to gain their attention.

It might sound like common sense - and indeed it is - to say that, for our pupils to learn, we must first gain their attention, but it's all too easy for learning to fail simply because we haven't stimulated our pupils' senses and therefore gained their attention, or because we have focused their attention on the wrong things.

I'm sure you're familiar with the Dancing Gorilla Awareness Test. If not, briefly: observers are asked to watch a video of a group of about eight people playing basketball and are told to count the number of passes made by the players dressed in white, ignoring the players in black. In the middle of the game, a man or woman in a gorilla suit dances across the court, weaving his or her way through the players. Most observers count the number of passes correctly but utterly fail to spot the gorilla. Their attention is not grabbed by the gorilla because they don't expect to see such an incongruous thing and are only focused on the ball as it passes from one player in white to another.

Sadly, this happens in our lessons all the time: our pupils miss what is at the end of their noses because either we've failed to gain the active attention of their working memories or have focused that active attention on the wrong things. For example, if I wanted a class to research the origins of two online encyclopaedias, Wikipedia and Microsoft's Encarta, and find out why Wikipedia - with no money and a reliance on volunteers to act as contributors - proved more successful than the encyclopaedia backed by big business, boasting an army of well-paid, qualified staff including Bill Gates, and asked them to do so on the internet, there's a danger that they would focus their attention on the act of researching rather than on the topic they'd been asked to research.

In other words, if I didn't explicitly teach them the skills needed to carry out the task and learn about Wikipedia, they would use all their working memory capacity on acquiring and using these skills and none, or very little, on the content.

They'd have to think about where to search, what search terms to use, how to sift information and make decisions about what was relevant and what was not, what was reliable and what was not. However, if I'd explicitly taught them how to conduct independent research - such as the use of three independent sources, skimming and scanning for key facts and names and dates, how to use quotations, how to detect inference and bias, etc., then modelled the process and got them to practice the skills until they become automatic – then they could have focused their attentions on the information they'd found out about Wikipedia (such as: In 2009, the year Encarta closed, only 1.27% of encyclopaedia searches in America were carried out using Encarta; Wikipedia meanwhile accounted for 97%) not on how to research that information.

This is important because if you don't think, you don't learn. We must gain pupils' active attentions and make them think hard in order for information to be processed in their working memories and then encoded in their long-term memories. And if we get them thinking hard about *how* to research, then they will process and encode this and learn nothing - or too little - about *what* they researched.

In short, stimulating pupils' sensory memories and focusing their attention on the right things is essential if our pupils are to engage their working memories.

Talking of which…

In order to help pupils utilise their limited working memories (depending on which research you read, it's thought that we can only handle between five and nine concepts in working memory at any one time - see, for example,

Miller 1956), we need to ensure they are made to think hard - are challenged with work that is difficult but achievable.

If the work is too easy, pupils will be able to complete it through habit and without thinking - this is called 'automaticity'. For example, as I explained in Chapter Twenty-One, if I asked you to calculate 2 x 10, you would do so automatically, through habit, without having to think about it because you likely mastered your times tables many years ago.

If the work's too hard, pupils will be unable to complete it because they will overpower their limited working memories with too much information (what's called 'cognitive overload') and the learning process will fail. For example, and again as I illustrated in Chapter Twenty-One, if I asked you to calculate 367 x 2892 in your head in a minute, you wouldn't be able to do so. Chances are, you'd do one of two things instead: Either you'd not attempt it because you'd quickly assess the task to be beyond your reach and therefore a pointless waste of energy; or you'd attempt it but be unable to hold so much information in your working memory and so would fail. Either way, you would be demotivated by your failure and, more importantly, you wouldn't have learnt or practiced anything, so the task would have been pointless.

Like Goldilocks, you need to find the bowl of porridge that's neither too hot nor too cold but is just right. In other words, you need to pitch your curriculum in the 'struggle zone', or what Robert Bjork calls the 'sweet spot' at the edge of pupils' current knowledge and abilities, albeit just within their reach. Lev Vygotsky defined this as the 'zone of proximal development' which is sandwiched between what pupils can do unaided and cannot yet do, in the area which is hard but achievable with time, effort and support.

But, in making pupils think hard, we also need to help them think efficiently. Thinking, as we have seen, will fail if pupils overload their working memories. As such, we need to help pupils cheat the limited space in their working memories (to mitigate cognitive overload) by learning new things within the context of what they already know (allowing them to 'chunk' information together to save space) and by teaching requisite knowledge and skills before they are applied because, as Daniel Willingham puts it in 'Why Students Don't Like School', "memory is the residue of thought".

Once pupils have been made to think hard but efficiently and have processed information in their working memories, we need to ensure they encode that information into their long-term memories and can easily retrieve it again later.

In order to help pupils store information in their practically limitless long-term memories (long term memory is so big, it will take more than a lifetime to fill it), we need to plan opportunities for deliberate practice, and we need to use two teaching strategies called spacing and interleaving.

Only by repeating learning and by doing so in a range of contexts, will we increase the storage strength of the information in long term memory. The better the storage strength, the more readily available will be our knowledge and skills.

Repeating learning - the very act of recalling prior knowledge and skills from long term memory - also improves their retrieval strength. The better the retrieval strength, the more easily, quickly and efficiently are knowledge and skills recalled from long term memory and brought into the working memory where they can be used.

The best form of repetition is purposeful practice which has well-defined, specific goals, is focused, involves feedback, and requires pupils to get out of their comfort zones because, if they don't push themselves beyond their comfort zones, they'll never improve. Getting out of their comfort zones means trying to do something that they couldn't do before. In this respect, the secret is not to "try harder" but rather to "try differently."

And so, in summary, there are – as I said earlier - three steps that we should take in order to ensure that our broad, balanced and ambitious curriculum is implemented in a way that leads to long-term learning:

1. Create a positive learning environment in order to stimulate sensory memory

2. Make pupils think hard but efficiently in order to gain the attention of - but cheat - working memory

3. Plan for deliberate practice in order to improve storage in, and retrieval from, long-term memory

I will explore these three steps – and much more besides – in Book Two of this series on **curriculum implementation**.

But we'e arrived at the destination of Book One. I hope you're enjoyed the ride and found it useful. Thank you for reading. And good luck with your own curriculum journey!

ABOUT THE AUTHOR

Matt Bromley is an education writer and consultant with over twenty years' experience in teaching and leadership including as headteacher. He also works as a public speaker, trainer, and adviser, and is a primary school governor.

Matt writes for various newspapers and magazines and is the author of numerous best-selling books for teachers. Matt's education blog, voted one of the UK's most influential, receives over 50,000 unique visitors a year.

He regularly speaks at national and international conferences and events, and provides education advice to charities, government agencies, training providers, colleges and multi-academy trusts. He works as a consultant and trainer with several companies and also provides a wide selection of direct-to-market consultancy and training services through his own company, Bromley Education, which he founded in 2012.

He lives in Yorkshire with his wife and three children. You can follow him on Twitter: @mj_bromley. You can find out more about him and read his blog at www.bromleyeducation.co.uk.

ALSO BY THE AUTHOR

The IQ Myth

The Art of Public Speaking

How to Become a School Leader

Teach

Teach 2

Making Key Stage 3 Count

The New Teacher Survival Kit

How to Lead

How to Learn

How to Teach

PUBLISHED BY

Spark Education Books UK

ISBN: 9781691220472

Printed in Great Britain
by Amazon